Plea Bargaining

The daring publisher, Universal Law Publishing Company, among the foremost in the law publishing field and progressive in venturing to bring out rare legal literature of avant garde *character has rightly enriched the* corpus juris *of India*

Justice V R Krishna Iyer
Random Reflections, page 14

Plea Bargaining

JUSTICE P. S. NARAYANA
Former Judge, Andhra Pradesh High Court

Universal
Law Publishing Co. Pvt. Ltd.
NEW DELHI - INDIA

2013 Edition

ISBN: 978-93-5035-381-3

Published by

Universal
Law Publishing Co. Pvt. Ltd.
NEW DELHI - INDIA

A-58, G.T. Karnal Road Industrial Area,
(Near Azadpur Metro Station), Delhi-110033
Tel. : 011-47082254, 27458529, 27215334 Fax : 011-27458529
e-mail: unilaw@vsnl.com

- Showroom : C-27, Connaught Place, New Delhi-110001
  e-mail: sales@unilawbooks.com
- Editorial : edit@unilawbooks.com
- Website : **www.unilawbooks.com**

Join us on Facebook www.facebook.com/unilawbooks

Recommended citation: Justice P.S. Narayana, *Plea Bargaining* (New Delhi: Universal Law Publishing Co. Pvt. Ltd., 2013).

Computer Typeset at Aesthetic and *Printed* at Deepak Printers, Delhi.

PREFACE

The concept of Plea Bargaining is a popular concept and the said concept had been adopted and being followed in several countries. It is reported that in a couple of countries this concept is working well in the administration of criminal justice system.

Initially our country had been reluctant to follow or adopt this concept and this is well reflected in certain decisions of the Apex Court too. However Chapter XXIA *i.e.* section 265A to section 265L of the Code of Criminal Procedure, 1973 was inserted in the aforesaid Code by Criminal Law Amendment Act, 2005 (Act 2 of 2006) dated 5-7-2006.

This brief commentary on the subject touches almost all the important aspects of the concept of certain provisions of the Code of Criminal Procedure, 1973 and even other than Chapter XXIA which may have some relevance with the aforesaid concept also had been dealt with.

I may be failing in my duty if I won't thank Sri P. Jagadish Chandra Prasad, Advocate, High Court of A.P. and Sri Tulasi Pemmasani, M.S. Finance, Bentley University, Boston, U.S.A. who had assisted me in collecting the relevant material. I do invite suggestions from all quarters for further improvement of this short commentary while releasing future editions.

JUSTICE P.S. NARAYANA

CONTENTS

TABLE OF CASES

A

C

D

E

I

K

L

M

R

T

W

Y

Z

CHAPTER 1
INTRODUCTION

Chapter XXIA of the Code of Criminal Procedure, 1973 was introduced by the Criminal Law Amendment Act, 2005, Act 2 of 2006 dated 5-7-2006. Sections 265A to 265L fall under Chapter XXIA referred to Supra. This Chapter is not applicable to any juvenile or child as defined in section 2(k) of the Juvenile Justice (Care and Protection of Children) Act, 2000, Act 56 of 2000. Section 2(k) aforesaid defines Juvenile or child as in this Act, unless the context otherwise requires "Juvenile" or "child" means a person who has not completed eighteenth year of age.

See *Ratan Lal* v. *State of Rajasthan,* 2003 (3) Raj LR 688: 2004 (1) WLC 159: 2004 Cr LJ 734 (Raj).

Suddarth v. *State of Bihar,* AIR 2005 SC 4352: 2005 Cr LJ 4499: 2005 AIR SCW 5010.

Balu v. *State of Tamil Nadu,* 2008 AIR SCW 1456: AIR 2008 SC 1434: 2008 Cr LJ 2066 (SC).

Charanjit Singh v. *State,* 2004 (4) Crimes 473 (Del).

Balkar Singh v. *State,* 2005 (2) Crimes 239 (P&H).

Krishna v. *Officer-in-Charge, Bandra P.S.,* 2006 (2) Crimes 192 (Bom).

Rafiq Khan v. *State,* 2004 (2) Crimes 106 (Raj).

Silak Ram v. *State of Haryana,* 2007 (3) ALT (Cri) 333 (SC).

Justin v. *State,* 2007 (3) Crimes 66 (Mad).

Satish Kumar v. *State of Andhra Pradesh,* 2009 (3) ALT (Cri) 86 (AP).

Pratap Singh v. *State of Jharkhand,* 2005 (1) Supreme 775: AIR 2005 SC 2731: 2005 Cr LJ 3091.

Parvathy v. *Superintendent Corporation Relief Centre,* 2002 (1) KLT 523.

Vimal Chadha v. *Vikas Choudhary,* 2008 (7) SCJ 80.

Vijay Singh v. *State of Delhi,* AIR 2012 SC 3437: 2012 Cr LJ 4527: 2012 AIR SCW 4877.

Om Prakash v. *State of Rajasthan,* AIR 2012 SC 1608: 2012 Cr LJ 2266: 2012 AIR SCW 2462.

Section 265A of the Code of Criminal Procedure, 1973 hereinafter referred to as the Code deals with Application of the Chapter. Likewise section 265B of the Code deals with Application for plea Bargaining.

The object of Juvenile Justice Act, 1986 has been discussed in *Abuzar Hussain* v. *State of West Bengal,* (2012) 10 SCC 489. Likewise the object of

Juvenile Justice (Care and Protection of Children) Act, 2000 was explained in *Om Prakash* v. *State of Rajasthan,* AIR 2012 SC 1608: 2012 Cr LJ 2266: 2012 AIR SCW 2462. See *Ramdeo Chauhan* v. *State of Assam,* (2001) 5 SCC 714: AIR 2001 SC 2231: 2001 Cr LJ 2902; *Abuzar Hussain* v. *State of West Bengal,* (2012) 10 SCC 489; *Vijay Singh* v. *State of Delhi,* AIR 2012 SC 3437: 2012 Cr LJ 4527: 2012 AIR SCW 4877. A claim of Juvenility may be raised at any stage even after the final disposal of the case *Abuzar Hussain* v. *State of West Bengal,* (2012) 10 SCC 489; *See* also *Pawan* v. *State of Uttaranchal,* (2009) 15 SCC 259; *Hari Ram* v. *State of Rajasthan,* (2009) 13 SCC 211.

Dayanand v. *State of Haryana,* (2011) 2 SCC 224: AIR 2011 SC 593: 2011 Cr LJ 1157.

Lakhan Lal v. *State of Bihar,* (2011) 2 SCC 251: AIR 2011 SC 842: 2011 Cr LJ 1116.

Shah Nawaz v. *State of Uttar Pradesh,* (2011) 13 SCC 751: AIR 2011 SC 3107: 2011 AIR SCW 4632.

In *Monohar Lal* v. *Vinesh Anand,* 2001 Cr LJ 2044: AIR 2001 SC 1820: 2001 AIR SCW 1590 (SC) while discussing with the concept of *Locus* it was held that the Doctrine of *Locus Standi* is foreign to Criminal Jurisprudence. See *A.R. Antulay* v. *Ramdas Sriniwas Nayak,* (1984) 2 SCC 500: AIR 1984 SC 718: 1984 Cr LJ 647. A judge to be identified with Justice, Justice done and nothing but Justice *S.P. Shenbagamoorthy* v. *Mu. Ka. Stalin,* 2003 Cr LJ 271 (Mad);

See also *Dr. Prem Chand* v. *Manak Lal,* AIR 1957 SC 415.

Ranjit Thakur v. *Union of India,* AIR 1987 SC 2386: JT 1987 (5) SC 93: (1987) 3 IJ Rep 658.

Sunil Kumar Pal v. *Phota Sheikh,* AIR 1984 SC 1591: 1984 Cri LR (SC) 374.

Rajender Kumar Jain v. *State,* AIR 1980 SC 1510: 1980 Cr LJ 1084: (1980) 3 SCC 435.

In *Lal Singh* v. *State of Gujarat,* 2001 AIR SCW 389: AIR 2001 SC 746: 2001 Cr LJ 978 (SC) it was held that in Criminal Jurisprudence the innocence of accused is presumed but the presumption to be Judged on the basis of Conceptions of Reasonable Prudent Man.

Though the primary duty of a public prosecutor is to ensure that an accused is punished, his duties extend to ensuring fairness in the proceedings and also to ensure that all relevant facts and circumstances are brought to the notice of the court for a just determination of the truth so that due justice prevails *V.K. Sasikala* v. *State,* (2012) 9 SCC 771: 2012 AIR SCW 5502. See *Sidhartha Vashisht @ Manu Sharma* v. *State (N.C.T. of Delhi),* (2010) 6 SCC 1: AIR 2010 SC 2352: 2010 AIR SCW 4302. The nature and status of the office of a public prosecutor had been dealt with by the apex court in *Centre for Public Interest Litigation* v. *Union of India,* (2012) 3 SCC 117: 2012 Cr LJ 1153; *See* also *Rajiv Ranjan Singh Lalan (8)* v. *Union of India,* (2006) 6 SCC 613: 2006

AIR SCW 4287. The meaning of Non-cognizable offence and Bailable offence has been explained in *Om Prakash* v. *Union of India,* AIR 2012 SC 545: 2012 Cr LJ 779: 2012 AIR SCW 112.

The normal canon of interpretation is that a remedial statute receives Liberal Construction where as a penal statute calls for strict construction. *R.P.F. Commissioner* v. *Hooghly Mills Co. Ltd.,* (2012) 2 SCC 489. When such strict construction may be deviated from had been dealt with in *Southern Electricity Supply Co. of Orissa Ltd.* v. *Sree Seetaram Rice Mills,* (2012) 2 SCC 108, but the settled rule of construction of a penal statute is strict interpretation.

Bijaya Kumar Agarwala v. *State of Orissa,* AIR 1996 SC 2531: 1996 Cr LJ 3577: 1996 AIR SCW 3144.

Niranjan Singh Karam Singh Punjabi v. *Jitendra Bhimraj Bijja,* AIR 1990 SC 1962: 1990 Cr LJ 1869: JT 1990 (3) SC 408.

Sakshi v. *Union of India,* AIR 2004 SC 3566: 2004 AIR SCW 3449: (2004) 5 SCC 518.

Surajmani Stella Kujur v. *Durga Charan Hansdah,* AIR 2001 SC 938: 2001 AIR SCW 711: (2001) 3 SCC 13.

Balram Kumawat v. *Union of India,* AIR 2003 SC 3268: 2003 AIR SCW 4658: (2003) 7 SCC 628.

If two possible and reasonable constructions can be put upon a penal provisions, the court must lean towards the construction which exempts the subject from penalty rather than the one which imposes penalty *Tolaram Relumal* v. *State of Bombay,* AIR 1954 SC 496: 1954 Cr LJ 1333: (1955) 1 SCR 158.

See also

Aslam Babalal Desai v. *State of Maharashtra,* 1992 AIR SCW 2621: AIR 1993 SC 1: 1992 Cr LJ 3712.

State of Madhya Pradesh v. *Azad Bharat Finance Company,* AIR 1967 SC 276: 1967 Cr LJ 285: 1967 (1) SCJ 815.

Dyke v. *Elliot,* (1872) LR 4 PC 184.

This rule of strict Construction may not be applicable in case of a procedural provisions held in *Iqbal Singh Marwah* v. *Meenakshi Marwah,* 2005 AIR SCW 1929: AIR 2005 SC 2119: 2005 Cr LJ 2161.

For Construction of penal Statutes. *See* the undernoted decisions

Suman Sethi v. *Ajay K. Churiwal,* AIR 2000 SC 828: 2000 AIR SCW 383: 2000 Cr LJ 1391.

M. Narayanan Nambiar v. *State of Kerala,* AIR 1963 SC 1116: (1963) 2 Cr LJ 186: 1963 (2) SCJ 582.

Government of Andhra Pradesh v. *P. Venku Reddy,* 2002 AIR SCW 3895: AIR 2002 SC 3346: 2002 Cr LJ 4333.

M.G. Wagh v. *Jay Engineering Works Ltd.*, AIR 1987 SC 670: (1987) 1 SCC 542: 1987 SCC (Cri) 202.

Standard Chartered Bank v. *Directorate of Enforcement,* (2005) 4 SCC 530: AIR 2005 SC 2622: 2005 Cr LJ 4917.

Enforcement Directorate v. *M. Samba Siva Rao,* AIR 2000 SC 2128: 2000 Cr LJ 3170: 2000 AIR SCW 2189.

State of Kerala v. *Mathai Verghese,* AIR 1987 SC 33: 1987 Cr LJ 308: (1986) 4 SCC 746.

Kisan Trimbak Kothula v. *State of Maharashtra,* AIR 1977 SC 435: 1977 Cr LJ 267: 1978 SC Cri R 92.

Murlidhar Meghraj Loya v. *State of Maharashtra,* AIR 1976 SC 1929: 1976 Cr LJ 1527: (1977) 1 SCR 1.

State of Bihar v. *Bhagirath Sharma,* AIR 1973 SC 2198: 1973 Cr LJ 1184: (1973) 2 SCC 257.

Seksaria Cotton Mills Ltd. v. *State of Bombay,* AIR 1953 SC 278: 1953 Cr LJ 1116: 1953 SCR 825.

R.M. Malkani v. *State of Maharashtra,* AIR 1973 SC 157: 1973 Cr LJ 238: (1973) 2 SCR 417.

Zahira Habibulla H. Sheikh v. *State of Gujarat,* AIR 2004 SC 3114: 2004 AIR SCW 2325: 2004 Cr LJ 2050.

Chief Inspector of Mines v. *Karam Chand Thapar,* AIR 1961 SC 838: (1962) 1 SCR 9: (1961) 2 Cr LJ 1.

State of Uttar Pradesh v. *Ramagya Sharma Vaidya,* AIR 1966 SC 78: 1966 Cr LJ 79: (1965) 3 SCR 161.

Ram Ratan Gupta v. *Director of Enforcement,* AIR 1966 SC 495: 1966 Cr LJ 457: 1966 (1) SCJ 670.

Shanti Prasad Jain v. *Director of Enforcement,* AIR 1962 SC 1764: (1963) 2 SCR 297: (1963) 1 SCA 524.

M.D. Shukla v. *State of Gujarat,* AIR 1971 SC 117: 1971 (1) SCJ 217: (1970) 3 SCR 515.

State of West Bengal v. *Moti Lal Kanoria,* AIR 1966 SC 1586: 1966 Cr LJ 1210: (1966) 3 SCR 933.

Intelligence Officer, Narcotic Control Bureau v. *Sambhu Sonkar,* 2001 AIR SCW 590: AIR 2001 SC 830: 2001 Cr LJ 1082.

Ganga Hire Purchase Pvt. Ltd. v. *State of Punjab,* AIR 2000 SC 449: 2000 Cr LJ 587: 1999 AIR SCW 4601.

State of Bihar v. *Kedar Sao,* AIR 2003 SC 3650: 2003 AIR SCW 4131: 2003 Cr LJ 4903.

State of West Bengal v. *Sujit Kumar Rana,* AIR 2004 SC 1851: 2004 AIR SCW 597: (2004) 1 SCALE 641.

Sanjay Dutt v. *State through C.B.I., Bombay,* 1994 AIR SCW 3857: 1995 Cr LJ 477: (1994) 5 SCC 410.

Divisional Forest Officer v. *G.V. Sudhakar Rao,* AIR 1986 SC 328: 1986 Cr LJ 357: (1985) 4 SCC 573.

Amery Pharmaceuticals v. *State of Rajasthan,* 2001 AIR SCW 1132: AIR 2001 SC 1303: 2001 Cr LJ 1686.

Kanwar Singh v. *Delhi Administration,* AIR 1965 SC 871: (1965) 1 SCR 7: 1965 (2) Cr LJ 1.

State of Uttar Pradesh v. *Chandrika,* AIR 2000 SC 164: 1999 AIR SCW 4251: 2000 Cr LJ 384.

Gurdeep Singh v. *State (Delhi Admn.),* AIR 1999 SC 3646: 1999 AIR SCW 3667: 1999 Cr LJ 4573.

NEPC Micon Ltd. v. *Magma Leasing Ltd.,* AIR 1999 SC 1952: 1999 AIR SCW 1637: 1999 Cr LJ 2883.

Pawan Kumar v. *State of Haryana,* AIR 1998 SC 958: 1998 AIR SCW 721: 1998 Cr LJ 1144.

N.K. Jain v. *C.K. Shah,* (1991) 2 SCC 495: AIR 1991 SC 1289: 1991 Cr LJ 1347.

State of Maharashtra v. *Natwarlal Damodardas Soni,* AIR 1980 SC 593: 1980 Cr LJ 429: (1980) 2 SCR 340.

Municipal Corporation of Delhi v. *Laxmi Narani Tandon,* (1976) 2 SCR 1050: AIR 1976 SC 621: 1976 Cr LJ 547.

Chitan J. Vaswani v. *State of West Bengal,* AIR 1975 SC 2473: (1976) 2 SCR 300: (1975) 2 SCC 829.

Swantraj v. *State of Maharashtra,* AIR 1974 SC 517: (1975) 3 SCC 322: 1974 Cr LJ 472.

Jayawant Dattatray Suryarao v. *State of Maharashtra,* 2001 AIR SCW 4717: AIR 2002 SC 143: 2002 Cr LJ 226.

Madan Singh v. *State of Bihar,* (2004) 4 SCC 622: AIR 2004 SC 3317: 2004 Cr LJ 2862.

State of Rajasthan v. *Babu Ram,* AIR 2007 SC 2018: 2007 AIR SCW 3799: (2007) 6 SCC 55.

B. Rama Raju v. *Union of India,* 2011 (3) Andh LT 443.

Radhey Shyam Kejiriwal v. *State of West Bengal,* (2011) 3 SCC 581.

Baldev Krishna Sahi v. *Shipping Corporation of India Ltd.,* AIR 1987 SC 2245: (1987) 4 SCC 361: 3 Crimes 449.

Lalita Jalan v. *Bombay Gas Co. Ltd.,* AIR 2003 SC 3157: 2003 AIR SCW 2175: 2003 Cr LJ 2514.

J.K. (Bombay) Ltd. v. *Mrs. Bharti Matha Mishra,* AIR 2001 SC 649: 2001 AIR SCW 282: 2001 Cr LJ 961.

Abhilash Vinod Kumar Jain v. *Cox and Kings (India) Ltd.,* AIR 1995 SC 1592: 1995 AIR SCW 2497: (1995) 3 SCC 732.

Reema Aggarwal v. *Anupam,* AIR 2004 SC 1418: 2004 AIR SCW 344: 2004 Cr LJ 892.

Prakash Kumar alias *Prakash Bhutto* v. *State of Gujarat*, AIR 2005 SC 1075: 2005 AIR SCW 493: (2005) 2 SCC 409.

Jameel Ahmed v. *State of Rajasthan*, 2003 AIR SCW 6078: AIR 2004 SC 588: (2003) 9 SCC 673.

Hari Chand Sarda v. *Mizo District Council*, AIR 1967 SC 829: (1967) 1 SCR 1012: 1968 (1) SCJ 59.

State of Himachal Pradesh v. *Associated Hotels of India Ltd.*, AIR 1972 SC 1131: (1972) 2 SCR 937: 1974 (1) SCJ 189.

Shivanarayan Kabra v. *The State of Madras*, AIR 1967 SC 986: (1967) 1 SCR 138: 1967 Cr LJ 946.

M.V. Joshi v. *M.U. Shimpi*, AIR 1961 SC 1494: 1961 (2) SCJ 571: (1961) 2 Cr LJ 696.

Sachidananda Banerjee Assistant Collector of Customs, Calcutta v. *Sitaram Agarawala*, (1966) 2 SCJ 111: 1966 Cr LJ 712: AIR 1966 SC 955.

Mansukhlal and Brothers v. *Commissioner of Income-tax, Bombay*, AIR 1969 SC 835: (1969) 1 SCR 970.

Vithal Kushnaraj Nuvendkar v. *Pandunau Ram Singh*, (1964) 1 Cr LJ 491.

Mohd. Ayub Dar v. *State of Jammu and Kashmir*, AIR 2010 SC 2864: 2010 Cr LJ 4389: 2010 AIR SCW 4625.

Mohd. Gausuddin v. *State of Maharashtra*, 2003 All MR (Cri) 1107: 2003 Cr LJ 2994 (Bom).

Shashikant Singh v. *Tarkeshwar Singh*, AIR 2002 SC 2031: 2002 Cr LJ 2806: 2002 AIR SCW 2079.

Ganesh Traders v. *District Collector, Karim Nagar*, 2002 Cr LJ 1105: 2002 (1) Andh LD 210: 2002 (1) Andh LT 611.

Hiten Sagar v. *IMC Ltd.*, 2001 (4) Civ LJ 252: 2001 (3) CCC 71: 2001 Cr LJ 4311 (Bom).

The introduction of the Concept of Plea Bargaining had been discouraged in *Kasambhai Abdulrehmanbhai Sheikh* v. *State of Gujarat*, AIR 1980 SC 854: 1980 (1) SCJ 549: 1980 Cr LJ 553; *Kachhia Patel Shantilal Koderlal* v. *State of Gujarat*, 1980 Cr LJ 553: (1980) 3 SCC 120: (1980) 1 FAC 216; *Murlidhar Meghraj Loya* v. *State of Maharashtra*, AIR 1976 SC 1929: 1976 Cr LJ 1527: (1977) 1 SCR 1; *State of Uttar Pradesh* v. *Chandrika*, AIR 2000 SC 164: 1999 AIR SCW 4251: 2000 Cr LJ 384. This concept however had been well accepted in countries like U.S.A., Canada, England and Wales, Victoria, Australia etc. with a view to reduce the delay in disposal of criminal cases, the Law Commissions of India in its 154th Report recommended the introduction of Plea Bargaining which has been re-affirmed by Justice Malimath Committee.

CHAPTER 2

APPLICATION OF CHAPTER XXIA OF CR PC

Section 265A of the Code dealing with Application of the Chapter reads:

265A. Application of the Chapter.—(1) This Chapter shall apply in respect of an accused against whom—

(a) the report has been forwarded by the officer in charge of the police station under section 173 alleging therein that an offence appears to have been committed by him other than an offence for which the punishment of death or of imprisonment for life or of imprisonment for a term exceeding seven years has been provided under the law for the time being in force; or

(b) a Magistrate has taken cognizance of an offence on complaint, other than an offence for which the punishment of death or of imprisonment for life or of imprisonment for a term exceeding seven years, has been provided under the law for the time being in force, and after examining complainant and witnesses under section 200, issued the process under section 204,

but does not apply where such offence affects the socio-economic condition of the country or has been committed against a woman, or a child below the age of fourteen years.

(2) For the purposes of sub-section (1), the Central Government shall, by notification, determine the offences under the law for the time being in force which shall be the offences affecting the socio-economic condition of the country.

Section 173 of the Code dealing with Report of police officer on completion of investigation reads.

173. Report of police officer on completion of investigation.—(1) Every investigation under this Chapter shall be completed without unnecessary delay.

(1A) The investigation in relation to rape of a child may be completed within three months from the date on which the information was recorded by the officer in charge of the police station.

(2) (i) As soon as it is completed, the officer in charge of the police station shall forward to a Magistrate empowered to take cognizance of the offence on a police report, a report in the form prescribed by the State Government, stating—

(a) the names of the parties;
(b) the nature of the information;
(c) the names of the persons who appear to be acquainted with the circumstances of the case;
(d) whether any offence appears to have been committed and, if so, by whom;
(e) whether the accused has been arrested;
(f) whether he has been released on his bond and, if so, whether with or without sureties;
(g) whether he has been forwarded in custody under section 170;
(h) whether the report of medical examination of the woman has been attached where investigation relates to an offence under section 376, 376A, 376B, 376C section 376D or section 376E of the Indian Penal Code (45 of 1860).

(ii) The officer shall also communicate, in such manner as may be prescribed by the State Government, the action taken by him, to the person, if any, by whom the information relating to the commission of the offence was first given.

(3) Where a superior officer of police has been appointed under section 158, the report, shall, in any case in which the State Government by general or special order so directs, be submitted through that officer, and he may, pending the orders of the Magistrate, direct the officer in charge of the police station to make further investigation.

(4) Whenever it appears from a report forwarded under this section that the accused has been released on his bond, the Magistrate shall make such order for the discharge of such bond or otherwise as he thinks fit.

(5) When such report is in respect of a case to which section 170 applies, the police officer shall forward to the Magistrate along with the report—

(a) all documents or relevant extracts thereof on which the prosecution proposes to rely other than those already sent to the Magistrate during investigation;
(b) the statements recorded under section 161 of all the persons whom the prosecution proposes to examine as its witnesses.

(6) If the police officer is of opinion that any part of any such statement is not relevant to the subject-matter of the proceedings or that its disclosure to the accused is not essential in the interests of justice and is inexpedient in the public interest, he shall indicate that part of the statement and append a note requesting the Magistrate to exclude that part from the copies to be granted to the accused and stating his reasons for making such request.

(7) Where the police officer investigating the case finds it convenient

so to do, he may furnish to the accused copies of all or any of the documents referred to in sub-section (5).

(8) Nothing in this section shall be deemed to preclude further investigation in respect of an offence after a report under sub-section (2) has been forwarded to the Magistrate and, where upon such investigation, the officer in charge of the police station obtains further evidence, oral or documentary, he shall forward to the Magistrate a further report or reports regarding such evidence in the form prescribed; and the provisions of sub-sections (2) to (6) shall, as far as may be, apply in relation to such report or reports as they apply in relation to a report forwarded under sub-section (2).

Section 200 of the Code falls under Chapter XV Complaints to Magistrates and deals with Examination of Complainant and the provision reads.

200. Examination of complainant.—A Magistrate taking cognizance of an offence on complaint shall examine upon oath the complainant and the witnesses present, if any, and the substance of such examination shall be reduced to writing and shall be signed by the complainant and the witnesses, and also by the Magistrate:

Provided that, when the complaint is made in writing, the Magistrate need not examine the complainant and the witnesses—

(a) if a public servant acting or purporting to act in the discharge of his official duties or a Court has made the complaint; or

(b) if the Magistrate makes over the case for inquiry or trial to another Magistrate under section 192:

Provided further that if the Magistrate makes over the case to another Magistrate under section 192 after examining the complainant and the witnesses, the latter Magistrate need not re-examine them.

Section 204 of the Code falls under Chapter XVI Commencement of proceedings before Magistrates and deals with issue of process and the provision reads.

204. Issue of process.—(1) If in the opinion of a Magistrate taking cognizance of an offence there is sufficient ground for proceeding, and the case appears to be—

(a) a summons-case, he shall issue his summons for the attendance of the accused, or

(b) a warrant-case, he may issue a warrant, or, if he thinks fit, a summons, for causing the accused to be brought or to appear at a certain time before such Magistrate or (if he has no jurisdiction himself) some other Magistrate having jurisdiction.

(2) No summons or warrant shall be issued against the accused under sub-section (1) until a list of the prosecution witnesses has been filed.

(3) In a proceeding instituted upon a complaint made in writing, every summons or warrant issued under sub-section (1) shall be

accompanied by a copy of such complaint.

(4) When by any law for the time being in force any process-fees or other fees are payable, no process shall be issued until the fees are paid and, if such fees are not paid within a reasonable time, the Magistrate may dismiss the complaint.

(5) Nothing in this section shall be deemed to affect the provisions of section 87.

The Central Government by S.O. 1042(E), dated 11-7-2006 specified offences under the following Laws for the time being in force which shall be the offences affecting the Socio Economic condition of the country for the purposes of section 265A(1) of the Code.

Dowry Prohibition Act, 1961.

The Commission of Sati Prevention Act, 1987.

The Indecent Representation of Woman (Prohibition) Act, 1986.

The Immoral Traffic (Prevention) Act, 1956.

The Protection of Woman From Domestic Violence Act, 2005.

The Infant Milk Substitutes Feeding Bottles and Infant Foods (Regulation of Production, Supply and Distribution) Act, 1992 provisions of Fruit Products Order, 1955.

Issued under the Essential Services Commodities Act, 1955

Provisions of Fruit Products Orders, 1973 issued under Essential Commodities Act, 1955 offences with respect of Animals that find place in Schedule I and Part II of the Schedule II as well as offences relating to altering of Boundaries of Protected Areas under the Wild Life (Protection) Act, 1972.

The Scheduled Castes, Scheduled Tribes (Prevention of Atrocities) Act, 1989 offences under the Protection of Civil Right Act, 1955.

Offences under sections 23 to 28 of the Juvenile Justice (Care and Protection of Children) Act, 2000.

The Army Act, 1950.

The Air Force Act, 1950.

The Navy Act, 1957.

Offences under sections 59 to 81 and 83 of the Delhi Metro Railway (Operation and Maintenance) Act, 2002.

The Explosives Act, 1884.

Offences under section 11 to 18 of the Cable Television Networks (Regulation) Act, 1995.

The Cinematograph Act, 1952.

CHAPTER 3

REPORT FORWARDED BY THE OFFICER-IN-CHARGE OF THE POLICE STATION UNDER SECTION 173

Section 265A(1)(a) of the Code says that this chapter shall apply in respect of an accused against whom the report has been forwarded by the officer-in-charge of the police station under section 173 of the Code alleging therein that an offence appears to have been committed by him other than an offence for which punishment of death or of imprisonment for life or of imprisonment for a term exceeding seven years has been provided under the Law for the time being in force. For offences under the Indian Penal Code, the punishment, cognizable or non-cognizable, bailable or non-bailable, by what court triable, are provided for under the First Schedule of the Code. Apart from the Indian Penal Code there are several penal legislations dealing with offences and punishment therefor. The First Schedule of the Code reads:

THE FIRST SCHEDULE

CLASSIFICATION OF OFFENCES

Explanatory Note.— (1) In regard to offences under the Indian Penal Code, the entries in the second and third columns against a section the number of which is given in the first column are not intended as the definition of, and the punishment prescribed for, the offence in the Indian Penal Code, but merely as indication of the substance of the section.

(2) In this Schedule, (i) the expressions "Magistrate of the first class" and "Any Magistrate" include Metropolitan Magistrates but not Executive Magistrates; (ii) the word "cognizable" stands for "a police officer may arrest without warrant"; and (iii) the word "non-cognizable" stands for "a police officer shall not arrest without warrant".

I.—OFFENCES UNDER THE INDIAN PENAL CODE

Section	Offence	Punishment	Cognizable or non-cognizable	Bailable or non-bailable	By what court triable
1	2	3	4	5	6
			CHAPTER V—ABETMENT		
109	Abetment of any offence, if the act abetted is committed in consequence, and where no express provision is made for its punishment.	Same as for offence abetted.	According as offence abetted is cognizable or non-cognizable.	According as offence abetted is bailable or non-bailable.	Court by which offence abetted is triable.
110	Abetment of any offence, if the person abetted does the act with a different intention from that of the abettor.	Same as for offence abetted.	According as offence abetted is cognizable or non-cognizable.	According as offence abetted is bailable or non-bailable.	Court by which offence abetted is triable.
111	Abetment of any offence, when one act is abetted and a different act is done; subject to the proviso.	Same for offence intended to be abetted.	According as offence abetted is cognizable or non-cognizable.	According as offence abetted is bailable or non-bailable.	Court by which offence abetted is triable.

Section	Offence	Punishment	Cognizable or non-cognizable	Bailable or non-bailable	By what court triable
1	2	3	4	5	6
113	Abetment of any offence, when an effect is caused by the act abetted different from that intended by the abettor.	Same as for offence committed.	According as offence abetted is cognizable or non-cognizable.	According as offence abetted is bailable or non-bailable.	Court by which offence abetted is triable.
114	Abetment of any offence, if abettor is present when offence is committed.	Same as for offence committed.	According as offence abetted is cognizable or non-cognizable.	According as offence abetted is bailable or non-bailable	Court by which offence abetted is triable.
115	Abetment of an offence, punishable with death or imprisonment for life, if the offence be not committed in consequence of the abetment.	Imprisonment for 7 years and fine.	According as offence abetted is cognizable or non-cognizable.	Non-bailable	Court by which offence abetted is triable.
	If an act which causes harm to be done in consequence of the abetment.	Imprisonment for 14 years and fine.	According as offence abetted is cognizable or non-cognizable.	Non-bailable	Court by which offence abetted is triable.
116	Abetment of an offence, punishable with imprisonment, if the offence be not committed in consequence of the abetment.	Imprisonment extending to a quarter part of the longest term provided for the offence, or fine, or both.	According as offence abetted is cognizable or non-cognizable.	According as offence abetted is bailable or non-bailable.	Court by which offence abetted is triable.
	If the abettor or the person abetted be a public servant whose duty it is to prevent the offence.	Imprisonment extending to half of the longest term provided for the offence, or fine or both.	According as offence abetted is cognizable or non-cognizable.	According as offence abetted is bailable or non-bailable.	Court by which offence abetted is triable.
117	Abetting the commission of an offence by the public, or by more than ten persons.	Imprisonment for 3 years, or fine, or both.	According as offence abetted is cognizable or non-cognizable.	According as offence abetted is bailable or non-bailable.	Court by which offence abetted is triable.

Section	Offence	Punishment	Cognizable or non-cognizable	Bailable or non-bailable	By what court triable
1	2	3	4	5	6
118	Concealing a design to commit an offence punishable with death or imprisonment for life, if the offence be committed.	Imprisonment for 7 years and fine.	According as offence abetted is cognizable or non-cognizable.	Non-bailable	Court by which offence abetted is triable.
	If the offence be not committed.	Imprisonment for 3 years and fine.	According as offence abetted is cognizable or non-cognizable.	Bailable	Court by which offence abetted is triable.
119	A public servant concealing a design to commit an offence which it is his duty to prevent, if the offence be committed.	Imprisonment extending to half of the longest term provided for the offence, or fine, or both.	According as offence abetted is cognizable or non-cognizable.	According as offence abetted is bailable or non-bailable.	Court by which offence abetted is triable.
	If the offence be punishable with death or imprisonment for life.	Imprisonment for 10 years.	According as offence abetted is cognizable or non-cognizable.	Non-bailable	Court by which offence abetted is triable.
	If the offence be not committed.	Imprisonment extending to a quarter part of the longest term provided for the offence, or fine, or both.	According as offence abetted is cognizable or non-cognizable.	Bailable	Court by which offence abetted is triable.
120	Concealing a design to commit an offence punishable with imprisonment, if offence be committed.	Imprisonment extending to a quarter part of the longest term provided for the offence, or fine, or both.	According as offence abetted is cognizable or non-cognizable.	According as offence abetted is bailable or non-bailable.	Court by which offence abetted is triable.
	If the offence be not committed.	Imprisonment extending to one-eighth part of the longest term provided for the offence, or fine, or both.	According as offence abetted is cognizable or non-cognizable.	Bailable	Court by which offence abetted is triable.

Section	Offence	Punishment	Cognizable or non-cognizable	Bailable or non-bailable	By what court triable
1	2	3	4	5	6
		CHAPTER VA—CRIMINAL CONSPIRACY			
120B	Criminal conspiracy to commit an offence punishable with death, imprisonment for life or rigorous imprisonment for a term of 2 years or upwards.	Same as for abetment of the offence which is the object of the conspiracy.	According as the offence which is the object of conspiracy is cognizable or non-cognizable.	According as offence which is object of conspiracy is bailable or non-bailable.	Court by which abetment of the offence which is the object of conspiracy is triable.
	Any other criminal conspiracy.	Imprisonment for 6 months, or fine, or both.	Non-cognizable	Bailable	Magistrate of the first class.
		CHAPTER VI—OFFENCES AGAINST THE STATE			
121	Waging or attempting to wage war, or abetting the waging of war, against the Government of India.	Death, or imprisonment for life and fine.	Cognizable	Non-bailable	Court of Session.
121A	Conspiring to commit certain offences against the State.	Imprisonment for life, or imprisonment for 10 years and fine.	Cognizable	Non-bailable	Court of Session.
122	Collecting arms, etc., with the intention of waging war against the Government of India.	Imprisonment for life, or imprisonment for 10 years and fine.	Cognizable	Non-bailable	Court of Session.
123	Concealing with intent to facilitate a design to wage war.	Imprisonment for 10 years and fine.	Cognizable	Non-bailable	Court of Session.
124	Assaulting President, Governor, etc., with intent to compel or restrain the exercise of any lawful power.	Imprisonment for 7 years and fine.	Cognizable	Non-bailable	Court of Session.

Section	Offence	Punishment	Cognizable or non-cognizable	Bailable or non-bailable	By what court triable
1	2	3	4	5	6
124A	Sedition.	Imprisonment for life and fine, or imprisonment for 3 years and fine, or fine.	Cognizable	Non-bailable	Court of Session.
125	Waging war against any Asiatic power in alliance or at peace with the Government of India, or abetting the waging of such war.	Imprisonment for life and fine, or imprisonment for 7 years and fine, or fine.	Cognizable	Non-bailable	Court of Session.
126	Committing depredation on the territories of any power in alliance or at peace with the Government of India.	Imprisonment for 7 years and fine, and forfeiture of certain property.	Cognizable	Non-bailable	Court of Session.
127	Receiving property taken by war or depredation mentioned in sections 125 and 126.	Imprisonment for 7 years and fine, and forfeiture of certain property.	Cognizable	Non-bailable	Court of Session.
128	Public servant voluntarily allowing prisoner of State or war in his custody to escape.	Imprisonment for life, or imprisonment for 10 years and fine.	Cognizable	Non-bailable	Court of Session.
129	Public servant negligently suffering prisoner of State or war in his custody to escape.	Simple imprisonment for 3 years and fine.	Cognizable	Bailable	Magistrate of the first class.
130	Aiding escape of, rescuing or harbouring, such prisoner, or offering any resistance to the recapture of such prisoner.	Imprisonment for life, or imprisonment for 10 years and fine.	Cognizable	Non-bailable	Court of Session.

Section	Offence	Punishment	Cognizable or non-cognizable	Bailable or non-bailable	By what court triable
1	2	3	4	5	6
		CHAPTER VII—OFFENCES RELATING TO THE ARMY, NAVY AND AIR FORCE			
131	Abetting mutiny, or attempting to seduce an officer, soldier, sailor or airman from his allegiance or duty.	Imprisonment for life, or imprisonment for 10 years and fine.	Cognizable	Non-bailable	Court of Session.
132	Abetment of mutiny, if mutiny is committed in consequence thereof.	Death, or imprisonment for life, or imprisonment for 10 years and fine.	Cognizable	Non-bailable	Court of Session.
133	Abetment of an assault by an officer, soldier, sailor or airman on his superior officer, when in the execution of his office.	Imprisonment for 3 years and fine.	Cognizable	Non-bailable	Magistrate of the first class.
134	Abetment of such assault, if the assault is committed.	Imprisonment for 7 years and fine.	Cognizable	Non-bailable	Magistrate of the first class.
135	Abetment of the desertion of an officer, soldier, sailor or airman.	Imprisonment for 2 years, or fine, or both	Cognizable	Bailable	Any Magistrate.
136	Harbouring such an officer, soldier, sailor or airman who has deserted.	Imprisonment for 2 years, or fine, or both	Cognizable	Bailable	Any Magistrate.
137	Deserter concealed on board merchant vessel, through negligence of master or person in charge thereof.	Fine of 500 rupees	Non-cognizable	Bailable	Any Magistrate.

Section	Offence	Punishment	Cognizable or non-cognizable	Bailable or non-bailable	By what court triable
1	2	3	4	5	6
138	Abetment of act of insubordination by an officer, soldier, sailor or airman, if the offence be committed in consequence.	Imprisonment for 6 months, or fine, or both.	Cognizable	Bailable	Any Magistrate.
140	Wearing the dress or carrying any token used by a soldier, sailor or airman with intent that it may be believed that he is such a soldier, sailor or airman.	Imprisonment for 3 months, or fine of 500 rupees, or both.	Cognizable	Bailable	Any Magistrate.
		CHAPTER VIII—OFFENCES AGAINST THE PUBLIC TRANQUILLITY			
143	Being member of an unlawful assembly.	Imprisonment for 6 months, or fine, or both.	Cognizable	Bailable	Any Magistrate.
144	Joining an unlawful assembly armed with any deadly weapon.	Imprisonment for 2 years, or fine, or both	Cognizable	Bailable	Any Magistrate.
145	Joining or continuing in an unlawful assembly, knowing that it has been commanded to disperse.	Imprisonment for 2 years, or fine, or both	Cognizable	Bailable	Any Magistrate.
147	Rioting.	Imprisonment for 2 years, or fine, or both.	Cognizable	Bailable	Any Magistrate.
148	Rioting armed with deadly weapon.	Imprisonment for 3 years, or fine or both.	Cognizable	Bailable	Magistrate of the first class.
149	If an offence be committed by any member of an unlawful assembly, every other member of such assembly shall be guilty of the offence.	The same as for the offence.	According as offence is cognizable or non-cognizable.	According as offence is bailable or non-bailable.	The Court by which the offence is triable.

Section	Offence	Punishment	Cognizable or non-cognizable	Bailable or non-bailable	By what court triable
1	2	3	4	5	6
150	Hiring, engaging or employing persons to take part in an unlawful assembly.	The same as for a member of such assembly, and for any offence committed by any member of such assembly.	Cognizable	According as offence is bailable or non-bailable.	The Court by which the offence is triable.
151	Knowingly joining or continuing in any assembly of five or more persons after it has been commanded to disperse.	Imprisonment for 6 months, or fine, or both.	Cognizable	Bailable	Any Magistrate.
152	Assaulting or obstructing public servant when suppressing riot, etc.	Imprisonment for 3 years, or fine, or both.	Cognizable	Bailable	Magistrate of the first class.
153	Wantonly giving provocation with intent to cause riot, if rioting be committed.	Imprisonment for 1 year, or fine, or both.	Cognizable	Bailable	Any Magistrate.
	If not committed.	Imprisonment for 6 months, or fine, or both.	Cognizable	Bailable	Magistrate of the first class.
153A	Promoting enmity between classes.	Imprisonment for 3 years, or fine, or both.	Cognizable	Non-Bailable	Magistrate of the first class.
	Promoting enmity between classes in place of worship, etc.	Imprisonment for 5 years and fine.	Cognizable	Non-Bailable	Magistrate of the first class.
[1][153AA	Knowingly carrying arms in any procession or organising or holding or taking part in any mass drill or mass training with arms.	Imprisonment for 6 months and fine of 2,000 rupees	Cognizable	Non-Bailable	Any Magistrate.]

1. Ins. by Act 25 of 2005, sec. 42(a) (effective date yet to be notified).

Section	Offence	Punishment	Cognizable or non-cognizable	Bailable or non-bailable	By what court triable
1	2	3	4	5	6
153B	Imputations, assertions prejudicial to national integration.	Imprisonment for 3 years, or fine, or both.	Cognizable	Non-Bailable	[1][Magistrate of the first class.]
	If committed in a place of public worship etc.	Imprisonment for 5 years and fine.	Cognizable	Non-Bailable	Magistrate of the first class.
154	Owner or occupier of land not giving information of riot, etc.	Fine of 1,000 rupees.	Non-cognizable	Bailable	Any Magistrate.
155	Person for whose benefit or on whose behalf a riot takes place not using all lawful means to prevent it.	Fine.	Non-cognizable	Bailable	Any Magistrate.
156	Agent of owner or occupier for whose benefit a riot is committed not using all lawful means to prevent it.	Fine.	Non-cognizable	Bailable	Any Magistrate.
157	Harbouring persons hired for an unlawful assembly.	Imprisonment for 6 months, or fine, or both.	Cognizable	Bailable	Any Magistrate.
158	Being hired to take part in an unlawful assembly or riot.	Imprisonment for 6 months, or fine, or both.	Cognizable	Bailable	Any Magistrate.
	Or to go armed.	Imprisonment for 2 years, or fine or both.	Cognizable	Bailable	Any Magistrate.
160	Committing affray.	Imprisonment for one month, or fine of 100 rupees, or both.	Cognizable	Bailable	Any Magistrate.

1. Subs. by Act 25 of 2005, sec. 42(b), for "Ditto" (enforcement date yet to be notified).

Section	Offence	Punishment	Cognizable or non-cognizable	Bailable or non-bailable	By what court triable
1	2	3	4	5	6
		CHAPTER IX—OFFENCES BY OR RELATING TO PUBLIC SERVANTS			
*161	Being or expecting to be a public servant, and taking a gratification other than legal remuneration in respect of an official act.	Imprisonment for 3 years, or fine, or both.	Cognizable	Non-Bailable	Magistrate of the first class.
*162	Taking a gratification in order, by corrupt or illegal means, to influence a public servant.	Imprisonment for 3 years, or fine, or both.	Cognizable	Non-Bailable	Magistrate of the first class.
*163	Taking a gratification for the exercise of personal influence with a public servant.	Simple imprisonment for 1 year, or fine, or both.	Cognizable	Non-Bailable	Magistrate of the first class.
*164	Abetment by public servant of the offences defined in the last two preceding clauses with reference to himself.	Imprisonment for 3 years, or fine, or both.	Cognizable	Non-Bailable	Magistrate of the first class.
*165	Public servant obtaining any valuable thing, without consideration, from a person concerned in any proceeding or business transacted by such public servant.	Imprisonment for 3 years, or fine, or both.	Cognizable	Non-Bailable	Magistrate of the first class.
*165A	Punishment for abetment of offences punishable under section 161 or section 165.	Imprisonment for 3 years, or fine, or both.	Cognizable	Non-Bailable	Magistrate of the first class.

*. Sections 161 to 165A of the Indian Penal Code (45 of 1860) repealed by the Prevention of Corruption Act, 1988 (49 of 1988), sec. 31 (w.e.f. 9-9-1988).

Section	Offence	Punishment	Cognizable or non-cognizable	Bailable or non-bailable	By what court triable
1	2	3	4	5	6
166	Public servant disobeying a direction of the law with intent to cause injury to any person.	Simple imprisonment for 1 year, or fine, or both.	Non-cognizable	Bailable	Magistrate of the first class.
[1][166A	Public servant disobeying direction under law	Imprisonment for minimum 6 months which may extend to 2 years and fine	Cognizable	Bailable	Magistrate of the first class.]
[1][166B	Non-treatment of victim by hospital	Imprisonment for 1 year or fine or both	Non-cognizable	Bailable	Magistrate of the first class.]
167	Public servant framing an incorrect document with intent to cause injury.	Imprisonment for 3 years, or fine or both.	Cognizable	Bailable	Magistrate of the first class.
168	Public servant unlawfully engaging in trade.	Simple imprisonment for 1 year, or fine, or both.	Non-cognizable	Bailable	Magistrate of the first class.
169	Public servant unlawfully buying or bidding for property.	Simple imprisonment for 2 years, or fine, or both and confiscation of property, if purchased.	Non-cognizable	Bailable	Magistrate of the first class.
170	Personating a Public servant.	Imprisonment for 2 years, or fine, or both.	Cognizable	Non-bailable	Any Magistrate.
171	Wearing garb or carrying token used by public servant with fraudulent intent.	Imprisonment for 3 months, or fine of 200 rupees, or both.	Cognizable	Bailable	Any Magistrate.
		CHAPTER IXA—OFFENCES RELATING TO ELECTIONS			
171E	Bribery.	Imprisonment for 1 year, or fine, or both, or if treating only, fine only.	Non-cognizable	Bailable	Magistrate of the first class.
171F	Undue influence at an election.	Imprisonment for 1 year, or fine, or both.	Non-cognizable	Bailable	Magistrate of the first class.

1. Ins. by Act 13 of 2013, sec. 24(a) (w.r.e.f. 3-2-2013).

Section	Offence	Punishment	Cognizable or non-cognizable	Bailable or non-bailable	By what court triable
1	2	3	4	5	6
	Personation at an election.	Imprisonment for 1 year, or fine, or both.	Cognizable	Bailable	Magistrate of the first class.
171G	False statement in connection with an election.	Fine.	Non-cognizable	Bailable	Magistrate of the first class.
171H	Illegal payments in connection with elections.	Fine of 500 rupees.	Non-cognizable	Bailable	Magistrate of the first class.
171-I	Failure to keep election accounts.	Fine of 500 rupees.	Non-cognizable	Bailable	Magistrate of the first class.
		CHAPTER X—CONTEMPTS OF THE LAWFUL AUTHORITY OF PUBLIC SERVANTS			
172	Absconding to avoid service of summons or other proceeding from a public servant.	Simple imprisonment for 1 month, or fine of 500 rupees, or both.	Non-cognizable	Bailable	Any Magistrate.
	If summons or notice require attendance in person, etc., in a Court of Justice.	Simple imprisonment for 6 months, or fine of 1,000 rupees, or both.	Non-cognizable	Bailable	Any Magistrate
173.	Preventing the service or the affixing of any summons of notice, or the removal of it when it has been affixed, or preventing a proclamation,	Simple imprisonment for 1 month or fine of 500 rupees, or both.	Non-cognizable	Bailable	Any Magistrate.
	If summons, etc., require attendance in person, etc., in a Court of Justice.	Simple imprisonment for 6 months, or fine of 1,000 rupees, or both.	Non-cognizable	Bailable	Any Magistrate.
174	Not obeying a legal order to attend at a certain place in person or by agent, or departing therefrom without authority.	Simple imprisonment for 1 month, or fine of 500 rupees, or both.	Non-cognizable	Bailable	Any Magistrate.

Section	Offence	Punishment	Cognizable or non-cognizable	Bailable or non-bailable	By what court triable
1	2	3	4	5	6
	If the order requires personal attendance, etc., in Court of Justice.	Simple imprisonment for 6 months, or fine of 1,000 rupees, or both.	Non-cognizable	Bailable	Any Magistrate.
[1][174A	Failure to appear at specified place and specified time as required by a proclamation published under sub-section (1) of section 82 of this Code.	Imprisonment for 3 years or with fine, or with both.	Cognizable	Non-bailable	Magistrate of the first class.
	In a case where declaration has been made under sub-section (4) of section 82 of this Code pronouncing a person as proclaimed offender.	Imprisonment for 7 years and fine.	Cognizable	Non-bailable	Magistrate of the first class.]
175	Intentionally omitting to produce a document to a public servant by a person legally bound to produce or deliver such document.	Simple imprisonment for 1 month, or fine of 500 rupees or both.	[2][Non-cognizable]	[3][Bailable]	The Court in which the offence is committed, subject to the provisions of Chapter XXVI; or, if not committed in a Court, any Magistrate.
	If the document is required to be produced in or delivered to a Court of Justice.	Simple imprisonment for 6 months, or fine of 1,000 rupees, or both.	Non-cognizable	Bailable	The Court in which the offence is committed, subject to the provision of Chapter XXVI; or, if not committed in a Court, any Magistrate.
176	Intentionally omitting to give notice or information to a public servant by a person legally bound to give such notice or information.	Simple imprisonment for 1 month, or fine of 500 rupees, or both.	Non-cognizable	Bailable	Any Magistrate.

1. Ins. by Act 25 of 2005, sec. 42(c) (w.e.f. 23-6-2006).

Section	Offence	Punishment	Cognizable or non-cognizable	Bailable or non-bailable	By what court triable
1	2	3	4	5	6
	If the notice or information required respects the commission of an offence, etc.	Simple imprisonment for 6 months, or fine of 1,000 rupees or both.	Non-cognizable	Bailable	Any Magistrate.
	If the notice or information is required by an order passed under sub-section (1) of section 356 of this Code.	Imprisonment for 6 months, or fine of 1,000 rupees, or both	Non-cognizable	Bailable	Any Magistrate.
177	Knowingly furnishing false information to a public servant.	Imprisonment for 6 months, or fine of 1,000 rupees, or both	Non-cognizable	Bailable	Any Magistrate.
	If the information required respects the commission of an offence, etc,	Imprisonment for 2 years, or fine, or both.	Non-cognizable	Bailable	Any Magistrate.
178	Refusing oath when duly required to take oath by a public servant.	Simple imprisonment for 6 months, or fine of 1,000 rupees, or both	Non-cognizable	Bailable	The Court in which the offence is committed, subject to the provisions of Chapter XXVI; or, if not committed in a Court, any Magistrate.
179	Being legally bound to state truth, and refusing to answer questions.	Simple imprisonment for 6 months, or fine of 1,000 rupees, or both.	Non-cognizable	Bailable	The Court in which the offence is committed, subject to the provision of Chapter XXVI; or, it not committed in a Court, any Magistrate.

Section	Offence	Punishment	Cognizable or non-cognizable	Bailable or non-bailable	By what court triable
1	2	3	4	5	6
180	Refusing to sign a statement made to a public servant when legally required to do so.	Simple imprisonment for 3 months, or fine of 500 rupees, or both.	Non-cognizable	Bailable	The Court in which the offence is committed, subject to the provision of Chapter XXVI; or, it not committed in a Court, any Magistrate.
181	Knowingly stating to a public servant, on oath as true that which is false.	Imprisonment for 3 years and fine.	Non-cognizable	Bailable	Magistrate of the first class.
182	Giving false information to a public servant in order to cause him to use his lawful power to the injury or annoyance of any person.	Imprisonment for 6 months, or fine of 1,000 rupees, or both.	Non-cognizable	Bailable	Any Magistrate.
183	Resistance to the taking of property by the lawful authority of a public servant.	Imprisonment for 6 months, or fine of 1,000 rupees, or both.	Non-cognizable	Bailable	Any Magistrate.
184	Obstructing sale of property offered for sale by authority of a public servant.	Imprisonment for 1 month, or fine of 500 rupees, or both.	Non-cognizable	Bailable	Any Magistrate.
185	Bidding, by a person under a legal incapacity to purchase it, for property at a lawfully authorised sale, or bidding without intending to perform the obligations incurred thereby.	Imprisonment for 1 month, or fine of 200 rupees, or both.	Non-cognizable	Bailable	Any Magistrate.

Section	Offence	Punishment	Cognizable or non-cognizable	Bailable or non-bailable	By what court triable
1	2	3	4	5	6
186	Obstructing public servant in discharge of his public functions.	Imprisonment for 3 months, or fine of 500 rupees, or both.	Non-cognizable	Bailable	Any Magistrate.

STATE AMENDMENT

Andhra Pradesh:

Offence under section 186 is cognizable.

[*Vide* A.P.G.O. Ms No. 732, dated 5th December, 1991.]

Section	Offence	Punishment	Cognizable or non-cognizable	Bailable or non-bailable	By what court triable
187	Omission to assist public servant when bound by law to give such assistance.	Simple imprisonment for 1 month, or fine of 200 rupees, or both.	Non-cognizable	Bailable	Any Magistrate.
	Wilfully neglecting to aid a public servant who demands aid in the execution of process, the prevention of offences, etc.	Simple imprisonment for 6 months, or fine of 500 rupees, or both.	Non-cognizable	Bailable	Any Magistrate.
188	Disobedience to an order lawfully promulgated by a public servant, if such disobedience causes obstruction, annoyance or injury to persons lawfully employed.	Simple imprisonment for one month, or fine of 200 rupees, or both.	Cognizable	Bailable	Any Magistrate.
	If such disobedience causes danger to human life, health or safety, etc.	Imprisonment for 6 months, or fine of 1,000 rupees, or both.	Cognizable	Bailable	Any Magistrate.

Section	Offence	Punishment	Cognizable or non-cognizable	Bailable or non-bailable	By what court triable
1	2	3	4	5	6
STATE AMENDMENT					
Andhra Pradesh:					
Offence under section 188 is non-bailable.					
[*Vide* A.P.G.O. Ms No. 732, dated 5th December, 1991.]					
189	Threatening a public servant with injury to him or one in whom he is interested, to induce him to do or forbear to do any official act.	Imprisonment for 2 years or fine, or both.	Non-cognizable	Bailable	Any Magistrate.
STATE AMENDMENT					
Andhra Pradesh:					
Offence under section 189 is cognizable.					
[*Vide* A.P.G.O. Ms No. 732, dated 5th December, 1991.]					
190	Threatening any person to induce him to refrain from making a legal application for protection from injury.	Imprisonment for 1 year, or fine, or both.	Non-cognizable	Bailable	Any Magistrate.
STATE AMENDMENT					
Andhra Pradesh:					
Offence under section 190 is cognizable.					
[*Vide* A.P.G.O. Ms No. 732, dated 5th December, 1991.]					
CHAPTER XI—FALSE EVIDENCE AND OFFENCES AGAINST PUBLIC JUSTICE					
193	Giving or fabricating false evidence in a judicial proceeding.	Imprisonment for 7 years and fine.	Non-cognizable	Bailable	Magistrate of the first class.

Section	Offence	Punishment	Cognizable or non-cognizable	Bailable or non-bailable	By what court triable
1	2	3	4	5	6
	Giving or fabricating false evidence in any other case.	Imprisonment for 3 years and fine.	Non-cognizable	Bailable	Any Magistrate.
194	Giving or fabricating false evidence with intent to cause any person to be convicted of a capital offence.	Imprisonment for life, or rigorous imprisonment for 10 years and fine.	Non-cognizable	Non-Bailable	Court of Session.
	If innocent person be thereby convicted and executed.	Death, or as above.	Non-cognizable	Non-Bailable	Court of Session.
195	Giving or fabricating false evidence with intent to procure conviction of an offence punishable with imprisonment for life or with imprisonment for 7 years or upwards.	The same as for the offence.	Non-cognizable	Non-Bailable	Court of Session.
[1][195A	Threatening any person to give false evidence.	Imprisonment for 7 years, or fine, or both.	Cognizable	Non-Bailable	Court by which offence of giving false evidence is triable.
	If innocent person is convicted and sentenced in consequence of false evidence with death, or imprisonment for more than seven years.	The same as for the offence.	Cognizable	Non-Bailable	Court by which offence of giving false evidence is triable.]
196	Using in a judicial proceeding evidence known to be false or fabricated.	The same as for giving or fabricating false evidence.	Non-cognizable	According as offence of giving such evidence is bailable or non-bailable.	Court by which offence of giving or fabricating false evidence is triable.

1. Ins. by Act 2 of 2006, sec. 7(a) (w.e.f. 16-4-2006).

Section	Offence	Punishment	Cognizable or non-cognizable	Bailable or non-bailable	By what court triable
1	2	3	4	5	6
197	Knowingly issuing or signing a false certificate relating to any fact of which such certificate is by law admissible in evidence.	The same as for giving or fabricating false evidence.	Non-cognizable	Bailable	Court by which offence of giving false evidence is triable.
198	Using as a true certificate one known to be false in a material point.	The same as for giving or fabricating false evidence.	Non-cognizable	Bailable	Court by which offence of giving false evidence is triable.
199	False statement made in any declaration which is by law receivable as evidence.	The same as for giving or fabricating false evidence.	Non-cognizable	Bailable	Court by which offence of giving false evidence is triable.
200	Using as true any such declaration known to be false.	The same as for giving or fabricating false evidence.	Non-cognizable	Bailable	Court by which offence of giving false evidence is triable.
201	Causing disappearance of evidence of an offence committed, or giving false information touching it to screen the offender, if a capital offence.	Imprisonment for 7 years and fine.	According as the offence in relation to which disappearance of evidence is caused is cognizable or non-cognizable.	Bailable	Court of Session.
	If punishable with imprisonment for life or imprisonment for 10 years.	Imprisonment for 3 years and fine.	Non-cognizable	Bailable	Magistrate of the first class.
	If punishable with less than 10 years' imprisonment.	Imprisonment for a quarter of the longest term provided for the offence, or fine, or both.	Non-cognizable	Bailable	Court by which the offence is triable.

Section	Offence	Punishment	Cognizable or non-cognizable	Bailable or non-bailable	By what court triable
1	2	3	4	5	6
202	Intentional omission to give information of an offence by a person legally bound to inform.	Imprisonment for 6 months, or fine, or both.	Non-cognizable	Bailable	Any Magistrate.
203	Giving false information respecting an offence committed.	Imprisonment for 2 years or fine, or both.	Non-cognizable	Bailable	Any Magistrate.
204	Secreting or destroying any document to prevent its production as evidence.	Imprisonment for 2 years or fine, or both.	Non-cognizable	Bailable	Magistrate of the first class.
205	False personation for the purpose of any act or proceeding in a suit or criminal prosecution, or for becoming bail or security.	Imprisonment for 3 years, or fine, or both.	Non-cognizable	Bailable	Magistrate of the first class.
206	Fraudulent removal or concealment, etc., of property to prevent its seizure as a forfeiture, or in satisfaction of a fine under sentence, or in execution of a decree.	Imprisonment for 2 years, or fine, or both.	Non-cognizable	Bailable	Any Magistrate.
207	Claiming property without right, or practising deception touching any right to it, to prevent its being taken as a forfeiture or in satisfaction of a fine under sentence, or in execution of a decree.	Imprisonment for 2 years, or fine, or both.	Non-cognizable	Bailable	Any Magistrate.

Section	Offence	Punishment	Cognizable or non-cognizable	Bailable or non-bailable	By what court triable
1	2	3	4	5	6
208	Fraudulently suffering a decree to pass for a sum not due, or suffering decree to be executed after it has been satisfied.	Imprisonment for 2 years, or fine, or both.	Non-cognizable	Bailable	Magistrate of the first class.
209	False claim in a Court of Justice.	Imprisonment for 2 years and fine.	Non-cognizable	Bailable	Magistrate of the first class.
210	Fraudulently obtaining a decree for a sum not due, or causing a decree to be executed after it has been satisfied.	Imprisonment for 2 years, or fine, or both.	Non-cognizable	Bailable	Magistrate of the first class.
211	False charge of offence made with intent to injure.	Imprisonment for 2 years, or fine, or both.	Non-cognizable	Bailable	Magistrate of the first class.
	If offence charged be punishable with imprisonment for 7 years or upwards.	Imprisonment for 7 years and fine.	Non-cognizable	Bailable	Magistrate of the first class.
	If offence charged be capital or punishable with imprisonment for life.	Imprisonment for 7 years and fine.	Non-cognizable	Bailable	Court of Session.
212	Harbouring an offender, if the offence be capital.	Imprisonment for 5 years and fine.	Cognizable	Bailable	Magistrate of the first class.
	If punishable with imprisonment for life or with imprisonment for 10 years,	Imprisonment for 3 years and fine.	Cognizable	Bailable	Magistrate of the first class.

Section	Offence	Punishment	Cognizable or non-cognizable	Bailable or non-bailable	By what court triable
1	2	3	4	5	6
	If punishable with imprisonment for 1 year and not for 10 years.	Imprisonment for a quarter of the longest term, and of the description, provided for the offence, or fine, or both.	Cognizable	Bailable	Magistrate of the first class.
213	Taking gift, etc., to screen an offender from punishment if the offence be capital.	Imprisonment for 7 years and fine.	Cognizable	Bailable	Magistrate of the first class.
	If punishable with imprisonment for life or with imprisonment for 10 years.	Imprisonment for 3 years and fine.	Cognizable	Bailable	Magistrate of the first class.
	If punishable with imprisonment for less than 10 years.	Imprisonment for a quarter of the longest term provided for the offence, or fine, or both	Cognizable	Bailable	Magistrate of the first class.
214	Offering gift or restoration of property in consideration of screening offender if the offence be capital.	Imprisonment for 7 years and fine.	Cognizable	Bailable	Magistrate of the first class.
	If punishable with imprisonment for life or with imprisonment for 10 years.	Imprisonment for 3 years and fine.	Non-cognizable	Bailable	Magistrate of the first class.
	If punishable with imprisonment for less than 10 years.	Imprisonment for a quarter of the longest term provided for the offence, or fine, or both.	Non-cognizable	Bailable	Magistrate of the first class.

Section	Offence	Punishment	Cognizable or non-cognizable	Bailable or non-bailable	By what court triable
1	2	3	4	5	6
215	Taking gift to help to recover movable property of which a person has been deprived by an offence without causing apprehension of offender.	Imprisonment for 2 years, or fine, or both.	Cognizable	Bailable	Magistrate of the first class.
216	Harbouring an offender who has escaped from custody, or whose apprehension has been ordered, if the offence be capital.	Imprisonment for 7 years and fine.	Cognizable	Bailable	Magistrate of the first class.
	If punishable with imprisonment for life or with imprisonment for 10 years.	Imprisonment for 3 years, with or without fine.	Cognizable	Bailable	Magistrate of the first class.
	If punishable with imprisonment for 1 year and not for 10 years.	Imprisonment for a quarter of the longest term provided for the offence, or fine, or both.	Cognizable	Bailable	Magistrate of the first class.
216A	Harbouring robbers or dacoits.	Rigorous imprisonment for 7 years and fine.	Cognizable	Bailable	Magistrate of the first class.
217	Public servant disobeying a direction of law with intent to save person from punishment, or property from forfeiture.	Imprisonment for 2 years, or fine or both.	Non-cognizable	Bailable	Any Magistrate.
218	Public servant framing an incorrect record or writing with intent to save person from punishment, or property from forfeiture.	Imprisonment for 3 years, or fine, or both.	Cognizable	Bailable	Magistrate of the first class.

Section	Offence	Punishment	Cognizable or non-cognizable	Bailable or non-bailable	By what court triable
1	2	3	4	5	6
219	Public servant in a judicial proceeding corruptly making and pronouncing an order, report, verdict, or decision which he knows to be contrary to law.	Imprisonment for 7 years, or fine, or both.	Non-cognizable	Bailable	Magistrate of the first class.
220	Commitment for trial or confinement by a person having authority, who knows that he is acting contrary to law.	Imprisonment for 7 years, or fine, or both.	Non-cognizable	Bailable	Magistrate of the first class.
221	Intentional omission to apprehend on the part of a public servant bound by law to apprehend an offender, if the offence be capital.	Imprisonment for 7 years, with or without fine.	According as the offence in relation to which such omission has been made is cognizable or non-cognizable.	Bailable	Magistrate of the first class.
	If punishable with imprisonment for life or imprisonment for 10 years.	Imprisonment for 3 years, with or without fine.	Cognizable	Bailable	Magistrate of the first class.
	If punishable with imprisonment for less than 10 years.	Imprisonment for 2 years, with or without fine.	Cognizable	Bailable	Magistrate of the first class.
222	Intentional omission to apprehend on the part of a public servant bound by law to apprehend person under sentence of a Court of Justice if under sentence of death.	Imprisonment for life, or imprisonment for 14 years, with or without fine.	Cognizable	Non-bailable	Court of Session.

Section	Offence	Punishment	Cognizable or non-cognizable	Bailable or non-bailable	By what court triable
1	2	3	4	5	6
	If under sentence of imprisonment for life or imprisonment for 10 years, or upwards	Imprisonment for 7 years, with or without fine.	Cognizable	Non-bailable	Magistrate of the first class.
	If under sentence of imprisonment for less than 10 years or lawfully committed to custody.	Imprisonment for 3 years, or fine, or both.	Cognizable	Bailable	Magistrate of the first class.
223	Escape from confinement negligently suffered by a public servant.	Simple imprisonment for 2 years or fine, or both.	Non-cognizable	Bailable	Any Magistrate.
224	Resistance or obstruction by a person to his lawful apprehension.	Imprisonment for 2 years, or fine or both.	Cognizable	Bailable	Any Magistrate.
225	Resistance or obstruction to the lawful apprehension of any person, or rescuing him from lawful custody.	Imprisonment for 2 years, or fine or both.	Cognizable	Bailable	Any Magistrate.
	If charged with an offence punishable with imprisonment for life or, imprisonment for 10 years.	Imprisonment for 3 years and fine.	Cognizable	Non-Bailable	Magistrate of the first class.
	If charged with a capital offence.	Imprisonment for 7 years and fine.	Cognizable	Non-Bailable	Magistrate of the first class.
	If the person is sentenced to imprisonment for life, or imprisonment for 10 years, or upwards.	Imprisonment for 7 years and fine.	Cognizable	Non-bailable	Magistrate of the first class.

Section	Offence	Punishment	Cognizable or non-cognizable	Bailable or non-bailable	By what court triable
1	2	3	4	5	6
	If under sentence of death.	Imprisonment for life, or imprisonment for 10 years and fine.	Cognizable	Non-bailable	Court of Session.
225A	Omission to apprehend, or sufferance of escape on part of public servant, in cases not otherwise provided for—				
	(a) in case of intentional omission or sufferance.	Imprisonment for 3 years, or fine, or both.	Non-cognizable	Bailable	Magistrate of the first class.
	(b) in case of negligent omission or sufferance.	Simple imprisonment for 2 years, or fine, or both.	Non-cognizable	Bailable	Any Magistrate.
225B	Resistance or obstruction to lawful apprehension, or escape or rescue in cases not otherwise provided for.	Imprisonment for 6 months, or fine, or both.	Cognizable	Bailable	Any Magistrate.
227	Violation of condition of remission of punishment.	Punishment of original sentence, or if part of the punishment has been undergone, the residue.	Cognizable	Non-bailable	The Court by which the original offence was triable.
228	Intentional insult or interruption to a public servant sitting in any stage of a judicial proceeding.	Simple imprisonment for 6 months, or fine of 1,000 rupees, or both	Non-cognizable	Bailable	The Court in which the offence is committed subject to the provisions of Chapter XXVI.

STATE AMENDMENT

Andhra Pradesh:

Offence under section 228 is cognizable.

[*Vide* A.P.G.O. Ms No. 732, dated 5th December, 1991.]

Section	Offence	Punishment	Cognizable or non-cognizable	Bailable or non-bailable	By what court triable
1	2	3	4	5	6
[1][228A	Disclosure of identity of the victim of certain offences, etc.	Imprisonment for two years and fine.	Cognizable	Bailable	Any Magistrate.
	Printing or publication of a proceeding without prior permission of court	Imprisonment for two years and fine.	Cognizable	Bailable	Any Magistrate.]
229	Personation of a juror or assessor.	Imprisonment for 2 years, or fine or both.	Non-cognizable	Bailable.	Magistrate of the first class.
[2][229A	Failure by person released on bail or bond to appear in Court.	Imprisonment for 1 year, or fine or both.	Cognizable	Non-bailable	Any Magistrate.]
	CHAPTER XII—OFFENCES RELATING TO COIN AND GOVERNMENT STAMPS				
231	Counterfeiting, or performing any part of the process of counterfeiting coin.	Imprisonment for 7 years and fine.	Cognizable	Non-bailable	Magistrate of the first class.
232	Counterfeiting, or performing any part of the process of counterfeiting Indian coin.	Imprisonment for life, or imprisonment for 10 years and fine.	Cognizable	Non-bailable	Court of Session.
233	Making, buying or selling instrument for the purpose of counterfeiting coin.	Imprisonment for 3 years and fine.	Cognizable	Non-bailable	Magistrate of the first class.
234	Making, buying or selling instrument for the purpose of counterfeiting Indian coin.	Imprisonment for 7 years and fine	Cognizable	Non-bailable	Court of Session.

1. Ins. by Act 43 of 1983, sec. 5(a) (w.e.f. 25-12-1983).
2. Ins. by Act 25 of 2005, sec. 42(e) (w.e.f. 23-6-2006).

Section	Offence	Punishment	Cognizable or non-cognizable	Bailable or non-bailable	By what court triable
1	2	3	4	5	6
235	Possession of instrument or material for the purpose of using the same for counterfeiting coin.	Imprisonment for 3 years and fine.	Cognizable	Non-bailable	Magistrate of the first class.
	If Indian coin.	Imprisonment for 10 years and fine.	Cognizable	Non-bailable	Court of Session.
236	Abetting, in India, the counterfeiting, out of India, of coin.	The punishment provided for abetting the counterfeiting of such coin within India.	Cognizable	Non-bailable	Court of Session.
237	Import or export of counterfeit coin, knowing the same to be counterfeit.	Imprisonment for 3 years and fine.	Cognizable	Non-bailable	Magistrate of the first class.
238	Import or export of counterfeit of Indian coin, knowing the same to be counterfeit.	Imprisonment for life, or Imprisonment for 10 years and fine.	Cognizable	Non-bailable	Court of Session.
239	Having any counterfeit coin known to be such when it came into possession, and delivering, etc., the same to any person.	Imprisonment for 5 years and fine.	Cognizable	Non-bailable	Magistrate of the first class.
240	Same with respect to Indian coin.	Imprisonment for 10 years and fine.	Cognizable	Non-bailable	Court of Session.
241	Knowingly delivering to another any counterfeit coin as genuine, which, when first possessed, the deliverer did not know to be counterfeit.	Imprisonment for 2 years, or fine, or 10 times the value of the coin counterfeited, or both.	Cognizable	Non-bailable	Any Magistrate

Section	Offence	Punishment	Cognizable or non-cognizable	Bailable or non-bailable	By what court triable
1	2	3	4	5	6
242	Possession of counterfeit coin by a person who knew it to be counterfeit when he became possessed thereof.	Imprisonment for 3 years and fine.	Cognizable	Non-bailable	Magistrate of the first class.
243	Possession of Indian coin by a person who knew it to be counterfeit when he became possessed thereof.	Imprisonment for 7 years and fine.	Cognizable	Non-bailable	Magistrate of the first class.
244	Person employed in a Mint causing coin to be of a different weight or composition from that fixed by law.	Imprisonment for 7 years and fine.	Cognizable	Non-bailable	Magistrate of the first class.
245	Unlawfully taking from a Mint any coining instrument.	Imprisonment for 7 years and fine.	Cognizable	Non-bailable	Magistrate of the first class.
246	Fraudulently diminishing the weight or altering the composition of any coin.	Imprisonment for 3 years and fine.	Cognizable	Non-bailable	Magistrate of the first class.
247	Fraudulently diminishing the weight or altering the composition of Indian coin.	Imprisonment for 7 years and fine.	Cognizable	Non-bailable	Magistrate of the first class.
248	Altering appearance of any coin with intent that it shall pass as a coin of a different description.	Imprisonment for 3 years and fine.	Cognizable	Non-bailable	Magistrate of the first class.

Section	Offence	Punishment	Cognizable or non-cognizable	Bailable or non-bailable	By what court triable
1	2	3	4	5	6
249	Altering appearance of Indian coin with intent that it shall pass as a coin of a different description.	Imprisonment for 7 years and fine.	Cognizable	Non-bailable	Magistrate of the first class.
250	Delivery to another of coin possessed with the knowledge that it is altered.	Imprisonment for 5 years and fine.	Cognizable	Non-bailable	Magistrate of the first class.
251	Delivery of Indian coin possessed with the knowledge that it is altered.	Imprisonment for 10 years and fine.	Cognizable	Non-bailable	Court of Session.
252	Possession of altered coin by a person who knew it to be altered when he became possessed thereof.	Imprisonment for 3 years and fine.	Cognizable	Non-bailable	Magistrate of the first class.
253	Possession of Indian coin by a person who knew it to be altered when he became possessed thereof.	Imprisonment for 5 years and fine.	Cognizable	Non-bailable	Magistrate of the first class.
254	Delivery to another of coin as genuine which, when first possessed, the deliverer did not know to be altered.	Imprisonment for 2 years, or fine, or 10 times the value of the coin.	Cognizable	Non-bailable	Any Magistrate.
255	Counterfeiting a Government stamp.	Imprisonment for life, or imprisonment for 10 years and fine.	Cognizable	Non-bailable	Court of Session.

Section	Offence	Punishment	Cognizable or non-cognizable	Bailable or non-bailable	By what court triable
1	2	3	4	5	6
256	Having possession of an instrument or material for the purpose of counterfeiting a Government stamp.	Imprisonment for 7 years and fine.	Cognizable	Non-bailable	Magistrate of the first class.
257	Making, buying or selling instrument for the purpose of counterfeiting a Government stamp.	Imprisonment for 7 years and fine.	Cognizable	Non-bailable	Magistrate of the first class.
258	Sale of counterfeit Government stamp.	Imprisonment for 7 years and fine.	Cognizable	Non-bailable	Magistrate of the first class.
259	Having possession of a counterfeit Government stamp.	Imprisonment for 7 years and fine.	Cognizable	Bailable	Magistrate of the first class.
260	Using as genuine a Government stamp known to be counterfeit.	Imprisonment for 7 years, or fine, or both.	Cognizable	Bailable	Magistrate of the first class.
261	Effacing any writing from a substance bearing a Government stamp, or removing from a document a stamp used for it, with intent to cause a loss to Government.	Imprisonment for 3 years, or fine, or both.	Cognizable	Bailable	Magistrate of the first class.
262	Using a Government stamp known to have been before used.	Imprisonment for 2 years, or fine, or both.	Cognizable	Bailable	Any Magistrate.
263	Erasure of mark denoting that stamps have been used.	Imprisonment for 3 years or fine, or both.	Cognizable	Bailable	Magistrate of the first class.

Section	Offence	Punishment	Cognizable or non-cognizable	Bailable or non-bailable	By what court triable
1	2	3	4	5	6
263A	Fictitious stamps.	Fine of 200 rupees.	Cognizable	Bailable	Any Magistrate.
		CHAPTER XIII—OFFENCES RELATING TO WEIGHTS AND MEASURES			
264	Fraudulent use of false instrument for weighing.	Imprisonment for 1 year, or fine, or both.	Non-cognizable	Bailable	Any Magistrate.
265	Fraudulent use of false weight or measure.	Imprisonment for 1 year, or fine, or both.	Non-cognizable	Bailable	Any Magistrate.
266	Being in possession of false weights or measures for fraudulent use.	Imprisonment for 1 year, or fine, or both.	Non-cognizable	Bailable	Any Magistrate.
267	Making or selling false weights or measures for fraudulent use.	Imprisonment for 1 year, or fine, or both.	Cognizable	Non-bailable	Any Magistrate.
		CHAPTER XIV—OFFENCES AFFECTING THE PUBLIC HEALTH, SAFETY, CONVENIENCE, DECENCY AND MORALS			
269	Negligently doing any act known to be likely to spread infection of any disease dangerous to life.	Imprisonment for 6 months, or fine, or both.	Cognizable	Bailable	Any Magistrate.
270	Malignantly doing any act known to be likely to spread infection of any disease dangerous to life.	Imprisonment for 2 years, or fine, or both.	Cognizable	Bailable	Any Magistrate.
271	Knowingly disobeying any quarantine rule.	Imprisonment for 6 months, or fine, or both.	Non-cognizable	Bailable	Any Magistrate.

Section	Offence	Punishment	Cognizable or non-cognizable	Bailable or non-bailable	By what court triable
1	2	3	4	5	6
272	Adulterating food or drink intended for sale, so as to make the same noxious.	Imprisonment for 6 months, or fine of 1,000 rupees, or both.	Non-cognizable	Bailable	Any Magistrate.
273	Selling any food or drink as food and drink, knowing the same to be noxious.	Imprisonment for 6 months, or fine of 1,000 rupees, or both.	Non-cognizable	Bailable	Any Magistrate.
274	Adulterating any drug or medical preparation intended for sale so as to lessen its efficacy, or to change its operation, or to make it noxious.	Imprisonment for 6 months, or fine of 1,000 rupees, or both.	Non-cognizable	[1][Non-bailable]	Any Magistrate.
275	Offering for sale or issuing from a dispensary any drug or medical preparation known to have been adulterated.	Imprisonment for 6 months, or fine of 1,000 rupees, or both.	Non-cognizable	[2][Bailable]	Any Magistrate.
276	Knowingly selling or issuing from a dispensary any drug or medical preparation as a different drug or medical preparation.	Imprisonment for 6 months, or fine of 1,000 rupees, or both.	Non-cognizable	Bailable	Any Magistrate.

STATE AMENDMENTS

Orissa:

For the entries relating to sections 272, 273, 274, 275 and 276, substitute the following entries, namely:—

"272	*Adulterating food or drink intended for sale, so as to make the same noxious.*	*Imprisonment for life, and fine.*	*Cognizable*	*Non-bailable*	*Court of Session.*

1. Subs. by Act 25 of 2005, sec. 42(f)(i), for "Bailable" (w.e.f. 23-6-2006).
2. Subs. by Act 25 of 2005, sec. 42(f)(ii), for "Ditto" (w.e.f. 23-6-2006).

Section	Offence	Punishment	Cognizable or non-cognizable	Bailable or non-bailable	By what court triable
1	2	3	4	5	6
273	*Selling any food or drink as food and drink, knowing the same to be noxious.*	*Imprisonment for life, and fine.*	*Cognizable*	*Non-bailable*	*Court of Session.*
274	*Adulterating any drug or medical preparation intended for sale so as to lessen its efficacy, or to change its operation, or to make it noxious.*	*Imprisonment for life, and fine.*	*Cognizable*	*Non-bailable*	*Court of Session.*
275	*Offering for sale or issuing from a dispensary any drug or medical preparation known to have been adulterated.*	*Imprisonment for life, and fine.*	*Cognizable*	*Non-bailable*	*Court of Session.*
276	*Knowingly selling or issuing from a dispensary any drug or medical preparation as a different drug or medical preparation.*	*Imprisonment for life, and fine.*	*Cognizable*	*Non-bailable*	*Court of Session."*

[*Vide* Orissa Act 6 of 2004, sec. 4.]

Uttar Pradesh:

For the entries relating to sections 272, 273, 274, 275 and 276, substitute the following entries, namely:—

"272	*Adulterating food or drink intended for sale, so as to make the same noxious.*	*Imprisonment for life, with or without fine*	*Cognizable*	*Non-bailable*	*Court of Session.*
273	*Selling any food or drink as food and drink, knowing the same to be noxious.*	*Imprisonment for life, with or without fine*	*Cognizable*	*Non-bailable*	*Court of Session.*

Section	Offence	Punishment	Cognizable or non-cognizable	Bailable or non-bailable	By what court triable
1	2	3	4	5	6
274	*Adulterating any drug or medical preparation intended for sale so as to lessen its efficacy, or to change its operation, or to make it noxious.*	*Imprisonment for life, with or without fine*	*Cognizable*	*Non-bailable*	*Court of Session.*
275	*Offering for sale or issuing from a dispensary any drug or medical preparation known to have been adulterated.*	*Imprisonment for life, with or without fine*	*Cognizable*	*Non-bailable*	*Court of Session.*
276	*Knowingly selling or issuing from a dispensary any drug or medical preparation as a different drug or medical preparation*	*Imprisonment for life, with or without fine*	*Cognizable*	*Non-bailable*	*Court of Session."*

[*Vide* Uttar Pradesh Act 47 of 1975, sec. 5 (w.e.f. 15-9-1975).]

West Bengal:

For the entries relating to sections 272, 273, 274, 275 and 276, substitute, the following entries, namely:—

Section	Offence	Punishment	Cognizable or non-cognizable	Bailable or non-bailable	By what court triable
"272	*Adulterating food or drink intended for sale, so as to make the same noxious.*	*Imprisonment for life, with or without fine.*	*Cognizable*	*Non-bailable*	*Court of Session.*
273	*Selling any food or drink, as food and drink, knowing the same to be noxious.*	*Imprisonment for life, with or without fine.*	*Cognizable*	*Non-bailable*	*Court of Session.*
274	*Adulterating any drug or medical preparation intended for sale so as to lessen its efficacy, or to change its operation, or to make it noxious.*	*Imprisonment for life, with or without fine.*	*Cognizable*	*Non-bailable*	*Court of Session.*

Section	Offence	Punishment	Cognizable or non-cognizable	Bailable or non-bailable	By what court triable
1	2	3	4	5	6
275	*Offering for sale or issuing from a dispensary any drug or medical preparation known to have been adulterated.*	*Imprisonment for life, with or without fine.*	*Cognizable*	*Non-bailable*	*Court of Session.*
276	*Knowingly selling or issuing from a dispensary any drug or medical preparation as a different drug or medical preparation.*	*Imprisonment for life, with or without fine.*	*Cognizable*	*Non-bailable*	*Court of Session."*
[*Vide* West Bengal Act 34 of 1974, sec. 5 (w.e.f. 16-7-1974).]					
277	Defiling the water of a public spring or reservoir.	Imprisonment for 3 months, or fine of 500 rupees, or both	Cognizable	Bailable	Any Magistrate.
278	Making atmosphere noxious to health.	Fine of 500 rupees	Non-cognizable	Bailable	Any Magistrate.
279	Driving or riding on a public way so rashly or negligently as to endanger human life, etc.	Imprisonment for 6 months, or fine of 1,000 rupees, or both.	Cognizable	Bailable	Any Magistrate.
280	Navigating any vessel so rashly or negligently as to endanger human life, etc.	Imprisonment for 6 months, or fine of 1,000 rupees, or both.	Cognizable	Bailable	Any Magistrate.
281	Exhibition of a false light, mark or buoy.	Imprisonment for 7 years, or fine, or both.	Cognizable	Bailable	Magistrate of the first class.
282	Conveying for hire any person by water, in a vessel in such a state, or so loaded, as to endanger his life.	Imprisonment for 6 months, or fine of 1,000 rupees, or both.	Cognizable	Bailable	Any Magistrate.

Section	Offence	Punishment	Cognizable or non-cognizable	Bailable or non-bailable	By what court triable
1	2	3	4	5	6
283	Causing danger, obstruction or, injury in any public way or line of navigation.	Fine of 200 rupees.	Cognizable	Bailable	Any Magistrate.
284	Dealing with any poisonous substance so as to endanger human life, etc.	Imprisonment for 6 months, or fine of 1,000 rupees, or both.	Cognizable	Bailable	Any Magistrate.
285	Dealing with fire or any combustible matter so as to endanger human life, etc.	Imprisonment for 6 months, or fine of 1,000 rupees, or both.	Cognizable	Bailable	Any Magistrate.
286	So dealing with any explosive substance.	Imprisonment for 6 months, or fine of 1,000 rupees, or both.	Cognizable	Bailable	Any Magistrate.
287	So dealing with any machinery.	Imprisonment for 6 months, or fine of 1,000 rupees, or both.	Non-cognizable	Bailable	Any Magistrate.
288	A person omitting to guard against probable danger to human life by the fall of any building over which he has a right entitling him to pull it down or repair it.	Imprisonment for 6 months, or fine of 1,000 rupees, or both.	Non-cognizable	Bailable	Any Magistrate.
289	A person omitting to take order with any animal in his possession, so as to guard against danger to human life, or of grievous hurt, from such animal.	Imprisonment for 6 months, or fine of 1,000 rupees, or both.	Cognizable	Bailable	Any Magistrate.
290	Committing a public nuisance.	Fine of 200 rupees.	Non-cognizable	Bailable	Any Magistrate.

Section	Offence	Punishment	Cognizable or non-cognizable	Bailable or non-bailable	By what court triable
1	2	3	4	5	6
291	Continuance of nuisance after injunction to discontinue.	Simple imprisonment for 6 months, or fine, or both.	Cognizable	Bailable	Any Magistrate.
292	Sale, etc., of obscene books, etc.	On first conviction, with imprisonment for 2 years, and with fine of 2,000 rupees and, in the event of second or subsequent conviction, with imprisonment for five years and with fine of 5,000 rupees	Cognizable	Bailable	Any Magistrate.

STATE AMENDMENTS

Orissa:

After the entries relating to section 292, insert the following entries, namely:—

"292A	*Printing*, etc. *of grossly indecent or scurrilous matter or matter intended for blackmail.*	*Imprisonment of either description for 2 years, or fine, or both.*	*Non-Cognizable*	*Bailable*	*Any Magistrate."*

[*Vide* Orissa Act 13 of 1962, sec. 3 (w.e.f. 16-5-1962).]

Tamil Nadu:

After the entries relating to section 292, insert the following entries, namely:—

"292A	*Printing*, etc. *of grossly indecent or scurrilous matter or matter intended for blackmail.*	*Imprisonment of either description for 2 years, or fine, or both.*	*Non-Cognizable*	*Bailable*	*Any Magistrate."*

[*Vide* Tamil Nadu Act 30 of 1984, sec. 3(ii) (w.e.f. 2-7-1984).] **Ed.** Earlier entries relating to section 292A and 293 were substituted by Tamil Nadu Act 13 of 1982, sec. 3(ii) (w.r.e.f. 21-9-1981).

Section	Offence	Punishment	Cognizable or non-cognizable	Bailable or non-bailable	By what court triable
1	2	3	4	5	6
293	Sale, etc., of obscene objects to young persons.	On first conviction with imprisonment for 3 years, and with fine of 2,000 rupees, and in the event of second or subsequent conviction, with imprisonment for 7 years, and with fine of 5,000 rupees.	Cognizable	Bailable	Any Magistrate.
294	Obscene songs.	Imprisonment for 3 months, or fine, or both	Cognizable	Bailable	Any Magistrate.
294A	Keeping a lottery office.	Imprisonment for 6 months, or fine, or both.	Non-cognizable	Bailable	Any Magistrate.
	Publishing proposals relating to lotteries.	Fine of 1,000 rupees.	Non-cognizable	Bailable	Any Magistrate.

STATE AMENDMENTS

Andhra Pradesh:

Entries relating to section 294A have been repealed.

[*Vide* Andhra Pradesh Act 16 of 1968, sec. 27.]

Gujarat:

Entries relating to section 294A have been repealed.

[*Vide* Bombay Act 82 of 1958.]

Maharashtra:

Entries relating to section 294A have been repealed

[*Vide* Bombay Act 82 of 1958.]

Section	Offence	Punishment	Cognizable or non-cognizable	Bailable or non-bailable	By what court triable
1	2	3	4	5	6

Mysore (Karnataka):

In its application to the whole of Mysore except Bellary District, entries relating to section 294A have been repealed.

[*Vide* Mysore Act 27 of 1951.]

Uttar Pradesh:

Entries relating to section 294A have been repealed.

[*Vide* Uttar Pradesh Act 24 of 1995, sec. 11.]

Chapter XV—Offences Relating to Religion

Section	Offence	Punishment	Cognizable or non-cognizable	Bailable or non-bailable	By what court triable
295	Destroying, damaging or defiling a place of worship or sacred object with intent to insult the religion of any class of persons.	Imprisonment for 2 years, or fine, or both.	Cognizable	Non-bailable	Any Magistrate.
295A	Maliciously insulting the religion or the religious beliefs of any class.	Imprisonment for 3 years, or fine, or both.	Cognizable	Non-bailable	Magistrate of the first class.

STATE AMENDMENT

Andhra Pradesh:

Offence under section 295A is cognizable.

[*Vide* A.P.G.O. Ms. No. 732, dated 5th December, 1991.]

Section	Offence	Punishment	Cognizable or non-cognizable	Bailable or non-bailable	By what court triable
296	Causing a disturbance to an assembly engaged in religious worship.	Imprisonment for 1 year, or fine or both.	Cognizable	Bailable	Any Magistrate.
297	Trespassing in place of worship or sepulchre, disturbing funeral with intention to wound the feelings or to insult the religion of any person, or offering indignity to a human corpse.	Imprisonment for 1 year, or fine or both.	Cognizable	Bailable	Any Magistrate.

Section	Offence	Punishment	Cognizable or non-cognizable	Bailable or non-bailable	By what court triable
1	2	3	4	5	6
298	Uttering any word or making any sound in the hearing or making any gesture, or placing any object in the sight of any person, with intention to wound his religious feelings.	Imprisonment for 1 year, or fine or both.	Non-cognizable	Bailable	Any Magistrate.

STATE AMENDMENT

Andhra Pradesh:

Offence under section 298 is cognizable.

[*Vide* A.P.G.O. Ms. No. 732, dated 5th December, 1991.]

CHAPTER XVI—OFFENCES AFFECTING THE HUMAN BODY

Section	Offence	Punishment	Cognizable or non-cognizable	Bailable or non-bailable	By what court triable
302	Murder.	Death, or imprisonment for life, and fine.	Cognizable	Non-bailable	Court of Session.
303	Murder by a person under sentence of imprisonment for life.	Death.	Cognizable	Non-bailable	Court of Session.
304	Culpable homicide not amounting to murder, if act by which the death is caused is done with intention of causing death, etc.	Imprisonment for life, or imprisonment for 10 years and fine.	Cognizable	Non-bailable	Court of Session.
	If act is done with knowledge that it is likely to cause death, but without any intention to cause death, etc.	Imprisonment for 10 years or fine, or both.	Cognizable	Non-bailable	Court of Session.
304A	Causing death by rash or negligent act.	Imprisonment for 2 years, or fine or both.	Cognizable	Bailable	Magistrate of the first class.

Section	Offence	Punishment	Cognizable or non-cognizable	Bailable or non-bailable	By what court triable
1	2	3	4	5	6
[1][304B	Dowry death.	Imprisonment of not less than 7 years but which may extend to imprisonment for life.	Cognizable	Non-bailable	Court of Session.]
305	Abetment of suicide committed by child or insane or delirious person or an idiot, or a person intoxicated.	Death, or imprisonment for life, or imprisonment for 10 years and fine.	Cognizable	Non-bailable	Court of Session.
306	Abetting the commission of suicide.	Imprisonment for 10 years and fine.	Cognizable	Non-bailable	Court of Session.
307	Attempt to murder.	Imprisonment for 10 years and fine.	Cognizable	Non-bailable	Court of Session.
	If such act causes hurt to any person.	Imprisonment for life or imprisonment for 10 years and fine.	Cognizable	Non-bailable	Court of Session.
	Attempt by life-convict to murder, if hurt is caused.	Death or imprisonment for 10 years, and fine,	Cognizable	Non-bailable	Court of Session.
308	Attempt to commit culpable homicide.	Imprisonment for 3 years or fine, or both.	Cognizable	Non-bailable	Court of Session.
	If such act causes hurt to any person.	Imprisonment for 7 years, or fine, or both.	Cognizable	Non-bailable	Court of Session.
309	Attempt to commit suicide.	Simple imprisonment for 1 year, or fine, or both.	Cognizable	Bailable	Any Magistrate.

1. Ins. by Act 43 of 1986, sec. 11 (w.e.f. 19-11-1986).

Section	Offence	Punishment	Cognizable or non-cognizable	Bailable or non-bailable	By what court triable
1	2	3	4	5	6
311	Being a thug.	Imprisonment for life and fine.	Cognizable	Non-bailable	Court of session.
312	Causing miscarriage.	Imprisonment for 3 years and fine or both.	Non-cognizable	Bailable	Magistrate of the first class.
	If the woman be quick with child.	Imprisonment for 7 years and fine.	Non-cognizable	Bailable	Magistrate of the first class.
313	Causing miscarriage without woman's consent.	Imprisonment for life, or imprisonment for 10 years and fine.	Cognizable	Non-bailable	Court of Session.
314	Death caused by an act done with intent to cause miscarriage.	Imprisonment for 10 years and fine.	Cognizable	Non-bailable	Court of Session.
	If act done without woman's consent.	Imprisonment for life, or as above.	Cognizable	Non-bailable	Court of Session.
315	Act done with intent to prevent a child being born alive, or to cause it to die after its birth.	Imprisonment for 10 years, or fine, or both.	Cognizable	Non-bailable	Court of Session.
316	Causing death of a quick unborn child by an act amounting to culpable homicide.	Imprisonment for 10 years, or fine.	Cognizable	Non-bailable	Court of Session.
317	Exposure of a child under 12 years of age by parent or person having care of it with intention of wholly abandoning it.	Imprisonment for 7 years, or fine, or both.	Cognizable	Bailable	Magistrate of the first class.

Section	Offence	Punishment	Cognizable or non-cognizable	Bailable or non-bailable	By what court triable
1	2	3	4	5	6
318	Concealment of birth by secret disposal of dead body.	Imprisonment for 2 years, or fine or both.	Cognizable	Bailable	Magistrate of the first class.

STATE AMENDMENT

Madhya Pradesh:

In the entries relating to sections 317 and 318, in column 6, for the words "Magistrate of the first class", substitute the words "Court of Session". [*Vide* The Code of Criminal Procedure (Madhya Pradesh Amendment) Act, 2007 (Madhya Pradesh Act 2 of 2008), sec. 4 (w.e.f. 14-2-2008).]

Section	Offence	Punishment	Cognizable or non-cognizable	Bailable or non-bailable	By what court triable
323	Voluntarily causing hurt.	Imprisonment for 1 year, or fine of 1,000 rupees, or both.	Non-cognizable	Bailable	Any Magistrate.
324	Voluntarily causing hurt by dangerous weapons or means.	Imprisonment for 3 years, or fine, or both.	Cognizable	[1][Non-bailable]	Any Magistrate.
325	Voluntarily causing grievous hurt.	Imprisonment for 7 years and fine.	Cognizable	[2][Bailable]	Any Magistrate.
326	Voluntarily causing grievous hurt by dangerous weapons or means.	Imprisonment for life, or imprisonment for 10 years and fine.	Cognizable	Non-bailable	Magistrate of the first class.
[3][326A	Voluntarily causing grievous hurt by use of acid, etc.	Imprisonment for not less than 10 years but which may extend to imprisonment for life and fine to be paid to the victim.	Cognizable	Non-bailable	Court of Session.]
[3][326B	Voluntarily throwing or attempting to throw acid.	Imprisonment for 5 years but which may extend to 7 years and with fine.	Cognizable	Non-bailable	Court of Session.]

1. Subs. by Act 25 of 2005, sec. 42(f)(iii), for "Bailable" (effective date yet to be notified).
2. Subs. by Act 25 of 2005, sec. 42(f)(iv), for "Ditto" (effective date yet to be notified).
3. Ins. by Act 13 of 2013, sec. 24(b) (w.r.e.f. 3-2-2013).

Section	Offence	Punishment	Cognizable or non-cognizable	Bailable or non-bailable	By what court triable
1	2	3	4	5	6

STATE AMENDMENT

Madhya Pradesh:

In the entries relating to section 326, in column 6, for the words "Magistrate of the first class", substitute the words "Court of Session".

[*Vide* The Code of Criminal Procedure (Madhya Pradesh Amendment) Act, 2007 (Madhya Pradesh Act 2 of 2008), sec. 4 (w.e.f. 14-2-2008).]

Section	Offence	Punishment	Cognizable or non-cognizable	Bailable or non-bailable	By what court triable
327	Voluntarily causing hurt to extort property or a valuable security, or to constrain to do anything which is illegal or which may facilitate the commission of an offence.	Imprisonment for 10 years and fine.	Cognizable	Non-bailable	Magistrate of the first class.
328	Administering stupefying drug with intent to cause hurt, etc.	Imprisonment for 10 years and fine.	Cognizable	Non-bailable	Court of Session.
329	Voluntarily causing grievous hurt to extort property or a valuable security, or to constrain to do anything which is illegal, or which may facilitate the commission of an offence.	Imprisonment for life, or imprisonment for 10 years and fine.	Cognizable	Non-bailable	Court of Session.
330	Voluntarily causing hurt to extort confession or information, or to compel restoration of property, etc.	Imprisonment for 7 years and fine.	Cognizable	Bailable	Magistrate of the first class.
331	Voluntarily causing grievous hurt to extort confession or information or to compel restoration of property, etc.	Imprisonment for 10 years and fine.	Cognizable	Non-bailable	Court of Session.

Section	Offence	Punishment	Cognizable or non-cognizable	Bailable or non-bailable	By what court triable
1	2	3	4	5	6
332	Voluntarily causing hurt to deter public servant from his duty.	Imprisonment for 3 years or fine, or both.	Cognizable	[1][Non-bailable]	Magistrate of the first class.
333	Voluntarily causing grievous hurt to deter public servant from his duty.	Imprisonment for 10 years and fine.	Cognizable	[2][Non-bailable]	Court of Session.
334	Voluntarily causing hurt on grave and sudden provocation, not intending to hurt any other than the person who gave the provocation.	Imprisonment for 1 month, or fine of 500 rupees, or both.	Non-cognizable	Bailable	Any Magistrate.
335	Causing grievous hurt on grave and sudden provocation, not intending to hurt any other than the person who gave the provocation.	Imprisonment for 4 years, or fine of 2,000 rupees, or both.	Cognizable	Bailable	Magistrate of the first class.
336	Doing any act which endangers human life or the personal safety of others.	Imprisonment for 3 months, or fine of 250 rupees, or both	Cognizable	Bailable	Any Magistrate.
337	Causing hurt by an act which endangers human life, etc.	Imprisonment for 6 months, or fine of 500 rupees, or both.	Cognizable	Bailable	Any Magistrate.
338	Causing grievous hurt by an act which endangers human life, etc.	Imprisonment for 2 years, or fine of 1,000 rupees, or both	Cognizable	Bailable	Any Magistrate.

1. Subs. by Act 25 of 2005, sec. 42(f)(v), for "Bailable" (w.e.f. 23-6-2006).
2. Subs. by Act 25 of 2005, sec. 42(f)(vi) (w.e.f. 23-6-2006).

Section	Offence	Punishment	Cognizable or non-cognizable	Bailable or non-bailable	By what court triable
1	2	3	4	5	6
341	Wrongfully restraining any person.	Simple imprisonment for 1 month, or fine of 500 rupees, or both.	Cognizable	Bailable	Any Magistrate.
342	Wrongfully confining any person.	Imprisonment for 1 year, or fine of 1,000 rupees, or both.	Cognizable	Bailable	Any Magistrate.
343	Wrongfully confining for 3 or more days.	Imprisonment for 2 years, or fine, or both.	Cognizable	Bailable	Any Magistrate.
344	Wrongfully confining for 10 or more days.	Imprisonment for 3 years and fine.	Cognizable	Bailable	Any Magistrate.
345	Keeping any person in wrongful confinement, knowing that a writ has been issued for his liberation.	Imprisonment for 2 years in addition to imprisonment under any other section.	Cognizable	Bailable	Magistrate of the first class.
346	Wrongful confinement in secret.	Imprisonment for 2 years in addition to imprisonment under any other section.	Cognizable	Bailable	Magistrate of the first class.
347	Wrongful confinement for the purpose of extorting property, or constraining to an illegal act, etc.	Imprisonment for 3 years and fine.	Cognizable	Bailable	Any Magistrate.
348	Wrongful confinement for the purpose of extorting confession or information, or of compelling restoration of property, etc.	Imprisonment for 3 years and fine.	Cognizable	Bailable	Any Magistrate.

Section	Offence	Punishment	Cognizable or non-cognizable	Bailable or non-bailable	By what court triable
1	2	3	4	5	6
352	Assault or use of criminal force otherwise than on grave provocation.	Imprisonment for 3 months, or fine of 500 rupees, or both.	Non-cognizable	Bailable	Any Magistrate.
353	Assault or use of criminal force to deter a public servant from discharge of his duty.	Imprisonment for 2 years, or fine, or both.	Cognizable	[1][Non-bailable]	Any Magistrate.
[2][354	Assault or use of criminal force to woman with intent to outrage her modesty.	Imprisonment of 1 year which may extend to 5 years, and with fine.	Cognizable	Non-bailable	Any Magistrate.]
[2][354A	Sexual harassment of the nature of unwelcome physical contact and advances or a demand or request for sexual favours, showing pornography	Imprisonment which may extend to 3 years or with fine or with both.	Cognizable	Bailable	Any Magistrate.
	Sexual harassment of the nature of making sexually coloured remark.	Imprisonment which may extend to 1 year or with fine or with both.	Cognizable	Bailable	Any Magistrate.]
[2][354B	Assault or use of criminal force to woman with intent to disrobe.	Imprisonment of not less than 3 years but which may extend to 7 years and with fine.	Cognizable	Non-bailable	Any Magistrate.]
[2][354C	Voyeurism.	Imprisonment of not less than 1 year but which may extend to 3 years and with fine for first conviction.	Cognizable	Bailable	Any Magistrate.

1. Subs. by Act 25 of 2005, sec. 42(f)(vii), for "Bailable" (w.e.f. 23-6-2006).
2. Subs. by Act 13 of 2013, sec. 24(c) (w.r.e.f. 3-2-2013).

Section	Offence	Punishment	Cognizable or non-cognizable	Bailable or non-bailable	By what court triable
1	2	3	4	5	6
		Imprisonment of not less than 3 years but which may extend to 7 years and with fine for second or subsequent conviction.	Cognizable	Non-bailable	Any Magistrate.]
[1][354D	Stalking.	Imprisonment up to 3 years and with fine for first conviction.	Cognizable	Bailable	Any Magistrate.
		Imprisonment up to 5 years and with fine for second or subsequent conviction	Cognizable	Non-bailable	Any Magistrate.]

STATE AMENDMENTS

Madhya Pradesh:

After the entries relating to section 354, insert the following entries, namely:—

"354A Asault or use of criminal force to woman with intend to disrobe her.	*Imprisonment of not less than one year but which may extend to ten years and fine.*	*Cognizable*	*Non-bailable*	*Court of Session."*

[*Vide* Madhya Pradesh Act 15 of 2004, sec. 5 (w.e.f. 26-11-2004).]

Orissa:

The offence under section 354 is Non-bailable.

[*Vide* Orissa Act 6 of 1995, sec. 3 (w.e.f. 10-3-1995).]

1. Subs. by Act 13 of 2013, sec. 24(c) (w.r.e.f. 3-2-2013).

Section	Offence	Punishment	Cognizable or non-cognizable	Bailable or non-bailable	By what court triable
1	2	3	4	5	6
355	Assault or criminal force with intent to dishonour a person, otherwise than on grave and sudden provocation.	Imprisonment for 2 years, or fine, or both.	Non-cognizable	Bailable	Any Magistrate.

STATE AMENDMENTS (Sections 354 and 355)

Andhra Pradesh:

For the entries relating to sections 354 and 355, substitute the following entries, namely:—

"*354*	*Assault or use of criminal force to a woman with intent to outrage her modesty*	*Imprisonment for 7 years and fine.*	*Cognizable*	*Non-bailable*	*Court of Session.*
355	*Assault or criminal force with intent to dishonour a person, otherwise than on grave and sudden provocations.*	*Imprisonment for 2 years, or fine, or both.*	*Non-cognizable*	*Bailable*	*Any Magistrate.*"

[*Vide* Andhra Pradesh Act 3 of 1992, sec. 2 (w.e.f. 15-2-1992).]

356	Assault or criminal force in attempt to commit theft of property worn or carried by a person.	Imprisonment for 2 years, or fine, or both.	Cognizable	Bailable	Any Magistrate.
357	Assault or use of criminal force in attempt wrongfully to confine a person.	Imprisonment for 1 year or fine of 1,000 rupees, or both.	Cognizable	Bailable	Any Magistrate.
358	Assault or use of criminal force on grave and sudden provocation.	Simple imprisonment for one month, or fine of 200 rupees, or both.	Non-cognizable	Bailable	Any Magistrate.

Section	Offence	Punishment	Cognizable or non-cognizable	Bailable or non-bailable	By what court triable
1	2	3	4	5	6
363	Kidnapping.	Imprisonment for 7 years, and fine.	Cognizable	Bailable	Magistrate of the first class.

STATE AMENDMENTS

Madhya Pradesh:

In the entries relating to sections 363, in column 6, for the words "Magistrate of the first class", substitute the words "Court of Session".

[*Vide* The Code of Criminal Procedure (Madhya Pradesh Amendment) Act, 2007 (Madhya Pradesh Act 2 of 2008), sec. 4 (w.e.f. 14-2-2008).]

Uttar Pradesh:

In the entries relating to section 363 in column 5, for the word "Bailable", substitute the word "Non-bailable".

[*Vide* Uttar Pradesh Act 1 of 1984, sec. 12 (w.e.f. 1-5-1984).]

Section	Offence	Punishment	Cognizable or non-cognizable	Bailable or non-bailable	By what court triable
363A	Kidnapping or obtaining the custody of a minor in order that such minor may be employed or used for purposes of begging.	Imprisonment for 10 years and fine.	Cognizable	Non-bailable	Magistrate of the first class.
	Maiming a minor in order that such minor may be employed or used for purposes of begging.	Imprisonment for life and fine.	Cognizable	Non-bailable	Court of Session.

STATE AMENDMENT

Madhya Pradesh:

In the entries relating to section 363A, in column 6, for the words "Magistrate of the first class", substitute the words "Court of Session".

[*Vide* The Code of Criminal Procedure (Madhya Pradesh Amendment) Act, 2007 (Madhya Pradesh Act 2 of 2008), sec. 4 (w.e.f. 14-2-2008).]

Section	Offence	Punishment	Cognizable or non-cognizable	Bailable or non-bailable	By what court triable
364	Kidnapping or abducting in order to murder.	Imprisonment for life, or rigorous imprisonment for 10 years and fine.	Cognizable	Non-bailable	Court of Session.
[1][364A	Kidnapping for ransom, etc.	Death, or imprisonment for life, and fine.	Cognizable	Non-bailable	Court of Session.]

1. Ins. by Act 42 of 1993, sec. 4 (w.e.f. 22-5-1993).

Section	Offence	Punishment	Cognizable or non-cognizable	Bailable or non-bailable	By what court triable
1	2	3	4	5	6
365	Kidnapping or abducting with intent secretly and wrongfully to confine a person.	Imprisonment for 7 years and fine.	Cognizable	Non-bailable	Magistrate of the first class.

STATE AMENDMENT

Madhya Pradesh:

In the entries relating to section 365, in column 6, for the words "Magistrate of the first class", substitute the words "Court of Session".

[*Vide* The Code of Criminal Procedure (Madhya Pradesh Amendment) Act, 2007 (Madhya Pradesh Act 2 of 2008), sec. 4 (w.e.f. 14-2-2008).]

Section	Offence	Punishment	Cognizable or non-cognizable	Bailable or non-bailable	By what court triable
366	Kidnapping or abducting a woman to compel her marriage or to cause her defilement etc.	Imprisonment for 10 years and fine.	Cognizable	Non-bailable	Court of Session.
366A	Procuration of minor girl.	Imprisonment for 10 years and fine.	Cognizable	Non-bailable	Court of Session.
366B	Importation of girl from foreign country.	Imprisonment for 10 years and fine.	Cognizable	Non-bailable	Court of Session.
367	Kidnapping or abducting in order to subject a person to grievous hurt, slavery, etc.	Imprisonment for 10 years and fine.	Cognizable	Non-bailable	Court of Session.
368	Concealing or keeping in confinement a kidnapped person.	Punishment for kidnapping or abduction.	Cognizable	Non-bailable	Court by which the kidnapping or abduction is triable.
369	Kidnapping or abducting a child with intent to take property from the person of such child.	Imprisonment for 7 years and fine.	Cognizable	Non-bailable	Magistrate of the first class.

Section	Offence	Punishment	Cognizable or non-cognizable	Bailable or non-bailable	By what court triable
1	2	3	4	5	6
[1][370	Trafficking of person	Imprisonment of not less than 7 years but which may extend to 10 years and with fine.	Cognizable	Non-bailable	Court of Session.
	Trafficking of more than one person.	Imprisonment of not less than 10 years but which may extend to imprisonment for life and with fine.	Cognizable	Non-bailable	Court of Session.
	Trafficking of a minor	Imprisonment of not less than 10 years but which may extend to imprisonment for life and with fine.	Cognizable	Non-bailable	Court of Session.
	Trafficking of more than one minor	Imprisonment of not less than 14 years but which may extend to imprisonment for life and with fine.	Cognizable	Non-bailable	Court of Session.
	Person convicted of offence of trafficking of minor on more than one occasion.	Imprisonment for life which shall mean the remainder of that person's natural life and with fine.	Cognizable	Non-bailable	Court of Session.
	Public servant or a police officer involved in trafficking of minor.	Imprisonment for life which shall mean the remainder of that person's natural life and with fine.	Cognizable	Non-bailable	Court of Session.]

1. Subs. by Act 13 of 2013, sec. 24(d), for section 370 (w.r.e.f. 3-2-2013).

Section	Offence	Punishment	Cognizable or non-cognizable	Bailable or non-bailable	By what court triable
1	2	3	4	5	6
[1][370A	Exploitation of a trafficked child.	Imprisonment of not less than 5 years but which may extend to 7 years and with fine.	Cognizable	Non-bailable	Court of Session.
	Exploitation of a trafficked person.	Imprisonment of not less than 3 years but which may extend to 5 years and with fine.	Cognizable	Non-bailable	Court of Session.]
371	Habitual dealing in slaves.	Imprisonment for life, or Imprisonment for 10 years and fine.	Cognizable	Non-bailable	Court of Session.
372	Selling or letting to hire a minor for purposes of prostitution, etc.	Imprisonment for 10 years and fine.	Cognizable	Non-bailable	Court of Session.
373	Buying or obtaining possession of a minor for the same purposes.	Imprisonment for 10 years and fine.	Cognizable	Non-bailable	Court of Session.
374	Unlawful compulsory labour.	Imprisonment for 1 year, or fine or both.	Cognizable	Bailable	Any Magistrate.
[2][376	Rape	Rigorous imprisonment of not less than 7 years but which may extend to imprisonment for life and with fine.	Cognizable	Non-bailable	Court of Session.

1. Subs. by Act 13 of 2013, sec. 24(d), for section 370 (w.r.e.f. 3-2-2013).
2. Subs. by Act 13 of 2013, sec. 24(e), for section 376 (w.r.e.f. 3-2-2013).

Section	Offence	Punishment	Cognizable or non-cognizable	Bailable or non-bailable	By what court triable
1	2	3	4	5	6
	Rape by a police officer or a public servant or members of armed forces or a person being on the management or on the staff of a jail, remand home or other place of custody or women's or children's institution or by a person on the management or on the staff of a hospital, and rape committed by a person in a position of trust or authority towards the person raped or by a near relative of the person raped.	Rigorous imprisonment of not less than 10 years but which may extend to imprisonment for life which shall mean the remainder of that person's natural life and with fine.	Cognizable	Non-bailable	Court of Session.]
[1][376A	Person committing an offence of rape and inflicting injury which causes death or causes the woman to be in a persistent vegetative state.	Rigorous imprisonment of not less than 20 years but which may extend to imprisonment for life which shall mean imprisonment for the remainder of that person's natural life or with death.	Cognizable	Non-bailable	Court of Session.]
[2][376B	Sexual intercourse by husband upon his wife during separation.	Imprisonment for not less than 2 years but which may extend to 7 years and with fine.	Cognizable (but only on the complaint of the victim)	Bailable	Court of Session.]

1. Subs. by Act 13 of 2013, sec. 24(e), for section 376A (w.r.e.f. 3-2-2013).
2. Subs. by Act 13 of 2013, sec. 24(e), for section 376B (w.r.e.f. 3-2-2013).

Section	Offence	Punishment	Cognizable or non-cognizable	Bailable or non-bailable	By what court triable
1	2	3	4	5	6
[1][376C	Sexual intercourse by a person in authority.	Rigorous imprisonment for not less than 5 years but which may extend to 10 years and with fine.	Cognizable	Non-bailable	Court of Session.]
[2][376D	Gang rape	Rigorous imprisonment for not less than 20 years but which may extend to imprisonment for life which shall mean imprisonment for the remainder of that person's natural life and with fine to be paid to the victim.	Cognizable	Non-bailable	Court of Session.]
[3][376E	Repeat offenders.	Imprisonment for life which shall mean imprisonment for the remainder of that person's natural life or with death.	Cognizable	Non-bailable	Court of Session.]
[4][377	Unnatural offences.	Imprisonment for life, or imprisonment for ten years and fine.	Cognizable	Non-bailable	Magistrate of the first class.]

1. Subs. by Act 13 of 2013, sec. 24(e), for sec. 376C (w.r.e.f. 3-2-2013).
2. Subs. by Act 13 of 2013, sec. 24(e), for sec. 376D (w.r.e.f. 3-2-2013).
3. Subs. by Act 13 of 2013, sec. 24(e) (w.r.e.f. 3-2-2013).
4. Subs. by Act 30 of 2001, sec. 3 and Second Schedule, for entries relating to section 377 (w.e.f. 3-9-2001).

Section	Offence	Punishment	Cognizable or non-cognizable	Bailable or non-bailable	By what court triable
1	2	3	4	5	6

STATE AMENDMENT

Madhya Pradesh:

In the entries relating to section 377, in column 6, for the words "Magistrate of the first class", substitute the words "Court of Session".

[*Vide* The Code of Criminal Procedure (Madhya Pradesh Amendment) Act, 2007 (Madhya Pradesh Act 2 of 2008), sec. 4 (w.e.f. 14-2-2008).]

CHAPTER XVII—OFFENCES AGAINST PROPERTY

Section	Offence	Punishment	Cognizable or non-cognizable	Bailable or non-bailable	By what court triable
379	Theft.	Imprisonment for 3 years, or fine or both	Cognizable	Non-bailable	Any Magistrate.
380	Theft in a building, tent or vessel.	Imprisonment for 7 years and fine.	Cognizable	Non-bailable	Any Magistrate.
381	Theft by clerk or servant of property in possession of master or employer.	Imprisonment for 7 years and fine.	Cognizable	Non-bailable	Any Magistrate.
382	Theft, after preparation having been made for causing death, or hurt, or restraint or fear of death, or of hurt or of restraint, in order to the committing of such theft, or to retiring after committing it, or to retaining property taken by it.	Rigorous imprisonment for 10 years and fine.	Cognizable	Non-bailable	Magistrate of the first class.
384	Extortion.	Imprisonment for 3 years, or fine, or both.	Cognizable	Non-bailable	Any Magistrate.
385	Putting or attempting to put in fear of injury, in order to commit extortion.	Imprisonment for 2 years, or fine, or both.	Cognizable	Bailable	Any Magistrate.

Section	Offence	Punishment	Cognizable or non-cognizable	Bailable or non-bailable	By what court triable
1	2	3	4	5	6
386	Extortion by putting a person in fear of death or grievous hurt.	Imprisonment for 10 years and fine.	Cognizable	Non-bailable	Magistrate of the first class.
387	Putting or attempting to put a person in fear of death or grievous hurt in order to commit extortion.	Imprisonment for 7 years and fine.	Cognizable	Non-bailable	Magistrate of the first class.
388	Extortion by threat of accusation of an offence punishable with death, imprisonment for life, or imprisonment for 10 years.	Imprisonment for 10 years and fine.	Cognizable	Bailable	Magistrate of the first class.
	If the offence threatened be an unnatural offence.	Imprisonment for life.	Cognizable	Bailable	Magistrate of the first class.
389	Putting a person in fear of accusation of an offence punishable with death, imprisonment for life, or imprisonment for 10 years in order to commit extortion.	Imprisonment for 10 years and fine.	Cognizable	Bailable	Magistrate of the first class.
	If the offence be an unnatural offence.	Imprisonment for life.	Cognizable	Bailable	Magistrate of the first class.
392	Robbery.	Rigorous imprisonment for 10 years and fine.	Cognizable	Non-bailable	Magistrate of the first class.
	If committed on the highway between sunset and sunrise.	Rigorous imprisonment for 14 years and fine.	Cognizable	Non-bailable	Magistrate of the first class.

Section	Offence	Punishment	Cognizable or non-cognizable	Bailable or non-bailable	By what court triable
1	2	3	4	5	6
393	Attempt to commit robbery.	Rigorous imprisonment for 7 years and fine.	Cognizable	Non-bailable	Magistrate of the first class.
394	Person voluntarily causing hurt in committing or attempting to commit robbery, or any other person jointly concerned in such robbery.	Imprisonment for life, or rigorous imprisonment for 10 years and fine.	Cognizable	Non-bailable	Magistrate of the first class.

STATE AMENDMENT

Madhya Pradesh:

In the entries relating to sections 392, 393 and 394, in column 6, for the words "Magistrate of the first class", substitute the words "Court of Session".

[*Vide* The Code of Criminal Procedure (Madhya Pradesh Amendment) Act, 2007 (Madhya Pradesh Act 2 of 2008), sec. 4 (w.e.f. 14-2-2008).]

Section	Offence	Punishment	Cognizable or non-cognizable	Bailable or non-bailable	By what court triable
395	Dacoity.	Imprisonment for life, or rigorous imprisonment for 10 years and fine.	Cognizable	Non-bailable	Court of Session.
396	Murder in Dacoity.	Death, Imprisonment for life, or rigorous imprisonment for 10 years and fine.	Cognizable	Non-bailable	Court of Session.
397	Robbery or dacoity, with attempt to cause death or grievous hurt.	Rigorous imprisonment for not less than 7 years.	Cognizable	Non-bailable	Court of Session.
398	Attempt to commit robbery or dacoity when armed with deadly weapons.	Rigorous imprisonment for not less than 7 years.	Cognizable	Non-bailable	Court of Session.
399	Making preparation to commit dacoity.	Rigorous imprisonment for 10 years and fine.	Cognizable	Non-bailable	Court of Session.

Section	Offence	Punishment	Cognizable or non-cognizable	Bailable or non-bailable	By what court triable
1	2	3	4	5	6
400	Belonging to a gang of persons associated for the purpose of habitually committing dacoity.	Imprisonment for life or rigorous imprisonment for 10 years and fine.	Cognizable	Non-bailable	Court of Session.
401	Belonging to a wandering gang of persons associated for the purpose of habitually committing thefts.	Rigorous imprisonment for 7 years and fine.	Cognizable	Non-bailable	Magistrate of the first class.
402	Being one of five or more persons assembled for the purpose of committing dacoity.	Rigorous imprisonment for 7 years and fine.	Cognizable	Non-bailable	Court of Session.
403	Dishonest misappropriation of movable property, or converting it to one's own use.	Imprisonment for 2 years, or fine, or both.	Non-cognizable	Bailable	Any Magistrate.
404	Dishonest misappropriation of property, knowing that it was in possession of a deceased person at his death, and that it has not since been in the possession of any person legally entitled to it.	Imprisonment for 3 years and fine.	Non-cognizable	Bailable	Magistrate of the first class.
	If by clerk or person employed by deceased.	Imprisonment for 7 years and fine.	Non-cognizable	Bailable	Magistrate of the first class.
406	Criminal breach of trust.	Imprisonment for 3 years or fine, or both	Cognizable	Non-bailable	Magistrate of the first class.
407	Criminal breach of trust by a carrier, wharfinger, etc.	Imprisonment for 7 years and fine.	Cognizable	Non-bailable	Magistrate of the first class.

Section	Offence	Punishment	Cognizable or non-cognizable	Bailable or non-bailable	By what court triable
1	2	3	4	5	6
408	Criminal breach of trust by a clerk or servant.	Imprisonment for 7 years and fine.	Cognizable	Non-bailable	Magistrate of the first class.
409	Criminal breach of trust by public servant or by banker, merchant or agent, etc.	Imprisonment for life, or imprisonment for 10 years and fine.	Cognizable	Non-bailable	Magistrate of the first class.

STATE AMENDMENT

Madhya Pradesh:

In the entries relating to section 409, in column 6, for the words "Magistrate of the first class", substitute the words "Court of Session".

[*Vide* The Code of Criminal Procedure (Madhya Pradesh Amendment) Act, 2007 (Madhya Pradesh Act 2 of 2008), sec. 4 (w.e.f. 14-2-2008).]

Section	Offence	Punishment	Cognizable or non-cognizable	Bailable or non-bailable	By what court triable
411	Dishonestly receiving stolen property knowing it to be stolen.	Imprisonment for 3 years, or fine, or both.	Cognizable	Non-bailable	Any Magistrate.
412	Dishonestly receiving stolen property, knowing that it was obtained by dacoity.	Imprisonment for life, or rigorous imprisonment for 10 years and fine.	Cognizable	Non-bailable	Court of Session.
413	Habitually dealing in stolen property.	Imprisonment for life, or imprisonment for 10 years and fine.	Cognizable	Non-bailable	Court of Session.
414	Assisting in concealment or disposal of stolen property, knowing it to be stolen.	Imprisonment for 3 years, or fine, or both.	Cognizable	Non-bailable	Any Magistrate.
417	Cheating.	Imprisonment for 1 year, or fine, or both.	Non-cognizable	Bailable	Any Magistrate.

Section	Offence	Punishment	Cognizable or non-cognizable	Bailable or non-bailable	By what court triable
1	2	3	4	5	6
418	Cheating a person whose interest the offender was bound, either by law or by legal contract, to protect.	Imprisonment for 3 years, or fine, or both.	Non-cognizable	Bailable	Any Magistrate.
419	Cheating by personation.	Imprisonment for 3 years, or fine, or both.	Cognizable	Bailable	Any Magistrate.
420	Cheating and thereby dishonestly inducing delivery of property, or the making, alteration or destruction of a valuable security.	Imprisonment for 7 years and fine.	Cognizable	Non-bailable	Magistrate of the first class.
421	Fraudulent removal or concealment of property, etc., to prevent distribution among creditors.	Imprisonment for 2 years, or fine, or both.	Non-cognizable	Bailable	Any Magistrate.
422	Fraudulently preventing from being made available for his creditors a debt or demand due to the offender.	Imprisonment for 2 years, or fine, or both.	Non-cognizable	Bailable	Any Magistrate.
423	Fraudulent execution of deed of transfer containing a false statement of consideration.	Imprisonment for 2 years, or fine, or both.	Non-cognizable	Bailable	Any Magistrate.
424	Fraudulent removal or concealment of property of himself or any other person or assisting in the doing thereof, or dishonestly releasing any demand or claim to which he is entitled.	Imprisonment for 2 years, or fine, or both.	Non-cognizable	Bailable	Any Magistrate.

Section	Offence	Punishment	Cognizable or non-cognizable	Bailable or non-bailable	By what court triable
1	2	3	4	5	6
426	Mischief.	Imprisonment for 3 months, or fine, or both	Non-cognizable	Bailable	Any Magistrate.
427	Mischief, and thereby causing damage to the amount of 50 rupees or upwards.	Imprisonment for 2 years, or fine, or both.	Non-cognizable	Bailable	Any Magistrate.
428	Mischief by killing, poisoning, maiming or rendering useless any animal of the value of 10 rupees or upwards.	Imprisonment for 2 years, or fine, or both.	Cognizable	Bailable	Any Magistrate.
429	Mischief by killing poisoning, maiming or rendering useless any elephant, camel, horse, etc., whatever may be its value or any other animal of the value of 50 rupees or upwards.	Imprisonment for 5 years or fine, or both.	Cognizable	Bailable	Magistrate of the first class.
430	Mischief by causing diminution of supply of water for agricultural purposes, etc.	Imprisonment for 5 years or fine, or both.	Cognizable	Bailable	Magistrate of the first class.
431	Mischief by injury to public road, bridge, navigable river, or navigable channel and rendering it impassable or less safe for travelling or conveying property.	Imprisonment for 5 years, or fine, or both.	Cognizable	Bailable	Magistrate of the first class.
432	Mischief by causing inundation or obstruction to public drainage attended with damage.	Imprisonment for 5 years or fine, or both.	Cognizable	Bailable	Magistrate of the first class.

Section	Offence	Punishment	Cognizable or non-cognizable	Bailable or non-bailable	By what court triable
1	2	3	4	5	6
433	Mischief by destroying or moving or rendering less useful a lighthouse or sea-mark, or by exhibiting false lights.	Imprisonment for 7 years, or fine, or both.	Cognizable	Bailable	Magistrate of the first class.
434	Mischief by destroying or moving, etc., a landmark fixed by public authority.	Imprisonment for 1 year, or fine, or both.	Non-cognizable	Bailable	Any Magistrate
435	Mischief by fire or explosive substance with intent to cause damage to an amount of 100 rupees or upwards, or, in case of agricultural produce, 10 rupees or upwards.	Imprisonment for 7 years and fine.	Cognizable	Bailable	Magistrate of the first class.

STATE AMENDMENT

Madhya Pradesh:

In the entries relating to section 435, in column 6, for the words "Magistrate of the first class", substitute the words "Court of Session".

[*Vide* The Code of Criminal Procedure (Madhya Pradesh Amendment) Act, 2007 (Madhya Pradesh Act 2 of 2008), sec. 4 (w.e.f. 14-2-2008).]

Section	Offence	Punishment	Cognizable or non-cognizable	Bailable or non-bailable	By what court triable
436	Mischief by fire or explosive substance with intent to destroy house, etc.	Imprisonment for life, or Imprisonment for 10 years and fine.	Cognizable	Non-bailable	Court of Session.
437	Mischief with intent to destroy or make unsafe a decked vessel or a vessel of 20 tonnes burden.	Imprisonment for 10 years and fine.	Cognizable	Non-bailable	Court of Session.
438	The mischief described in the last section when committed by fire or any explosive substance.	Imprisonment for life, or imprisonment for 10 years, and fine.	Cognizable	Non-bailable	Court of Session.

Section	Offence	Punishment	Cognizable or non-cognizable	Bailable or non-bailable	By what court triable
1	2	3	4	5	6
439	Running vessel ashore with intent to commit theft, etc.	Imprisonment for 10 years and fine.	Cognizable	Non-bailable	Court of Session.
440	Mischief committed after preparation made for causing death, or hurt, etc.	Imprisonment for 5 years and fine.	Cognizable	Bailable	Magistrate of the first class.
447	Criminal trespass.	Imprisonment for 3 months, or fine of 500 rupees or both.	Cognizable	Bailable	Any Magistrate.
448	House-trespass.	Imprisonment for one year, or fine of 1,000 rupees or both.	Cognizable	Bailable	Any Magistrate.
449	House-trespass in order to the commission of an offence punishable with death.	Imprisonment for life, or rigorous imprisonment for 10 years and fine.	Cognizable	Non-bailable	Court of Session.
450	House-trespass in order to the commission of an offence punishable with imprisonment for life.	Imprisonment for 10 years and fine.	Cognizable	Non-bailable	Court of Session.
451	House-trespass in order to the commission of an offence punishable with imprisonment.	Imprisonment for 2 years and fine.	Cognizable	Bailable	Any Magistrate.
	If the offence is theft.	Imprisonment for 7 years and fine.	Cognizable	Non-bailable	Any Magistrate.

Section	Offence	Punishment	Cognizable or non-cognizable	Bailable or non-bailable	By what court triable
1	2	3	4	5	6
452	House-trespass, having made preparation for causing hurt, assault, etc.	Imprisonment for 7 years and fine.	Cognizable	Non-bailable	Any Magistrate.
453	Lurking house trespass or house-breaking.	Imp⁻isonment for 2 years and fine.	Cognizable	Non-bailable	Any Magistrate.
454	Lurking house-trespass or house-breaking in order to the commission of an offence punishable with imprisonment.	Imprisonment for 3 years and fine.	Cognizable	Non-bailable	Any Magistrate.
	If the offence be theft.	Imprisonment for 10 years and fine.	Cognizable	Non-bailable	Magistrate of the first class.
455	Lurking house-trespass or house-breaking after preparation made for causing hurt, assault, etc.	Imprisonment for 10 years and fine.	Cognizable	Non-bailable	Magistrate of the first class.
456	Lurking house-trespass or house-breaking by night.	Imprisonment for 3 years and fine.	Cognizable	Non-bailable	Any Magistrate.
457	Lurking house-trespass or house -breaking by night in order to the commission of an offence punishable with imprisonment.	Imprisonment for 5 years and fine.	Cognizable	Non-bailable	Magistrate of the first class.
	If the offence is theft.	Imprisonment for 14 years and fine.	Cognizable	Non-bailable	Magistrate of the first class.

Section	Offence	Punishment	Cognizable or non-cognizable	Bailable or non-bailable	By what court triable
1	2	3	4	5	6
458	Lurking house-trespass or house-breaking by night, after preparation made for causing hurt, etc.	Imprisonment for 14 years and fine.	Cognizable	Non-bailable	Magistrate of the first class.
459	Grievous hurt caused whilst committing lurking house-trespass or house-breaking.	Imprisonment for life or imprisonment for 10 years and fine.	Cognizable	Non-bailable	Court of Session.
460	Death or grievous hurt caused by one of several persons jointly concerned in house-breaking by night, etc.	Imprisonment for life or imprisonment for 10 years and fine.	Cognizable	Non-bailable	Court of Session.
461	Dishonestly breaking open or unfastening any closed receptacle containing or supposed to contain property.	Imprisonment for 2 years, or fine or both.	Cognizable	Non-bailable	Any Magistrate.
462	Being entrusted with any closed receptacle containing or supposed to contain any property, and fraudulently opening the same.	Imprisonment for 3 years, or fine, or both.	Cognizable	Bailable	Any Magistrate.
	Chapter XVIII—Offences Relating to Documents and to Property Marks				
465	Forgery	Imprisonment for 2 years, or fine, or both.	Non-cognizable	Bailable	Magistrate of the first class.
466	Forgery of a record of a Court of Justice or of a Registrar of Births, etc., kept by a public servant.	Imprisonment for 7 years and fine.	Non-cognizable	Non-Bailable	Magistrate of the first class.

Section	Offence	Punishment	Cognizable or non-cognizable	Bailable or non-bailable	By what court triable
1	2	3	4	5	6
467	Forgery of a valuable security, will or authority to make or transfer any valuable security, or to receive any money, etc.	Imprisonment for life, or imprisonment for 10 years and fine.	Non-cognizable	Non-Bailable	Magistrate of the first class.
	When the valuable security is a promissory note of the Central Government.	Imprisonment for life, or imprisonment for 10 years and fine.	Cognizable	Non-Bailable	Magistrate of the first class.
468	Forgery for the purpose of cheating.	Imprisonment for 7 years and fine.	Cognizable	Non-Bailable	Magistrate of the first class.

STATE AMENDMENT

Madhya Pradesh:

In the entries relating to sections 466, 467 and 468, in column 6, for the words "Magistrate of the first class", substitute the words "Court of Session".

[*Vide* The Code of Criminal Procedure (Madhya Pradesh Amendment) Act, 2007 (Madhya Pradesh Act 2 of 2008), sec. 4 (w.e.f. 14-2-2008).]

Section	Offence	Punishment	Cognizable or non-cognizable	Bailable or non-bailable	By what court triable
469	Forgery for the purpose of harming the reputation of any person or knowing that it is likely to be used for that purpose.	Imprisonment for 3 years and fine.	Cognizable	Bailable	Magistrate of the first class.
471	Using as genuine a forged document which is known to be forged.	Punishment for forgery of such document.	Cognizable	Bailable	Magistrate of the first class.
	When the forged document is a promissory note of the Central Government.	Punishment for forgery of such document.	Cognizable	Bailable	Magistrate of the first class.

Section	Offence	Punishment	Cognizable or non-cognizable	Bailable or non-bailable	By what court triable
1	2	3	4	5	6
472	Making or counterfeiting a seal, plate, etc., with intent to commit a forgery punishable under section 467 of the Indian Penal Code, or possessing with like intent any such seal, plate, etc. knowing the same to be counterfeit.	Imprisonment for life, or imprisonment for 7 years and fine.	Cognizable	Bailable	Magistrate of the first class.
473	Making or counterfeiting a seal, plate, etc., with intent to commit a forgery punishable otherwise than under section 467 of the Indian Penal Code, or possessing with like intent any such seal, plate, etc., knowing the same to be counterfeit.	Imprisonment for 7 years and fine.	Cognizable	Bailable	Magistrate of the first class.
474	Having possession of a document, knowing it to be forged, with intent to use it as genuine; if the document is one of the description mentioned in section 466 of the Indian Penal Code.	Imprisonment for 7 years and fine.	Cognizable	Bailable	Magistrate of the first class..
	If the document is one of the description mentioned in section 467 of the Indian Penal Code.	Imprisonment for life, or imprisonment for 7 years and fine.	Non-cognizable	Bailable	Magistrate of the first class.

Section	Offence	Punishment	Cognizable or non-cognizable	Bailable or non-bailable	By what court triable
1	2	3	4	5	6

STATE AMENDMENT

Madhya Pradesh:

In the entries relating to sections 471, 472, 473 and 474 in column 6, for the words "Magistrate of the first class", substitute the words "Court of Session".

[*Vide* The Code of Criminal Procedure (Madhya Pradesh Amendment) Act, 2007 (Madhya Pradesh Act 2 of 2008), sec. 4 (w.e.f. 14-2-2008).]

Section	Offence	Punishment	Cognizable or non-cognizable	Bailable or non-bailable	By what court triable
475	Counterfeiting a device or mark used for authenticating documents described in section 467 of the Indian Penal Code, or possessing counterfeit marked material.	Imprisonment for life, or imprisonment for 7 years and fine.	Non-cognizable	Bailable	Magistrate of the first class.
476	Counterfeiting a device or mark used for authenticating documents other than those described in section 467 of the Indian Penal Code, or possessing counterfeit marked material.	Imprisonment for 7 years and fine.	Non-cognizable	Non-bailable	Magistrate of the first class.
477	Fraudulently destroying or defacing, or attempting to destroy or deface, or secreting, a Will, etc.	Imprisonment for life, or imprisonment for 7 years and fine.	Non-cognizable	Non-bailable	Magistrate of the first class.
477A	Falsification of accounts.	Imprisonment for 7 years, or fine, or both.	Non-cognizable	Bailable	Magistrate of the first class.

STATE AMENDMENT

Madhya Pradesh:

In the entries relating to sections 475, 476, 477 and 477A, in column 6, for the words "Magistrate of the first class", substitute the words "Court of Session".

[*Vide* The Code of Criminal Procedure (Madhya Pradesh Amendment) Act, 2007 (Madhya Pradesh Act 2 of 2008), sec. 4 (w.e.f. 14-2-2008).]

Section	Offence	Punishment	Cognizable or non-cognizable	Bailable or non-bailable	By what court triable
1	2	3	4	5	6
482	Using a false property mark with intent to deceive or injure any person.	Imprisonment for 1 year, or fine, or both.	Non-cognizable	Bailable	Any Magistrate.
483	Counterfeiting a property mark used by another, with intent to cause damage or injury.	Imprisonment for 2 years, or fine, or both.	Non-cognizable	Bailable	Any Magistrate.
484	Counterfeiting a property mark used by a public servant, or any mark used by him to denote the manufacture, quality, etc., of any property.	Imprisonment for 3 years and fine.	Non-cognizable	Bailable	Magistrate of the first class.
485	Fraudulently marking or having possession of any die, plate or other instrument for counterfeiting any public or private property mark.	Imprisonment for 3 years, or fine, or both.	Non-cognizable	Bailable	Magistrate of the first class.
486	Knowingly selling goods marked with a counterfeit property mark.	Imprisonment for 1 year, or fine, or both.	Non-cognizable	Bailable	Any Magistrate.
487	Fraudulently marking a false mark upon any package or receptacle containing goods, with intent to cause it to be believed that it contains goods which it does not contain, etc.	Imprisonment for 3 years, or fine, or both.	Non-cognizable	Bailable	Any Magistrate.

Section	Offence	Punishment	Cognizable or non-cognizable	Bailable or non-bailable	By what court triable
1	2	3	4	5	6
488	Making use of any such false mark.	Imprisonment for 3 years, or fine, or both.	Non-cognizable	Bailable	Any Magistrate.
489	Removing, destroying or defacing property mark with intent to cause injury.	Imprisonment for 1 year, or fine, or both.	Non-cognizable	Bailable	Any Magistrate.
489A	Counterfeiting currency-notes or bank-notes.	Imprisonment for life, or imprisonment for 10 years and fine.	Cognizable	Non-bailable	Court of Session.
489B	Using as genuine forged or counterfeit currency-notes or bank-notes.	Imprisonment for life, or imprisonment for 10 years and fine.	Cognizable	Non-bailable	Court of Session.
489C	Possession of forged or counterfeit currency-notes or bank-notes.	Imprisonment for 7 years, or fine, or both.	Cognizable	Bailable	Court of Session.
489D	Making or possessing machinery, instrument or material for forging or counterfeiting currency-notes or bank-notes.	Imprisonment for life, or imprisonment for 10 years and fine.	Cognizable	Non-bailable	Court of Session.
489E	Making or using documents resembling currency-notes or bank-notes.	Fine of 100 rupees.	Non-cognizable	Bailable	Any Magistrate.
	On refusal to disclose the name and address of the printer.	Fine of 200 rupees.	Non-cognizable	Bailable	Any Magistrate.

Section	Offence	Punishment	Cognizable or non-cognizable	Bailable or non-bailable	By what court triable
1	2	3	4	5	6
		CHAPTER XIX—CRIMINAL BREACH OF CONTRACTS OF SERVICE			
491	Being bound to attend on or supply the wants of a person who is helpless from youth, unsoundness of mind or disease, and voluntarily omitting to do so.	Imprisonment for 3 months, or fine of 200 rupees or both.	Non-cognizable	Bailable	Any Magistrate.
		CHAPTER XX—OFFENCES RELATING TO MARRIAGE			
493	A man by deceit causing a woman not lawfully married to him to believe that she is lawfully married to him and to cohabit with him in that belief.	Imprisonment for 10 years and fine.	Non-cognizable	Non-bailable	Magistrate of the first class.
494	Marrying again during the lifetime of a husband or wife.	Imprisonment for 7 years and fine.	Non-cognizable	Bailable	Magistrate of the first class.
495	Same offence with concealment of the former marriage from the person with whom subsequent marriage is contracted.	Imprisonment for 10 years and fine.	Non-cognizable	Bailable	Magistrate of the first class.
496	A person with fraudulent intention going through the ceremony of being married knowing that he is not thereby lawfully married.	Imprisonment for 7 years and fine.	Non-cognizable	Bailable	Magistrate of the first class.

Section	Offence	Punishment	Cognizable or non-cognizable	Bailable or non-bailable	By what court triable
1	2	3	4	5	6

STATE AMENDMENTS

Andhra Pradesh:

Offences under sections 494, 495 and 496 are cognizable and non-bailable.

[*Vide* Andhra Pradesh Act 3 of 1992, sec. 2 (w.e.f. 15-2-1992).]

Section	Offence	Punishment	Cognizable or non-cognizable	Bailable or non-bailable	By what court triable
497	Adultery.	Imprisonment for 5 years, or fine, or both.	Non-cognizable	Bailable	Magistrate of the first class.

STATE AMENDMENTS

Andhra Pradesh:

Offence under section 497 is non-cognizable and bailable.

[*Vide* Andhra Pradesh Act 3 of 1993.]

Section	Offence	Punishment	Cognizable or non-cognizable	Bailable or non-bailable	By what court triable
498	Enticing or taking away or detaining with a criminal intent a married woman.	Imprisonment for 2 years, or fine, or both.	Non-cognizable	Bailable	Any Magistrate.

[1][CHAPTER XXA—OF CRUELTY BY HUSBAND OR RELATIVES OF HUSBAND

Section	Offence	Punishment	Cognizable or non-cognizable	Bailable or non-bailable	By what court triable
498A	Punishment for subjecting a married woman to cruelty.	Imprisonment for three years and fine.	Cognizable if information relating to the commission of the offence is given to an officer in charge of a police station by the person aggrieved by the offence or by any person related to her by blood, marriage or adoption or if there in no such relative, by any public servant belonging to such class or category as may be notified by the State Government in this behalf.	Non-bailable	Magistrate of the first class.]

1. Ins. by Act 46 of 1983, sec. 6 (w.e.f. 25-12-1983).

Section	Offence	Punishment	Cognizable or non-cognizable	Bailable or non-bailable	By what court triable
1	2	3	4	5	6
		CHAPTER XXI—DEFAMATION			
500	Defamation against the President or the Vice-president or the Governor of a State or Administrator of a Union territory or a Minister in respect of his conduct in the discharge of his public functions when instituted upon a complaint made by the Public Prosecutor.	Simple imprisonment for 2 years, or fine, or both.	Non-cognizable	Bailable	Court of Session.
	Defamation in any other case.	Simple imprisonment for 2 years, or fine, or both.	Non-cognizable	Bailable	Magistrate of the first class.
501	(a) Printing or engraving matter knowing it to be defamatory against the President or the Vice-President or the Governor of a State or Administrator of a Union territory or a Minister in respect of his conduct in the discharge of his public functions when instituted upon a complaint made by the Public Prosecutor.	Simple imprisonment for 2 years, or fine, or both.	Non-cognizable	Bailable	Court of Session.
	(b) Printing or engraving matter knowing it to be defamatory, in any other case.	Simple imprisonment for 2 years, or fine, or both.	Non-cognizable	Bailable	Magistrate of the first class.

Section	Offence	Punishment	Cognizable or non-cognizable	Bailable or non-bailable	By what court triable
1	2	3	4	5	6
502	(a) Sale of printed or engraved substance containing defamatory matter, knowing it to contain such matter against the President or the Vice-President or the Governor of a State or Administrator of a Union territory or a Minister in respect of his conduct in the discharge of his public functions when instituted upon a complaint made by the Public Prosecutor.	Simple imprisonment for 2 years, or fine, or both.	Non-cognizable	Bailable	Court of Session.
	(b) Sale of printed or engraved substance containing defamatory matter, knowing it to contain such matter in any other case.	Simple imprisonment for 2 years, or fine, or both.	Non-cognizable	Bailable	Magistrate of the first class.
		CHAPTER XXII—CRIMINAL INTIMIDATION, INSULT AND ANNOYANCE			
504	Insult intended to provoke breach of the peace.	Imprisonment for 2 years, or fine, or both.	Non-cognizable	Bailable	Any Magistrate.
505	False statement, rumour, etc,. circulated with intent to cause mutiny or offence against the public peace.	Imprisonment for 3 years, or fine, or both.	Non-cognizable	Non-bailable	Any Magistrate.

Section	Offence	Punishment	Cognizable or non-cognizable	Bailable or non-bailable	By what court triable
1	2	3	4	5	6
	False statement, rumour, etc., with intent to create enmity, hatred or ill-will between different classes.	Imprisonment for 3 years, or fine, or both.	Cognizable	Non-bailable	Any Magistrate.
	False statement, rumour, etc, made in place of worship etc., with intent to create enmity, hatred or ill-will.	Imprisonment for 5 years and fine.	Cognizable	Non-bailable	Any Magistrate.

STATE AMENDMENT

Andhra Pradesh:

Offences under section 505 are Cognizable.

[*Vide* A.P.G.O. Ms. No. 732, dated 5th December, 1991.]

Section	Offence	Punishment	Cognizable or non-cognizable	Bailable or non-bailable	By what court triable
506	Criminal intimidation.	Imprisonment for 2 years, or fine, or both.	Non-cognizable	Bailable	Any Magistrate.
	If threat be to cause death or grievous hurt, etc.	Imprisonment for 7 years or fine, or both.	Non-cognizable	Bailable	Magistrate of the first class.

STATE AMENDMENTS

Andhra Pradesh:

Offences under section 506 are cognizable and non-bailable.

[*Vide* A.P.G.O. Ms. No. 732, dated 5th December, 1991.]

Uttar Pradesh:

The offence under section 506 are cognizable and non-bailable.*

[*Vide* Notification. No. 777/VIII 9-4(2)-87, dated 31st July, 1989, published in U.P. Gazette, Extra., Part A, Section (Kha), dated 2nd August, 1989.]

* The offence is bailable and non-cognizable as decided in *Virendra Singh* v. *State of Uttar Pradesh*, 2002 Cr LJ 4265 (All).

Section	Offence	Punishment	Cognizable or non-cognizable	Bailable or non-bailable	By what court triable
1	2	3	4	5	6
507	Criminal intimidation by anonymous communication or having taken precaution to conceal whence the threat comes.	Imprisonment for 2 years, in addition to the punishment under above section.	Non-cognizable	Bailable	Magistrate of the first class.

STATE AMENDMENT

Andhra Pradesh:

Offence under section 507 is cognizable.

[*Vide* A.P.G.O. Ms. No. 732, dated 5th December, 1991.

Section	Offence	Punishment	Cognizable or non-cognizable	Bailable or non-bailable	By what court triable
508	Act caused by inducing a person to believe that he will be rendered an object of Divine displeasure.	Imprisonment for 1 year, or fine, or both.	Non-cognizable	Bailable	Any Magistrate.
509	Uttering any word or making any gesture intended to insult the modesty of a woman, etc.	[1][Simple imprisonment for 3 years and with fine.]	Cognizable	Bailable	Any Magistrate.
510	Appearing in a public place, etc., in a state of intoxication, and causing annoyance to any person.	Simple imprisonment for 24 hours, or fine of 10 rupees, or both.	Non-cognizable	Bailable	Any Magistrate.
	CHAPTER XXIII—ATTEMPTS TO COMMIT OFFENCES				
511	Attempting to commit offences punishable with imprisonment for life or imprisonment, and in such attempt doing any act towards the commission of the offence.	Imprisonment for life or imprisonment not exceeding half of the longest term provided for the offence, or fine, or both.	According as the offence is cognizable or non-cognizable.	According as the offence attempted by the offender is bailable or not.	The court by which the offence attempted is triable.

1. Subs. by Act 13 of 2013, sec. 24(f), for "Simple imprisonment for one year, or fine, or both" (w.r.e.f. 3-2-2013).

II - Classification of offences Against Other Laws

Offence	Cognizable or non-cognizable	Bailable or non-bailable	By what court triable
1	2	3	4
If punishable with death, imprisonment for life, or imprisonment for more than 7 years,	Cognizable	Non-bailable	Court of Session.
If punishable with imprisonment for 3 years, and upwards but not more than 7 years.	Cognizable	Non-bailable	Magistrate of the first class.
If punishable with imprisonment for less than 3 years or with fine only.	Non-cognizable	Bailable	Any Magistrate.

Section 2(o) of the Code defines officer-in-charge of a police station as in this Code unless the context otherwise requires "Officer-in-charge of a police station" includes when the officer in-charge of the police station in absent from the station- house or unable from illness or other cause to perform his duties, the police officer present at the station-house who is next in rank to such officer or is above the rank of a constable or when the State Government so directs, any other police officer so present. Section 2(n) of the Code defines offence as in this Code unless the context otherwise requires "offence" means any act or omission made punishable by any law for the time being in force and includes any act in respect of which a complaint may be made under section 20 of the Cattle Trespass Act, 1871. Section 3(38) of the General Clauses Act, 1897 defines offence as in this Act and in all Central Acts and Regulations made after the commencement of this Act unless there is anything repugnant in the subject or context offence shall mean any act or omission made punishable by any law for the time being in force. Under the Indian Penal Code offence means.

> *40. "Offence".*—Except in the Chapters and sections mentioned in clauses 2 and 3 of this section, the word "offence" denotes a thing made punishable by this Code.
>
> In Chapter IV, Chapter VA and in the following sections, namely, sections 64, 65, 66, 67, 71, 109, 110, 112, 114, 115, 116, 117, 118, 119, 120, 187, 194, 195, 203, 211, 213, 214, 221, 222, 223, 224, 225, 327, 328, 329, 330, 331, 347, 348, 388, 389 and 445, the word "offence" denotes a thing punishable under this Code, or under any special or local law as hereinafter defined.
>
> And in sections 141, 176, 177, 201, 202, 212, 216 and 441, the word "offence" has the same meaning when the thing punishable under the special or local law is punishable under such law with imprisonment for a term of six months or upwards, whether with or without fine.

Certain penal Legislation contemplate separate procedure, certain of them specify certain provisions in addition to the Code and certain of such Legislations adopting the procedure under the Code. *See* also section 5 of the Code dealing with saving.

In *Central Bureau of Investigation through S.P., Jaipur* v. *State of Rajasthan,* AIR 2001 SC 668: 2001 AIR SCW 305: 2001 Cr LJ 968 (SC) it was held that a Magistrate may direct an officer-in-charge of a police station to conduct investigation under section 156(3) of the Code and this power cannot be exercised by directing CBI to conduct Investigations. In *Dr. A.V. Mohan Rao* v. *M. Kishan Rao,* 2000 (1) ALT (Cri) 532 (AP) while dealing with definition of offence it was held that it does not stipulate that an offence necessarily should take place within the territory of India. In *Vasanti Dubey* v. *State of Madhya Pradesh,* (2012) 2 SCC 731: 2012 Cr LJ 1309: 2012 AIR SCW 962 it was held that even if police report indicates that no case is made out, the

Magistrate can ignore the same and can take cognizance on applying his mind independently to the case and can

(1) Take cognizance so as to proceed under sections 202 and 203 of the Code,

(2) take cognizance under section 190 of the Code at once if be disagrees with the adverse police report but the special Judge or the Magistrate cannot straight away direct submissions of the charge-sheet by the police.

See *H.S. Bains* v. *State,* 1980 Cr LJ 1308: AIR 1980 SC 1883: (1980) 4 SCC 631.

Ram Naresh Prasad v. *State of Jharkhand,* (2009) 11 SCC 299: AIR 2009 SC (Supp) 219: 2009 AIR SCW 1672.

Abhinandan Jha v. *Dinesh Mishra,* AIR 1968 SC 117: (1967) 3 SCR 668: 1968 Cr LJ 97.

Nupur Talwar v. *CBI,* AIR 2012 SC 1921: 2012 (3) Crimes 31: (2012) 5 SCALE 744.

Subramaniam Swamy v. *Manmohan Singh,* AIR 2012 SC 1185: 2012 AIR SCW 1249: 2012 Cr LJ 1519.

The aspect of further investigation was dealt with in *Hasanbhai Valibhai Qureshi* v. *State of Gujarat,* (2004) 5 SCC 347: AIR 2004 SC 2078: 2004 Cr LJ 2018; see *Gururaja Rao* v. *C.I. Alampur,* 2006 (2) ALT (Cri) 121 (AP).

Subramanyam v. *Seshadri,* 2006 (2) ALT (Cri) 206 (AP).

Hemant Dhasmana v. *CBI,* AIR 2001 SC 2721: 2001 Cr LJ 4190: 2001 AIR SCW 3064.

J. Prabhavathiamma v. *State of Kerala,* 2008 (1) Ker LJ 9: 2007 (4) Ker LT 601: 2008 Cr LJ 455 (Ker).

The ordering of Reinvestigation had fallen for conideration in *Union Public Service Commission* v. *S. Papaiah,* AIR 1997 SC 3876: 1997 AIR SCW 3801: 1997 Cr LJ 4636 (SC). Non-forwarding of Documents and Statements under section 173(5) of the Code along with charge-sheet is a curable irregularily observed in *Md. Yusuf Rather* v. *State of West Bengal,* 1998 Cal Cri LR 469: (1999) 1 Cal LJ 389: (1998) 3 Crimes 436 (Cal). For the ambit of section 173 of the Code.

See *Sadhu Narayana* v. *S.H.O.,* 2006 (5) AIR Bom R 880 (NOC): 2006 (1) ALD (Crl) 867: 2006 Cr LJ 3038 (AP).

State of Bihar v. *Chandra Bhushan Singh,* AIR 2001 SC 429: 2001 AIR SCW 16: 2001 Cr LJ 702 (SC).

Moreshwar Savey v. *State of Uttar Pradesh,* 2001 (43) All Cri C 73: 2001 (3) All Cri R 2094: 2001 Cr LJ 1765 (All).

Central Bureau of Investigation v. *M. Thomas,* 2001 (1) Ker LJ 928: 2001 (2) Ker LT 349: 2001 Cr LJ 3167 (Ker).

Anoop Kumar v. *State of Uttar Pradesh,* 2005 (51) All Cri C 505: 2005 (1) All Cri R 844: 2005 Cr LJ 2775 (All).

Ghanashyam Jena v. *State of Orissa,* 2004 (2) All Cri LR 244: 2004 (1) Rec Cri R 671: 2003 Cr LJ 4794 (Ori).

K.M. Natarajan v. *Sasidharan,* 2002 (1) Ker LJ 280: 2002 (1) Ker LT 499: 2002 Cr LJ 1672 (Ker).

Vikas Gupta v. *State of Punjab,* 2002 (2) DMC 45: 2002 (2) Rec Cri R 12: 2002 Cr LJ 4165 (P&H).

Rajneesh Kumar Singhal v. *State,* 2001 (2) Crimes 346: 2001 (89) DLT 511: 2001 Cr LJ 1192 (Del).

T.T. Anthony v. *State of Kerala,* 2001 Cr LJ 3329: AIR 2001 SC 2637: 2001 (5) Supreme 131: 2001 AIR SCW 2571.

Vikram Malhotra v. *CBI,* 2004 (2) Crimes 442 (J&K).

Gangadhar Janardan Mhatre v. *State of Maharashtra,* AIR 2004 SC 4753: 2004 Cr LJ 4623: 2004 AIR SCW 5414 (SC).

Prakash Singh Badal v. *State of Punjab,* 2006 (4) Crimes 388 (SC).

Dinesh Dalmia v. *CBI,* AIR 2008 SC 78: 2008 Cr LJ 337: 2007 (4) Crimes 33 (SC).

Central Bureau of Investigation v. *R.S. Pai,* AIR 2002 SC 1644: 2002 Cr LJ 2029: 2002 AIR SCW 1562.

Resham Lal Yadav v. *State of Bihar,* 1981 BLJ 338: 1981 BLJR 647: 1981 Cr LJ 976 (Pat).

K. Ramasubbu v. *State,* 1987 (1) Crimes 914: 1987 Mad LW (Cri) 79: 1988 Cr LJ 214 (Mad).

Dr. Kapil Garg v. *State,* 2004 Crimes 100 (Del).

Bhagwant Singh v. *Commissioner of Police,* AIR 1985 SC 1285: 1985 Cr LJ 1521: (1985) 2 SCC 537.

Kashmiri Lal Khera v. *State of Haryana,* 1996 (1) Cri CJ 408: 1996 (1) Rec Cri R 410: 1996 Cr LJ 915 (P&H).

Sukhdas v. *State of Rajasthan,* 2001 (1) Raj Cri C 576: 2001 (3) Raj LW 1716: 2001 Cr LJ 3138 (Raj).

Meenakshi Agrawal v. *State of Uttar Pradesh,* 2000 (41) All Cri C 777: 2000 (29) All Cri R 2061: 2001 Cr LJ 395 (All).

State of Delhi v. *Gyan Devi,* 2001 Cr LJ 124: AIR 2001 SC 40: 2000 AIR SCW 3844 (SC).

Brij Mohan Aggarwal v. *State,* 2005 (2) Crimes 219 (All).

Shaji Raghavan Pillai v. *State of Kerala,* 2003 (2) Ker LJ 127: 2003 (2) Ker LT 929: 2004 Cr LJ 187 (Ker).

Leela Das v. *CBI,* 2005 (25) All Ind Cas 911: 2001 Cr LJ 2684 (Cal).

Dr. Neela Lohitha Dasan Nadar v. *State of Kerala,* 2003 (1) Ker LJ 423: 2003 (1) Ker LT 844: 2003 Cr LJ 3327 (Ker).

State v. *Dinakar Balkrishna Palande,* 2005 (2) Crimes 455 (Bom).

State of Bihar v. *Chandra Bhushan Singh,* AIR 2001 SC 429: 2001 AIR SCW 16: 2001 Cr LJ 702 (SC).

Chittappa v. *State,* 2001 AIR Kant HCR 1730: 2001 Cr LJ 3555 (Kant).

Rameshwar Singh v. *State of Bihar,* 2006 (4) East Cri C 378: 2006 (4) Pat LJR 338: 2006 Cr LJ 4427 (Pat).

Harinder Pal Singh v. *State of Punjab,* 2004 (3) All Cri LR 10: 2004 (2) Rec Cri R 307: 2004 Cr LJ 2648 (P&H).

Vijay Narayan Uttekar v. *State of Maharashtra,* 2005 (2) Bom CR (Cri) 952: 2005 (4) Cur Cri R 61: 2005 Cr LJ 4452 (Bom).

Gurtej Singh v. *State,* 2005 (3) Crimes 705 (Raj).

R. Rathinasabapathy v. *State,* 2005 (1) Mad LW (Cri) 229: 2004 (3) Rec Cri R 869: 2004 Cr LJ 2737 (Mad).

K. Muralidharan v. *State of Kerala,* ILR (2006) 4 Ker 512: 2006 (3) Ker LJ 605: 2007 Cr LJ 417 (Ker).

Jeevan Singh v. *State of Rajasthan,* 2005 Cri LR (Raj) 1377: 2004 (4) Rec Cri R 7172: 2004 Cr LJ 3469 (Raj).

State of Punjab v. *Kasturi Lal,* 2005 AIR SCW 3306: AIR 2005 SC 4135: 2005 Cr LJ 3200 (SC).

Ramachandran v. *Udaya Kumar,* 2008 (2) Crimes 379 (SC).

CHAPTER 4

ISSUE OF THE PROCESS UNDER SECTION 204, AFTER EXAMINING COMPLAINANT AND WITNESS UNDER SECTION 200,

Section 265A(1)(b) of the Code says that the Chapter shall apply in respect of an accused against whom a Magistrate has taken cognizance of an offence on complaint other than an offence for which the punishment of death or of imprisonment for life or of imprisonment for a term exceeding seven years has been provided under the Law for the time being in force and after examining complainant and witnesses under section 200 issued the process under section 204 of the Code but does not apply where such offence affects the Socio-economic condition of the country or has been committed against a woman or a child below the age of Fourteen years.

See the First Schedule of the Code.

Section 2(d) of the Code defines "complaint" as in this Code unless the context otherwise requires "complaint" means any allegation made orally or in writing to a Magistrate with a view to his taking action under the Code that some person whether known or unknown has committed an offence but does not include a police report. The *Explanation* says that a report made by a police officer is a case which discloses, after investigation, the commission of a non cognizable offence shall be deemed to be a complaint and the police officer by whom such report is made shall be deemed to be the complaint.

See *Mohan Rao* v. *Murali Krishna,* 2007 (2) ALT (Cri).

Suraj Lal Jaiswal v. *State of Uttar Pradesh,* 2006 (2) DMC 1: 2007 (2) Marri LJ 50: 2006 Cr LJ 3323 (All).

Roy Joseph Creado v. *Sk. Tamisuddin,* 2009 (2) Civ LJ 377: 2008 (3) CCC 443: 2008 Cr LJ 1509 (Bom).

Mohanan v. *Sub-Inspector of Police, Koipuram Police Station,* 2008 (1) Ker LJ 445: 2008 (1) Ker LT 560: 2008 Cr LJ 1709 (Ker).

Sailender Pradhan v. *Uppaisla Jyothi,* 2006 (1) Crimes 156 (Ori).

In *Jitendra Chandrakant Mehta* v. *Shamrock Impex Pvt. Ltd.,* 2006 (3) Bom LR 2211: 2006 (4) Mah LJ 355: 2006 Cr LJ 3131 (Bom) it was held that absence of prayer to take action against accused according to law, will not affect the legality or validity of the complaint. In *James Sebastian* v. *State of Assam,* 2008 (3) Gau LT 713: 2009 (3) Gau LR 85: 2008 Cr LJ 3634 (Gau) it was held that when a complaint is made to a Magistrate whether is the form of a petition or otherwise such a complaint must be registered as a complaint and thereafter only the Magistrate may pass if be deems necessary, orders directing the police to register the complaint as FIR and investigate the case. When an information is given to a Magistrate and even whom such an information does not amount to a complaint within the meaning of section 2(d) of the Code, it would nevertheless be legally permissible for the Magistrate to take cognizance of the offences which such information may reveal to have been committed.

In *Mohd. Yousuf* v. *Afaq Jahan*, AIR 2006 SC 705: 2006 AIR SCW 95: 2006 Cr LJ 788, the apex court held that since there is no particular format of a complaint, a petition addressed to the Magistrate containing an allegation that an offence has been committed and ending with a prayer that the cutpoints be dealt with suitably, is a complaint.

In *Thethavusamy* v. *Radha Krishnan*, 2007 (2) Crimes 166 (Mad) while dealing with joint complaint it was held that where a complaint is filed by two persons relating to one and same occurrence or transaction, jointly, such complaint is not valid. Inquiry and investigation and the distinction has been dealt with in *Birendra Singh* v. *State of Jharkhand*, 2004 (1) BLJR 241: 2004 (3) Cur Cri R 82: 2004 Cr LJ 1913 (Jhar).

Section 2(h) of the Code defines investigation as in this Code unless the context otherwise requires "Investigation" includes all the proceedings under this Code for the collection of evidence conducted by a police officer or by any person other than a Magistrate who is authorised by a Magistrate in this behalf. For Definition of Evidence *see* section 3 of the Indian Evidence Act, 1872. for Investigation see *E. Seshaiah* v. *State of Andhra Pradesh*, 2000 (2) ALT (Cri) 91 (AP). For cognizable offence *see* section 2(c) of the Code. For non-cognizable offence *see* section 2(l) of the Code. Section 190 of the Code dealing with cognizance of offences by Magistrates reads:

> *190. Cognizance of offences by Magistrates.*—(1) Subject to the provisions of this Chapter, any Magistrate of the first class, and any Magistrate of the second class specially empowered in this behalf under sub-section (2), may take cognizance of any offence—
>
> (a) upon receiving a complaint of facts which constitute such offence;
>
> (b) upon a police report of such facts;
>
> (c) upon information received from any person other than a police officer, or upon his own knowledge, that such offence has been committed.
>
> (2) The Chief Judicial Magistrate may empower any Magistrate of the second class to take cognizance under sub-section (1) of such offences as are within his competence to inquire into or try.

Section 193 of the Code dealing with Cognizance of offences by courts of session reads:

> *193. Cognizance of offences by Courts of Session.*—Except as otherwise expressly provided by this Code or by any other law for the time being

in force, no Court of Session shall take cognizance of any offence as a Court of original jurisdiction unless the case has been committed to it by a Magistrate under this Code.

In *Bhushan Kumar* v. *State, (NCT of Delhi),* AIR 2012 SC 1747: (2012) 5 SCC 424: 2012 Cr LJ 2286 it was held that the expression "Cognizance" in section 190 and section 204 of the Code is entirely a different thing from innovation of proceedings rather it is the condition precedent to the innovation of proceedings by the Magistrate or the Judge. Cognizance is taken of cases and not of persons. Under section 190 of the Code it is the application of the judicial mind to the averments in the complaint that constitutes cognizance.

See *Subramaniam Swamy* v. *Manmohan Singh,* AIR 2012 SC 1185: 2012 AIR SCW 1249: 2012 Cr LJ 1519.

Nupur Talwar v. *C.B.I.,* AIR 2012 SC 847: 2012 Cr LJ 954: 2012 AIR SCW 579.

Helios and Matheson Information Technology Ltd. v. *Rajeev Sawhney,* AIR 2012 SC 660: 2012 Cr LJ 1248: (2012) 1 SCC 699.

Geeta Mehrotra v. *State of Uttar Pradesh,* (2012) 10 SCC 741.

Ramesh v. *State of Tamil Nadu,* (2005) 3 SCC 507: AIR 2005 SC 1989: 2005 Cr LJ 1732.

State of Karnataka v. *Pastor P. Raju,* (2006) 6 SCC 728: AIR 2006 SC 2825: 2006 Cr LJ 4045.

R.R. Chari v. *State of Uttar Pradesh,* AIR 1951 SC 207: 1951 SCJ 302: 52 Cr LJ 775.

State of West Bengal v. *Mohd Khalid,* (1995) 1 SCC 684: 1995 AIR SCW 559: AIR 1995 SC 785.

In *S.K. Sinha, Chief Enforcement Officer* v. *Videocon International Ltd.,* AIR 2008 SC 1213: 2008 AIR SCW 1203: 2008 Cr LJ 1636, it was held that taking cognizance does not involve any formal action of any kind and it occurs as soon as a Magistrate applies his mind to the suspected commission of an offence and cognizance is taken prior to the commencement of criminal proceedings. Taking of cognizance is thus a *sine qua non* or condition precedent for holding a valid trial. Cognizance is taken of an offence and not of an offender. Whether or not a Magistrate has taken cognizance of an offence depends on the facts and circumstances of each case and no rule of universal application can be laid down as to when a Magistrate can be said to have taken cognizance.

In *Sanjay Bansal* v. *Jawaharlal Vats,* AIR 2008 SC 207: 2008 Cr LJ 428: 2008 (2) SCJ 665 it was held that the Magistrate can ignore the conclusion arrived at by the investigating officer and independently apply his mind to the facts emerging from the Investigation and taken cognizance of the case if he thinks fit, exercise his powers under section 190(1)(b) of the Code and direct the issue of process to the accused. The Magistrate is not bound in such a situation to follow the procedure laid down in sections 200 and 202 of the Code for taking cognizance of a case under section 190(1)(a) of the Code though it is open to him to act under section 200 or section 202 of the Code also.

In *K. Neelaveni* v. *State rep. by Inspector of Police,* AIR 2010 SC 3191: 2010 Cr LJ 2819: 2010 AIR SCW 2760 it was held that when a report is submitted to the Magistrate, he is required to be *prima facie,* satisfied that the facts disclosed therein constitute an offence. In *Court on its Own motion* v. *Union of India,* 2001 (1) Rec Civ R 203: 2001 (3) Cur Cri R 212: 2001 Cr LJ 225 (P&H) it was held that High Court cannot direct Magistrate to take cognizance of an offence said to have been committed by Election Commissioner in view of the bar under section 197 of the Code.

For cognizance *see*

C.R.E.F. Finance Ltd. v. *Shree Shanthi Homes Pvt. Ltd.,* (2005) 7 SCC 467: AIR 2005 SC 4284: 2005 Cr LJ 4524.

Charanjit Singh v. *DB. Merchant Banking Services Ltd.,* 2001 (3) ICC 412: 2001 (90) DLT 484: 2001 Cr LJ 2276 (Del).

Mahesh Chand v. *B. Janardhan Reddy,* 2003 Cr LJ 866: 2002 AIR SCW 5385: (2003) 1 SCC 734.

Mahendra Pal Sharma v. *State of Uttar Pradesh,* 2002 (3) All Cri R 2452: 2003 (1) Crimes 208: 2003 Cr LJ 698 (All).

Dy. Chief Controller of Imports and Exports v. *Roshanlal Agarwal of Imports and Exports,* AIR 2003 SC 1900: 2003 AIR SCW 1377: 2003 Cr LJ 1698 (SC).

Musaraf Hossain Khan v. *Bhagheeratha Engg. Ltd.,* AIR 2006 SC 1288: 2006 Cr LJ 1683: 2006 AIR SCW 1137.

Fakhruddin Ahmad v. *State of Uttaranchal,* 2008 AIR SCW 5881: 2009 (1) Civ LJ 34: 2008 Cr LJ 4377 (SC).

Vinayak Steels Ltd. v. *State of Andhra Pradesh,* 2005 (2) ALD (Crl) 723: 2006 (1) Rec Cri R 375: 2005 Cr LJ 4337 (AP).

Dilawar Singh v. *State of Delhi,* 2007 Cr LJ 4709: AIR 2007 SC 3234: 2007 AIR SCW 5899.

Anuram Rastogi v. *State of Uttar Pradesh,* 2007 (2) Crimes 33 (SC).

D.K. Pattanaik v. *S.H.O.,* 2008 (1) ALD (Crl) 692: 2008 (2) Andh LT 541: 2008 Cr LJ 2287 (AP).

It is not necessary for the Magistrate to specifically state in his order that he has taken cognizance of the offences since it can be inferred from the facts and the other material on record.

V.S. Joshi v. *N.G. Bhat Chitrigi,* 2006 (2) AIR Kar R 103: 2006 (2) All Cri LR 347: 2006 Cr LJ 1566 (Kant).

In *Sabitha Ramamurthy* v. *R.B.S. Channabasavaradhya*, AIR 2006 SC 3086: 2006 AIR SCW 4582: 2006 Cr LJ 4602 it was held by the apex court that in terms of section 200 of the Code, the complainant is bound to make statement on oath as to how the offence has been committed and how the accused are responsible in relation thereto. In *Nova Electricals, Jalgaon* v. *State of Maharashtra*, 2007 (4) Bank Cas 59: 2007 (1) Bom CR (Cri) 291: 2007 Cr LJ 535 (Bom) it was held that verification is not a mere formality and the Magistrate has to ascertain whether the complaint is genuine or frivolous. Payment of expenses to witnesses had fallen for consideration in *Satish Tyagi* v. *Radha Kishan Tyagi*, 2008 (4) AIR Bom R 647 (NOC): 2008 (1) MPHT 87: 2008 Cr LJ 1327 (MP).

In *P. Vasanth Kumar* v. *Commissioner of Police*, 2007 (1) ALD (Crl) 879: 2007 (3) Andh LT 136: 2007 Cr LJ 2013 (AP) it was held that in the event of the police officer failing to register FIR or failing to receive written information by entering into the General Dairy, it is open to such person to file a complaint before the Magistrate under section 200 of the Code and hence it may not be just and proper for the petition to straight away approach High Court for issuance of a writ of *Mandamus* directing the SHO to register FIR and investigate the matter. In *Nupur Talwar* v. *CBI*, AIR 2012 SC 1921: 2012 (3) Crimes 31: (2012) 5 SCALE 744 it was observed that once the order of Magistrate taking cognizance and issuing process against the petitioner and her husband had been affirmed there is so scope for granting the relief of further investigation for the purpose of finding out whether someone other than the petitioner and her husband had committed offences in respect of deceased persons.

In *Vidavaluru Balaramaiah* v. *State of Andhra Pradesh*, 2003 (1) ALD (Crl) 543: 2004 (1) Rec Cri R 882: 2003 Cr LJ 3192 (AP) it was held that cognizance can be taken even after examination of witnesses and complainant. In *Ram Babu Gupta* v. *State of Uttar Pradesh*; 2001 (44) All LR 558: 2001 (3) Cur Cri R 477: 2001 Cr LJ 3363 (All) it was held that where an application stating facts constituting cognizable offence had been made, such complaint does not cease to be a complaint even if there is defective prayer or no prayer against known or unknown accused. In *K. Venkataramaiah* v. *Katterao S. Deshpande*, 2008 (2) AIR Kar R 284: 2008 (2) All Cri LR 844: 2008 Cr LJ 1547 (Kant) it was held that the specific procedure contemplated under section 200 of the Code cannot be devoted by adopting some other procedure not prescribed in *Bhushan Kumar* v. *State, (NCT of Delhi)*, AIR 2012 SC 1747: (2012) 5 SCC 424: 2012 Cr LJ 2286, it was observed by the apex court that a summons is a process issued by a court calling upon a person to appear before a Magistrate. It is used for the purpose of notifying an individual of his legal obligation to appear before the Magistrate as a response to the violation of law. Where the facts of a given case make out an offence, the availability of a civil remedy is not a bar to a criminal case *Shakuntala Devi* v. *State of*

Uttar Pradesh, 2002 (45) All Cri C 1091: 2002 (3) All Cri R 2477: 2003 Cr LJ 687 (All); *Pratibha Rani* v. *Suraj Kumar,* 1985 Cr LJ 817: AIR 1985 SC 628: (1985) 2 SCC 370.

In *Tula Ram* v. *Kishore Singh,* AIR 1977 SC 2401: 1978 Cr LJ 8: (1977) 4 SCC 459 it was held that where the Magistrate had kept the complaint with himself and ordered the statements of complaint and witnesses be recorded, later on complaint cannot be sent to police for investigation since he had taken cognizance of the complaint.

For ambit of section 200 of the Code

See also

Pramod v. *C.K. Velayudhan,* 2006 (2) Civ LJ 813: 2006 (1) CCC 731: 2005 Cr LJ 4572 (Ker).

Manojbhai Bhagwandas Shah v. *State of Gujarat,* 2001 (3) Guj LH 482: 2002 (2) Guj LR 1052: 2002 Cr LJ 2134 (Guj).

Dilip Saharan v. *State of Rajasthan,* 2003 (2) Raj LW 964: 2003 (3) Rec Cri R 213: 2002 Cr LJ 4169 (Raj).

Shiv Dayal Arora v. *Renu Arora,* 2007 (2) Marri LJ 270: 2007 (3) Rec Cri R 10: 2007 Cr LJ 2972 (P&H).

R.P.S. Rekhy v. *State (U.T.), Chandigarh,* 2008 Cr LJ 4292 (P&H).

Narain Singh v. *State of Uttar Pradesh,* 2008 (62) All Cri C 628: 2008 (3) All Cri R 2762: 2008 Cr LJ 4553 (All).

Mohammed Kutty v. *Mohammed,* 2007 (2) Civ LJ 779: 2007 (2) Cur Cri R 144: 2006 Cr LJ 3601 (Ker).

Ajay Kant v. *Alka Sharma,* 2007 (4) MPLJ 193: 2009 (1) Marri LJ 723: 2008 Cr LJ 264 (MP).

L.M.L. Ltd. v. *Kailash Narain Rai,* 2008 (3) MPHT 416: 2008 (66) All Ind Cas 333: 2008 Cr LJ 1718 (MP).

Tulsidas v. *State of Rajasthan,* 2007 (57) All Ind Cas 554: 2007 (2) Crimes 403: 2007 Cr LJ 1343 (Raj).

Adimul Hossain Khan v. *State of Orissa,* 2008 (3) AIR Bom R 422 (NOC): 2007 (38) OCR 716: 2008 Cr LJ 655 (Ori).

K. Gopalakrishnan v. *Karunakaran,* 2007 (2) CCC 559: 2007 (1) Cur Cri R 222: 2006 Cr LJ 4365 (Mad).

Dilawar Singh v. *State of Delhi,* 2007 Cr LJ 4709: AIR 2007 SC 3234: 2007 AIR SCW 5899.

K.L. Chawla v. *S.M. Agarwal,* 2001 (1) All Cri LR 349: 2000 (87) DLT 202: 2001 Cr LJ 2116 (Raj).

Raghuveer Singh v. *Phoolmal,* 2003 (7) All Ind Cas 396: 2003 (2) Cur Cri R 408: 2003 Cr LJ 3411 (MP).

K. Janaki Manoharan v. *Gayatri Sugar Complex Ltd.,* 2000 (4) Civ LJ 603: 2000 (3) CCC 566: 2001 Cr LJ 52 (AP).

Roy Joseph Creado v. *Sk. Tamisuddin,* 2009 (2) Civ LJ 377: 2008 (3) CCC 443: 2008 Cr LJ 1509 (Bom).

State of Haryana v. *Bhajan Lal,* AIR 1992 SC 604: 1992 AIR SCW 237: 1992 Cr LJ 527.

T.T. Anthony v. *State of Kerala,* 2001 Cr LJ 3329: AIR 2001 SC 2637: 2001 (5) Supreme 131: 2001 AIR SCW 2571.

B.A. Srinivasa Gupta v. *State of Karnataka,* 2002 (3) All Cri LR 760: 2003 (2) Kant LJ 445: 2002 Cr LJ 4540 (Kant).

Tulsidas v. *State of Rajasthan,* 2007 (57) All Ind Cas 554: 2007 (2) Crimes 403: 2007 Cr LJ 1343 (Raj).

S.K. Agarwal v. *Manoj Dalmia,* 2001 (4) Crimes 437: 2002 (1) Cur Cri R 128: 2001 Cr LJ 3343 (All).

L. Ramesh Kumar v. *L. Lalitha,* 2004 (1) DMC 771: 2003 (4) Rec Cri R 593: 2003 Cr LJ 2477 (AP).

Prabhanshu Kamal v. *Awadhesh Singh Bhadoriya,* 2003 (1) All Ind Cas 378: 2002 (4) Cur Cri R 281: 2002 Cr LJ 4532 (MP).

Hotline Shares and Securities Ltd. v. *Dinesh Ganeshmal Shah,* 2003 (1) Civ LJ 85: 2002 (2) CCC 581: 2002 Cr LJ 3291 (Kant).

Dharmendra Singh v. *State of Orissa,* 2000 (19) OCR 565: 2001 Cr LJ 439 (Ori).

Maharaja Developers v. *Udaysingh Pratapsinghrao Bhonsle,* 2007 CLC 873: 2007 (4) CCC 212: 2007 Cr LJ 2207 (Bom).

Md. Abdullah Khan v. *State of Bihar,* 2002 (1) East Cri C 302: 2002 (1) Pat LJR 639: 2002 Cr LJ 3875 (Pat).

Section 204 of the Code does not mandate the Magistrate to explicitly state the reasons for issuance of summons. Section 204 of the Code mandates the Magistrate to form an opinion as to whether there exists a sufficient ground for summons to be issued but it is no where mentioned in section 204 of the Code that the explicit narration of the same is mandatory, meaning thereby that it is not prerequisite for deciding the validity of the summons issued *Bhushan Kumar* v. *State, (NCT of Delhi),* AIR 2012 SC 1747: (2012) 5 SCC 424: 2012 Cr LJ 2286.

See:

Everest Advertising Pvt. Ltd. v. *State Government of NCT of Delhi,* 2007 AIR SCW 2510: AIR 2007 SC 1650: 2007 Cr LJ 2442.

S.K. Sinha, Chief Enforcement Officer v. *Videocon International Ltd.,* AIR 2008 SC 1213: 2008 AIR SCW 1203: 2008 Cr LJ 1636.

Magistrate issuing process, is an order of interlocutory nature observed in *Subramanium Sethuraman* v. *State of Maharashtra,* AIR 2004 SC 4711: 2004 AIR SCW 5326: 2004 (6) Supreme 662.

In *Ramesh* v. *A. Ramanujam,* 1998 Cr LJ 1959: 1998 (1) Bank Cas 481: 1998 (1) Crimes 334 it was held that in a private complaint, summons or warrant shall be accompanied by a copy of the complaint.

In *C.P. Yogeshwara* v. *Registrar Karnataka Lokayukta,* 2007 (5) AIR Kar R 97: 2008 (61) All Ind Cas 361: 2007 Cr LJ 3806 (Kant) it was observed that taking cognizance by the court itself is an act of application of mind cancellation of the process issued against the accused when may be proper, had fallen for consideration in *Mahendra Kumar Mishra* v. *Chandra Shekhar Prasad Mishra,* 2001 Cri LR (SC and MP) MPJ 280: 2001 Cr LJ 3455 (Kant). In *Bhiku Yeshwant Dhangat* v. *Baban Maruti Barate,* 2001 (5) Bom CR 69: 2001 (4) Bom LR 654: 2001 Cr LJ 295 (Bom) it was held that when complaint had been filed without lust of witnesses, taking cognizance of the same would be improper.

See *Fakirappa* v. *Shiddalingappa,* 2002 (2) Civ LJ 169: 2002 (1) CCC 275: 2002 Cr LJ 1926 (Kant).

Pramila Mahesh Shah v. *Employees' State Insurance,* 2002 (2) Mah LJ 100: 2002 (3) Mah LR 436: 2002 Cr LJ 2454 (Bom).

For ambit of section 204 of the Code.

See:

S.K. Agarwal v. *Manoj Dalmia,* 2001 (4) Crimes 437: 2002 (1) Cur Cri R 128: 2001 Cr LJ 3343 (All).

Vidavaluru Balaramaiah v. *State of Andhra Pradesh,* 2003 (1) ALD (Crl) 543: 2004 (1) Rec Cri R 882: 2003 Cr LJ 3192 (AP).

Joginder Kumar v. *Shamsher Singh Malik,* 2007 (2) Crimes 591 (Del).

Sagar Suri v. *State,* 2003 (106) DLT 439: 2003 (71) DRJ 49: 2004 Cr LJ 212 (Del).

Appollo Tyres Ltd. v. *Dr. Shashitai Bhagwan Ahire,* 2008 (4) AIR Bom R 768: 2008 All MR (Crl) 1794: 2008 Cr LJ 3758 (Bom).

Sunil Vassudev Pednekar v. *Bicholim Urban Co-operative Bank Ltd.,* 2006 (3) CCC 659: 2006 (4) Crimes 434: 2006 Cr LJ 3114 (Bom).

Poonam Chand Jain v. *Fazru,* AIR 2005 SC 38: 2004 AIR SCW 6222: 2005 Cr LJ 100 (SC).

Avtar Singh v. *Andrew Yule and Company Ltd.,* 2007 (4) Gau LT 6612: 2007 (4) Gau LR 24: 2007 Cr LJ 3915 (Gau).

Bhor Industries Ltd. v. *Anil Mahajan,* 2003 All MR (Cri) 2518: 2004 Cr LJ 1330 (Bom).

Prahalad Singh v. *State,* 2006 (1) Crimes 820 (Raj).

Tom Thomas v. *Abdul Lathief E.,* 2007 (1) Ker LJ 36: 2006 (4) Ker LT 1009: 2007 Cr LJ 1143 (Ker).

Kushua Murthy v. *Deep Chand Agarwal,* 2005 (4) Crimes 493 (AP).

Md. Mustafa v. *State of Jharkhand,* 2005 (3) BLJR 2363: 2005 (4) East Cri C 374: 2006 Cr LJ 786 (Jhar).

Palarwappa v. *Rawchandran,* 2006 (4) Crimes 511 (Mad).

Anand Swaroop v. *State of Uttar Pradesh,* 2006 (55) All Cri C 442: 2006 (2) All Cri R 1944: 2006 Cr LJ 2602 (All).

Sharda Prasad Tiwari v. *State of Uttar Pradesh,* 2006 (2) All Cri R 1831: 2006 (2) Hindu LR 646: 2006 Cr LJ 3319 (All).

R. Babu Shankar v. *State of Karnataka,* 2004 (2) KCCR 1251: 2004 (4) Kant LJ 51: 2004 Cr LJ 321 (Ker).

Jancy Nelson D'Souza v. *Nelson D'Souza,* 2004 (2) All Cri LR 361: 2003 All MR (Cri) 1875: 2004 Cr LJ 1690 (Bom).

Rakesh Devi v. *State of Uttar Pradesh,* 2002 (1) Crimes 540: 2002 (2) Rec Cri R 157: 2002 Cr LJ 1225 (All).

Kulwant Singh v. *Surjit Kaur,* 2002 (2) Marri LJ 491: 2002 (3) Rec Cri R 261: 2002 Cr LJ 3443 (P&H).

Shriniwas Mulchand Ladniya v. *Laxminarayan Jainarayan Rathi,* 2004 (1) Civ LJ 264: 2003 (2) Mah LJ 813: 2003 Cr LJ 3795 (Bom).

Sub-section (2)

Sub-section (2) of section 265A of the Code says that for the purposes of section 265A(1) of the Code, the Central Government shall by notification, determine the offences under the law for the time being in force which shall be the offences affecting the socio-economic condition of the country. In *Edward Mills Co. Ltd.* v. *State of Ajmer,* AIR 1955 SC 25: 1955 SCJ 42: 1955 SCR 735, it was held that the Orders and Notifications to have the force of law should be of Legislative character.

See *Madhorao Phalke* v. *State of Madhya Bharat,* AIR 1961 SC 298: (1961) 1 SCR 957: 1961 (2) SCJ 477.

Jayantilal Amratlal Shodhan v. *F.N. Rana,* AIR 1964 SC 648: (1964) 2 SCA 284: (1964) 5 SCR 294.

Union of India v. *Cynamide India Ltd.,* AIR 1987 SC 1802: (1987) 2 SCC 720: JT 1987 (3) SC 107.

Ajay Kumar Bhuyan v. *State of Orissa,* (2003) 1 SCC 707: 2002 AIR SCW 4866: 2003 Lab IC 78.

Union of India v. *Majji Jangammayya,* AIR 1977 SC 757: (1977) 1 SCC 606: (1977) 2 SCR 28.

Meghraj Kothari v. *Delimitation Commission,* AIR 1967 SC 669: 1967 (2) SCJ 248: (1967) 1 SCR 400.

State of Punjab v. *Tehal Singh,* AIR 2002 SC 533: 2002 AIR SCW 105: (2002) 2 SCC 7.

Ramesh Chandra v. *State of Maharashtra,* AIR 1981 SC 1127: 1981 BBCJ (SC) 106: (1981) 2 SCC 722.

West Bengal Electricity Regulatory Commission v. *C.E.S.C. Ltd.,* AIR 2002 SC 3588: 2002 AIR SCW 4212: (2002) 8 SCC 715.

H.S.S.K. Niyami v. *Union of India,* AIR 1990 SC 2128: (1990) 4 SCC 516.

Kalyani Stores v. *State of Orissa,* AIR 1966 SC 1686: 1966 (2) SCJ 367: (1966) 1 SCR 865.

State of Bombay v. *F.N. Balsara,* AIR 1951 SC 318: 1951 SCJ 478: 1951 SCR 682.

Kailash Nath v. *State of Uttar Pradesh,* AIR 1957 SC 790: (1957) 8 STC 358.

John Vallamattom v. *Union of India,* AIR 2003 SC 2902: 2003 AIR SCW 3536: 2003 (4) Civ LJ 429.

Builders Supply Corporation v. *The Union of India,* AIR 1965 SC 1061: 1965 (1) SCJ 402: (1965) 2 SCR 289.

Dena Bank v. *Bhikhabhai Prabhudas Parekh and Co.,* AIR 2000 SC 3654: 2000 AIR SCW 4237: (2000) 5 SCC 694.

K.M. Chikkaputtaswamy v. *State of Andhra Pradesh,* AIR 1985 SC 956: (1985) 1 Cur CC 1093: (1985) 2 Land LR 158.

Video Electronics Pvt Ltd. v. *State of Punjab,* AIR 1990 SC 820: (1990) 3 SCC 87: 1989 Supp (2) SCR 731.

Tilkayat Shri Govindlalji Maharaj v. *State of Rajasthan,* AIR 1963 SC 1638: (1963) 2 SCA 518: (1964) 1 SCR 561.

Promod Chandra Deb v. *State of Orissa,* AIR 1962 SC 1288: 1962 (1) SCJ 1: 1962 Supp (1) SCR 405.

Maharaja Shree Umaid Mills Ltd. v. *Union of India,* AIR 1963 SC 953: 1964 (1) SCJ 699: 1963 Supp (2) SCR 515.

Bengal Nagpur Cotton Mills Ltd. v. *Board of Revenue,* AIR 1964 SC 888: (1963) 2 SCWR 392: (1964) 4 SCR 190.

Raj Kumar Narsing Pratap Singh Deo v. *The State of Orissa,* AIR 1964 SC 1793: 1965 (1) SCJ 421: (1964) 7 SCR 112.

Union of India v. *Gwalior Rayon Silk Mfg. (Wvg.) Co. Ltd.,* AIR 1964 SC 1903: 1965 (1) SCJ 41: (1964) 7 SCR 892.

Maharaj Dhiraj Himmatsinghji v. *State of Rajasthan,* AIR 1987 SC 82: (1987) 1 SCC 52: 1987 (1) Supreme 19.

State of Madhya Pradesh v. *Lal Bhargavendra Singh,* AIR 1966 SC 704: (1969) 2 SCR 56: 1967 (1) SCJ 526.

CHAPTER 5

APPLICATION FOR PLEA BARGAINING

Section 265B of the Code dealing with Application for Plea Bargaining reads:

265B. Application for plea bargaining.—(1) A person accused of an offence may file application for plea bargaining in the Court in which such offence is pending for trial.

(2) The application under sub-section (1) shall contain a brief description of the case relating to which the application is filed including the offence to which the case relates and shall be accompanied by an affidavit sworn by the accused stating therein that he has voluntarily preferred, after understanding the nature and extent of punishment provided under the law for the offence, the plea bargaining in his case and that he has not previously been convicted by a Court in a case in which he had been charged with the same offence.

(3) After receiving the application under sub-section (1), the Court shall issue notice to the Public Prosecutor or the complainant of the case, as the case may be, and to the accused to appear on the date fixed for the case.

(4) When the Public Prosecutor or the complainant of the case, as the case may be, and the accused appear on the date fixed under sub-section (3), the Court shall examine the accused *in camera*, where the other party in the case shall not be present, to satisfy itself that the accused has filed the application voluntarily and where—

(a) the Court is satisfied that the application has been filed by the accused voluntarily, it shall provide time to the Public Prosecutor or the complainant of the case, as the case may be, and the accused to work out a mutually satisfactory disposition of the case which may include giving to the victim by the accused the compensation and other expenses during the case and thereafter fix the date for further hearing of the case;

(b) the Court finds that the application has been filed involuntarily by the accused or he has previously been convicted by a Court in a case in which he had been charged with the same offence, it shall proceed further in accordance with the provisions of this Code from the stage such application has been filed under sub-section (1).

Section 2(u) of the Code defines public prosecutor as in this Code unless the context otherwise requires "public prosecutor" means any person appointed under section 24 and includes any person acting under the directions of a public prosecutor. Section 24 of the Code dealing with public prosecutors says:

> 24. *Public Prosecutors.*—(1) For every High Court, the Central Government or the State Government shall, after consultation with the High Court, appoint a Public Prosecutor and may also appoint one or more Additional Public Prosecutors, for conducting in such Court, any prosecution, appeal or other proceeding on behalf of the Central Government or State Government, as the case may be.
>
> (2) The Central Government may appoint one or more Public Prosecutors for the purpose of conducting any case or class of cases in any district or local area.
>
> (3) For every district, the State Government shall appoint a Public Prosecutor and may also appoint one or more Additional Public Prosecutors for the district:
>
> Provided that the Public Prosecutor or Additional Public Prosecutor appointed for one district may be appointed also to be a Public Prosecutor or an Additional Public Prosecutor, as the case may be, for another district.
>
> (4) The District Magistrate shall, in consultation with the Sessions Judge, prepare a panel of names of persons, who are, in his opinion fit to be appointed as Public Prosecutors or Additional Public Prosecutors for the district.
>
> (5) No person shall be appointed by the State Government as the Public Prosecutor or Additional Public Prosecutor for the district unless his name appears in the panel of names prepared by the District Magistrate under sub-section (4).
>
> (6) Notwithstanding anything contained in sub-section (5), where in a State there exists a regular Cadre of Prosecuting Officers, the State Government shall appoint a Public Prosecutor or an Additional Public Prosecutor only from among the persons constituting such Cadre:
>
> Provided that where, in the opinion of the State Government, no suitable person is available in such Cadre for such appointment that Government may appoint a person as Public Prosecutor or Additional Public Prosecutor, as the case may be, from the panel of names prepared by the District Magistrate under sub-section (4).
>
> *Explanation.*—For the purposes of this sub-section,—
>
> (a) "regular Cadre of Prosecuting Officers" means a Cadre of Prosecuting Officers which includes therein the post of a Public Prosecutor, by whatever name called, and which provides for promotion of

Assistant Public Prosecutors, by whatever name called, to that post;

(b) "Prosecuting Officer" means a person, by whatever name called, appointed to perform the functions of a Public Prosecutor, an Additional Public Prosecutor or an Assistant Public Prosecutor under this Code.

(7) A person shall be eligible to be appointed as a Public Prosecutor or an Additional Public Prosecutor under sub-section (1) or sub-section (2) or sub-section (3) or sub-section (6), only if he has been in practice as an advocate for not less than seven years.

(8) The Central Government or the State Government may appoint, for the purposes of any case or class of cases, a person who has been in practice as an advocate for not less than ten years as a Special Public Prosecutor:

Provided that the Court may permit the victim to engage an advocate of his choice to assist the prosecution under this sub-section.

(9) For the purposes of sub-section (7) and sub-section (8), the period during which a person has been in practice as a pleader, or has rendered (whether before or after the commencement of this Code) service as a Public Prosecutor or as an Additional Public Prosecutor or Assistant Public Prosecutor or other Prosecuting Officer, by whatever name called, shall be deemed to be the period during which such person has been in practice as an advocate.

Section 39 of the Indian Penal Code defines voluntarily as a person is said to cause an effect "Voluntarily" when he causes it by means whereby he intended to cause it or by means, which, at the time of employing those means, be know or had reasons to believe to be likely to cause it.

The *illustration* reads:

Illustration

A attacks *Z* under such circumstances of grave provocation that his killing of *Z* would be only culpable homicide not amounting to murder. *B*, having ill-will towards *Z* and intending to kill him, and not having been subject to the provocation, assists *A* in killing *Z*. Here, though *A* and *B* are both engaged in causing *Z's* death, *B* is guilty of murder, and *A* is guilty only of culpable homicide.

Section 2(y) of the Code says that in this Code unless the context otherwise requires words and expressions used herein and not defined but defined in the Indian Penal Code have the meanings respectively assigned in them in that Code. Section 53 of the Indian Penal Code, 1860 dealing with punishments says.

53. *Punishments*.—The punishments to which offenders are liable under the provisions of this Code are—

First.—Death;

Secondly.—Imprisonment for life;

Fourthly.—Imprisonment, which is of two descriptions, namely:—

(1) Rigorous, that is, with hard labour;

(2) Simple;

Fifthly.—Forfeiture of property;

Sixthly.—Fine.

Sections 357, 357A, 358 of the Code read as hereunder:

357. *Order to pay compensation.*—(1) When a Court imposes a sentence of fine or a sentence (including a sentence of death) of which fine forms a part, the Court may, when passing judgment order the whole or any part of the fine recovered to be applied—

(a) in defraying the expenses properly incurred in the prosecution;

(b) in the payment to any person of compensation for any loss or injury caused by the offence, when compensation is, in the opinion of the Court, recoverable by such person in a Civil Court;

(c) when any person is convicted of any offence for having caused the death of another person or of having abetted the commission of such an offence, in paying compensation to the persons who are, under the Fatal Accidents Act, 1855 (13 of 1855), entitled to recover damages from the person sentenced for the loss resulting to them from such death;

(d) when any person is convicted of any offence which includes theft, criminal misappropriation, criminal breach of trust, or cheating, or of having dishonestly received or retained, or of having voluntarily assisted in disposing of, stolen property knowing or having reason to believe the same to be stolen, in compensating any *bona fide* purchaser of such property for the loss of the same if such property is restored to the possession of the person entitled thereto.

(2) If the fine is imposed in a case which is subject to appeal, no such payment shall be made before the period allowed for presenting the appeal has elapsed, or if an appeal be presented, before the decision of the appeal.

(3) When a Court imposes a sentence, of which fine does not form a part, the Court may, when passing judgment order the accused person to pay, by way of compensation such amount as may be specified in the order to the person who has suffered any loss or injury by reason of the act for which the accused person has been so sentenced.

(4) An order under this section may also be made by an Appellate Court or by the High Court or Court of Session when exercising its powers of revision.

(5) At the time of awarding compensation in any subsequent civil suit relating to the same matter, the Court shall take into account any sum paid or recovered as compensation under this section.

357A. Victim compensation scheme.—(1) Every State Government in co-ordination with the Central Government shall prepare a scheme for providing funds for the purpose of compensation to the victim or his dependents who have suffered loss or injury as a result of the crime and who require rehabilitation.

(2) Whenever a recommendation is made by the Court for compensation, the District Legal Service Authority or the State Legal Service Authority, as the case may be, shall decide the quantum of compensation to be awarded under the scheme referred to in sub-section (1).

(3) If the trial Court, at the conclusion of the trial, is satisfied that the compensation awarded under section 357 is not adequate for such rehabilitation, or where the cases end in acquittal or discharge and the Victim has to be rehabilitated, it may make recommendation for compensation.

(4) Where the offender is not traced or identified, but the victim is identified, and where no trial takes place, the victim or his dependents may make an application to the State or the District Legal Services Authority for award of compensation.

(5) On receipt of such recommendations or on the application under sub-section (4), the State or the District Legal Services Authority shall, after due enquiry award adequate compensation by completing the enquiry within two months.

(6) The State or the District Legal Services Authority, as the case may be, to alleviate the suffering of the victim, may order for immediate first-aid facility or medical benefits to be made available free of cost on the certificate of the police officer not below the rank of the officer in charge of the police station or a Magistrate of the area concerned, or any other interim relief as the appropriate authority deems fit.

358. Compensation to persons groundlessly arrested.—(1) Whenever any person causes a police officer to arrest another person, if it appears to the Magistrate by whom the case is heard that there was no sufficient ground of causing such arrest, the Magistrate may award such compensation, not exceeding one thousand rupees, to be paid by the person so causing the arrest to the person so arrested, for his loss of time and expenses in the matter, as the Magistrate thinks fit.

(2) In such cases, if more persons than one are arrested, the Magistrate may, in like manner, award to each of them such compensation, not exceeding one thousand rupees, as such Magistrate thinks fit.

(3) All compensation awarded under this section may be recovered as if it were a fine, and, if it cannot be so recovered, the person by whom it is payable shall be sentenced to simple imprisonment for such

term not exceeding thirty days as the Magistrate directs, unless such sum is sooner paid.

Section 250 of the Code reads:

250. Compensation for accusation without reasonable cause.—(1) If, in any case instituted upon complaint or upon information given to a police officer or to a Magistrate, one or more persons is or are accused before a Magistrate of any offence triable by a Magistrate, and the Magistrate by whom the case is heard discharges or acquits all or any of the accused, and is of opinion that there was no reasonable ground for making the accusation against them or any of them, the Magistrate may, by his order of discharge or acquittal, if the person upon whose complaint or information the accusation was made is present, call upon him forthwith to show cause why he should not pay compensation to such accused or to each or any of such accused when there are more than one or, if such person is not present, direct the issue of a summons to him to appear and show cause as aforesaid.

(2) The Magistrate shall record and consider any cause which such complainant or informant may show, and if he is satisfied that there was no reasonable ground for making the accusation, may, for reasons to be recorded, make an order that compensation to such amount not exceeding the amount of fine he is empowered to impose, as he may determine, be paid by such complainant or informant to the accused or to each or any of them.

(3) The Magistrate may, by the order directing payment of the compensation under sub-section (2) further order that, in default of payment, the person ordered to pay such compensation shall under go simple imprisonment for a period not exceeding thirty days.

(4) When any person is imprisoned under sub-section (3), the provisions of sections 68 and 69 of the Indian Penal Code (45 of 1860) shall, so far as may be, apply.

(5) No person who has been directed to pay compensation under this section shall, by reason of such order, be exempted from any civil or criminal liability in respect of the complaint made or information given by him:

Provided that any amount paid to an accused person under this section shall be taken into account in awarding compensation to such person in any subsequent civil suit relating to the same matter.

(6) A complainant or informant who has been ordered under sub-section (2) by a Magistrate of the second class to pay compensation exceeding one hundred rupees, may appeal from the order, as if such complainant or informant had been convicted on a trial held by such Magistrate.

(7) When an order for payment of compensation to an accused person is made in a case which is subject to appeal under sub-section (6), the compensation shall not be paid to him before the period allowed for the presentation of the appeal has elapsed, or, if an appeal is presented, before the appeal has been decided; and where such order is made in a case which is not so subject to appeal the compensation shall not be paid before the expiration of one month from the date of the order.

(8) The provisions of this section apply to summons-cases as well as to warrant cases.

CHAPTER 6

APPLICATION FOR PLEA BARGAINING MAY BE FILED IN THE COURT IN WHICH SUCH OFFENCE IS PENDING FOR TRIAL

Sub-section (1) of section 265B of the Code says that a person accused of an offence may file application for Plea Bargaining in the court in which such offence is pending for trial. Section 3 of the Indian Evidence Act, 1872 defines court as "Court" includes all Judges and Magistrates and all persons, except Arbitrators, legally authorised to take evidence. Section 4 of the Code dealing with trial of offences under the Indian Penal Code and other laws reads:

> 4. *Trial of offences under the Indian Penal Code and other laws.*—(1) All offences under the Indian Penal Code (45 of 1860) shall be investigated, inquired into, tried, and otherwise dealt with according to the provisions hereinafter contained.
>
> (2) All offences under any other law shall be investigated, inquired into, tried, and otherwise dealt with according to the same provisions, but subject to any enactment for the time being in force regulating the manner or place of investigating, inquiring into, trying or otherwise dealing with such offences.

Section 26 of the Code dealing with Courts by which offences are triable reads:

> 26. *Courts by which offences are triable.*—Subject to the other provisions of this Code,—
>
> (a) any offence under the Indian Penal Code (45 of 1860) may be tried by—
>
> (i) the High Court, or
>
> (ii) the Court of Session, or
>
> (iii) any other Court by which such offence is shown in the First Schedule to be triable;
>
> Provided that any offence under section 376, section 376A, section 376B, section 376C, section 376D or section 376E of the Indian Penal Code (45 of 1860) shall be tried as far as practicable by a Court presided over by a woman.
>
> (b) any offence under any other law shall, when any Court is mentioned in this behalf in such law, be tried by such Court and when no Court is so mentioned, may be tried by—

(i) the High Court, or

(ii) any other Court by which such offence is shown in the First Schedule to be triable.

Chapter II of the Code deals with Constitution of Criminal Courts and offices to have better understanding of criminal court, it may be desirable to have a glance at sections 6 to 23 of the Code. Sections 6 to 23 of the Code read:

> 6. *Classes of Criminal Courts.*—Besides the High Courts and the Courts constituted under any law, other than this Code, there shall be, in every State, the following classes of Criminal Courts, namely:—
>
> (i) Courts of Session;
>
> (ii) Judicial Magistrates of the first class and, in any metropolitan area, Metropolitan Magistrates;
>
> (iii) Judicial Magistrates of the second class; and
>
> (iv) Executive Magistrates.
>
> 7. *Territorial divisions.*—(1) Every State shall be a sessions division or shall consist of sessions divisions; and every sessions division shall, for the purposes of this Code, be a district or consist of districts:
>
> Provided that every metropolitan area shall, for the said purposes, be a separate sessions division and district.
>
> (2) The State Government may, after consultation with the High Court, alter the limits or the number of such divisions and districts.
>
> (3) The State Government may, after consultation with the High Court, divide any district into sub-divisions and may alter the limits or the number of such sub-divisions.
>
> (4) The sessions divisions, districts and sub-divisions existing in a State at the commencement of this Code, shall be deemed to have been formed under this section.
>
> 8. *Metropolitan areas.*—(1) The State Government may, by notification, declare that, as from such date as may be specified in the notification, any area in the State comprising a city or town whose population exceeds one million shall be a metropolitan area for the purposes of this Code.
>
> (2) As from the commencement of this Code, each of the Presidency-towns of Bombay, Calcutta and Madras and the city of Ahmedabad shall be deemed to be declared under sub-section (1) to be a metropolitan area.
>
> (3) The State Government may, by notification, extend, reduce or alter the limits of a metropolitan area but the reduction or alteration shall not be so made as to reduce the population of such area to less than one million.

(4) Where, after an area has been declared, or deemed to have been declared to be, a metropolitan area, the population of such area falls below one million, such area shall, on and from such date as the State Government may, by notification, specify in this behalf, cease to be a metropolitan area; but notwithstanding such cesser, any inquiry, trial or appeal pending immediately before such cesser before any Court or Magistrate in such area shall continue to be dealt with under this Code, as if such cesser had not taken place.

(5) Where the State Government reduces or alters, under sub-section (3), the limits of any metropolitan area, such reduction or alteration shall not affect any inquiry, trial or appeal pending immediately before such reduction or alteration before any Court or Magistrate, and every such inquiry, trial or appeal shall continue to be dealt with under this Code as if such reduction or alteration had not taken place.

Explanation.—In this section, the expression "population" means the population as ascertained at the last preceding census of which the relevant figures have been published.

9. Court of Session.—(1) The State Government shall establish a Court of Session for every sessions division.

(2) Every Court of Session shall be presided over by a Judge, to be appointed by the High Court.

(3) The High Court may also appoint Additional Sessions Judges and Assistant Sessions Judges to exercise jurisdiction in a Court of Session.

(4) The Sessions Judge of one sessions division may be appointed by the High Court to be also an Additional Sessions Judge of another division, and in such case he may sit for the disposal of cases at such place or places in the other division as the High Court may direct.

(5) Where the office of the Sessions Judge is vacant, the High Court may make arrangements for the disposal of any urgent application which is, or may be, made or pending before such Court of Session by an Additional or Assistant Sessions Judge, or, if there be no Additional or Assistant Sessions Judge, by a Chief Judicial Magistrate, in the sessions division; and every such Judge or Magistrate shall have jurisdiction to deal with any such application.

(6) The Court of Sessions shall ordinarily hold its sitting at such place or places as the High Court may, by notification, specify; but, if, in any particular case, the Court of Session is of opinion that it will tend to the general convenience of the parties and witnesses to hold its sittings at any other place in the sessions division, it may, with the consent of the prosecution and the accused, sit at that place for the disposal of the case or the examination of any witness or witnesses therein.

Explanation.—For the purposes of this Code, "appointment" does not include the first appointment, posting or promotion of a person by the Government to any Service, or post in connection with the affairs of the Union or of a State, where under any law, such appointment, posting or promotion is required to be made by Government.

10. Subordination of Assistant Sessions Judges.—(1) All Assistant Sessions Judges shall be subordinate to the Sessions Judge in whose Court they exercise jurisdiction.

(2) The Sessions Judge may, from time to time, make rules consistent with this Code, as to the distribution of business among such Assistant Sessions Judges.

(3) The Sessions Judge may also make provision for the disposal of any urgent application, in the event of his absence or inability to act, by an Additional or Assistant Sessions Judge, or, if there be no Additional or Assistant Sessions Judge, by the Chief Judicial Magistrate, and every such Judge or Magistrate shall be deemed to have jurisdiction to deal with any such application.

11. Courts of Judicial Magistrates.—(1) In every district (not being a metropolitan area), there shall be established as many Courts of Judicial Magistrates of the first class and of the second class, and at such places, as the State Government may, after consultation with the High Court, by notification, specify:

Provided that the State Government may, after consultation with the High Court, establish, for any local area, one or more Special Courts of Judicial Magistrates of the first class or of the second class to try any particular case or particular class of cases, and where any such Special Court is established, no other Court of Magistrate in the local area shall have jurisdiction to try any case or class of cases for the trial of which such Special Court of Judicial Magistrate has been established.

(2) The presiding officers of such Courts shall be appointed by the High Court.

(3) The High Court may, whenever it appears to it to be expedient or necessary, confer the powers of a Judicial Magistrate of the first class or of the second class on any member of the Judicial Service of the State, functioning as a Judge in a Civil Court.

12. Chief Judicial Magistrate and Additional Chief Judicial Magistrate, etc.—(1) In every district (not being a metropolitan area), the High Court shall appoint a Judicial Magistrate of the first class to be the Chief Judicial Magistrate.

(2) The High Court may appoint any Judicial Magistrate of the first class to be an Additional Chief Judicial Magistrate, and such Magistrate shall have all or any of the powers of a Chief Judicial Magistrate under

this Code or under any other law for the time being in force as the High Court may direct.

(3) (a) The High Court may designate any Judicial Magistrate of the first class in any sub-division as the Sub-divisional Judicial Magistrate and relieve him of the responsibilities specified in this section as occasion requires.

(b) Subject to the general control of the Chief Judicial Magistrate, every Sub-divisional Judicial Magistrate shall also have and exercise, such powers of supervision and control over the work of the Judicial Magistrates (other than Additional Chief Judicial Magistrates) in the sub-division as the High Court may, by general or special order, specify in this behalf.

13. Special Judicial Magistrates.—(1) The High Court may, if requested by the Central or State Government so to do, confer upon any person who holds or has held any post under the Government, all or any of the powers conferred or conferrable by or under this Code on a Judicial Magistrate of the first class or of the second class, in respect to particular cases or to particular classes of cases, in any local area, not being a metropolitan area:

Provided that no such power shall be conferred on a person unless he possesses such qualification or experience in relation to legal affairs as the High Court may, by rules, specify.

(2) Such Magistrates shall be called Special Judicial Magistrates and shall be appointed for such term, not exceeding one year at a time, as the High Court may, by general or special order, direct.

(3) The High Court may empower a Special Judicial Magistrate to exercise the powers of a Metropolitan Magistrate in relation to any metropolitan area outside his local jurisdiction.

14. Local Jurisdiction of Judicial Magistrates.—(1) Subject to the control of the High Court, the Chief Judicial Magistrate may, from time to time, define the local limits of the areas within which the Magistrates appointed under section 11 or under section 13 may exercise all or any of the powers with which they may respectively be invested under this Code:

Provided that the Court of a Special Judicial Magistrate may hold its sitting at any place within the local area for which it is established.

(2) Except as otherwise provided by such definition, the jurisdiction and powers of every such Magistrate shall extend throughout the district.

(3) Where the local jurisdiction of a Magistrate, appointed under section 11 or section 13 or section 18, extends to an area beyond the district, or the metropolitan area, as the case may be, in which he ordinarily holds Court, any reference in this Code to the Court of

Session, Chief Judicial Magistrate or the Chief Metropolitan Magistrate shall, in relation to such Magistrate, throughout the area within his local jurisdiction, be construed, unless the context otherwise requires, as a reference to the Court of Session, Chief Judicial Magistrate, or Chief Metropolitan Magistrate, as the case may be, exercising jurisdiction in relation to the said district or metropolitan area.

15. Subordination of Judicial Magistrates.—(1) Every Chief Judicial Magistrate shall be subordinate to the Sessions Judge; and every other Judicial Magistrate shall, subject to the general control of the Sessions Judge, be subordinate to the Chief Judicial Magistrate.

(2) The Chief Judicial Magistrate may, from time to time, make rules or give special orders, consistent with this Code, as to the distribution of business among the Judicial Magistrates subordinate to him.

16. Courts of Metropolitan Magistrates.—(1) In every metropolitan area, there shall be established as many Courts of Metropolitan Magistrates, and at such places, as the State Government may, after consultation with the High Court, by notification, specify.

(2) The presiding officers of such Courts shall be appointed by the High Court.

(3) The jurisdiction and powers of every Metropolitan Magistrate shall extend throughout the metropolitan area.

17. Chief Metropolitan Magistrate and Additional Chief Metropolitan Magistrate.—(1) The High Court shall, in relation to every metropolitan area within its local jurisdiction, appoint a Metropolitan Magistrate to be the Chief Metropolitan Magistrate for such metropolitan area.

(2) The High Court may appoint any Metropolitan Magistrate to be an Additional Chief Metropolitan Magistrate, and such Magistrate shall have all or any of the powers of a Chief Metropolitan Magistrate under this Code or under any other law for the time being in force as the High Court may direct.

18. Special Metropolitan Magistrates.—(1) The High Court may, if requested by the Central or State Government so to do, confer upon any person who holds or has held any post under the Government, all or any of the powers conferred or conferrable by or under this Code on a Metropolitan Magistrate, in respect to particular cases or to particular classes of cases in any metropolitan area within its local jurisdiction:

Provided that no such power shall be conferred on a person unless he possesses such qualification or experience in relation to legal affairs as the High Court may, by rules, specify.

(2) Such Magistrates shall be called Special Metropolitan Magistrates and shall be appointed for such term, not exceeding one year at a time, as the High Court may, by general or special order, direct.

(3) The High Court or the State Government, as the case may be, may empower any Special Metropolitan Magistrate to exercise, in any local area outside the metropolitan area, the powers of a Judicial Magistrate of the first class.

19. Subordination of Metropolitan Magistrates.—(1) The Chief Metropolitan Magistrate and every Additional Chief Metropolitan Magistrate shall be subordinate to the Sessions Judge; and every other Metropolitan Magistrate shall, subject to the general control of the Sessions Judge, be subordinate to the Chief Metropolitan Magistrate.

(2) The High Court may, for the purposes of this Code, define the extent of the subordination, if any, of the Additional Chief Metropolitan Magistrates to the Chief Metropolitan Magistrate.

(3) The Chief Metropolitan Magistrate may, from time to time, make rules or give special orders, consistent with this Code, as to the distribution of business among the Metropolitan Magistrates and as to the allocation of business to an Additional Chief Metropolitan Magistrate.

20. Executive Magistrates.—(1) In every district and in every metropolitan area, the State Government may appoint as many persons as it thinks fit to be Executive Magistrates and shall appoint one of them to be the District Magistrate.

(2) The State Government may appoint any Executive Magistrate to be an Additional District Magistrate, and such Magistrate shall have such of the powers of a District Magistrate under this Code or under any other law for the time being in force, as may be directed by the State Government.

(3) Whenever, in consequence of the office of a District Magistrate becoming vacant, any officer succeeds temporarily to the executive administration of the district, such officer shall, pending the orders of the State Government, exercise all the powers and perform all the duties respectively conferred and imposed by this Code on the District Magistrate.

(4) The State Government may place an Executive Magistrate in charge of a sub-division and may relieve him of the charge as occasion requires; and the Magistrate so placed in charge of a sub-division shall be called the Sub-divisional Magistrate.

(4A) The State Government may, by general or special order and subject to such control and directions as it may deem fit to impose, delegate its powers under sub-section (4) to the District Magistrate.

(5) Nothing in this section shall preclude the State Government from conferring under any law for the time being in force, on a Commissioner of Police, all or any of the powers of an Executive Magistrate in relation to a metropolitan area.

21. Special Executive Magistrates.—The State Government may appoint, for such term as it may think fit, Executive Magistrates, to be known as Special Executive Magistrates for particular areas or for the performance of particular functions and confer on such Special Executive Magistrates such of the powers as are conferrable under this Code on Executive Magistrates, as it may deem fit.

22. Local Jurisdiction of Executive Magistrates.—(1) Subject to the control of the State Government, the District Magistrate may, from time to time, define the local limits of the areas within which the Executive Magistrates may exercise all or any of the powers with which they may be invested under this Code.

(2) Except as otherwise provided by such definition, the jurisdiction and powers of every such Magistrate shall extend throughout the district.

23. Subordination of Executive Magistrates.—(1) All Executive Magistrates, other than the Additional District Magistrate, shall be subordinate to the District Magistrate, and every Executive Magistrate (other than the Sub-divisional Magistrate) exercising powers in a sub-division shall also be subordinate to the Sub-divisional Magistrate, subject, however, to the general control of the District Magistrate.

(2) The District Magistrate may, from time to time, make rules or give special orders, consistent with this Code, as to the distribution of business among the Executive Magistrates subordinate to him and as to the allocation of business to an Additional District Magistrate.

Police Commissioner can be appointed as Executive Magistrate, observed by the apex court in *A.N. Roy* v. *Suresh Sham Singh*, AIR 2006 SC 2677: 2006 Cr LJ 3614: (2006) 5 SCC 745 where a special court had been constituted no other court can try cases of such special court.

Raghunath Rai v. *State of Uttar Pradesh*, 1993 (1) Cr LJ 1001 (All).

See

State of Assam v. *Keising James*, 2007 (1) Gau LT 644: 2007 (1) Gau LR 644: 2007 Cr LJ 897 (Gau).

Ashwani Dhingra v. *Central Bureau of Investigation*, 2001 (42) All Cri C 166: 2001 (1) All Cri R 17: 2001 Cr LJ 946 (All).

Mohd. Aslam v. *State of Uttar Pradesh*, AIR 2007 SC 1901: 2007 Cr LJ 3200: 2007 AIR SCW 3402.

Moleswar Savey v. *State of Uttar Pradesh*, 2001 All LJ 638 (All).

For Jurisdiction of the Criminal Courts for inquires and Trials

See Sections 177 to 189 of the Code.

For Trial before a Court of Session

See sections 225 to 237 of the Code.

For trial of warrant cases by Magistrates

See sections 238 to 250 of the Code.

For trial of Summons Cases by Magistrates

See Sections 251 to 259 of the Code.

For summary trials.

See sections 260 to 265 of the Code.

The words "in the Court in which such offence is pending for trial" indicate the courts before which applications for plea bargaining may be filed by persons accused of an offence or offences.

For Terminal Jurisdiction. See *Hiralal Agarwal* v. *State of Orissa,* 2006 Cr LJ 3809: 2006 (2) DMC 624: 2006 (2) Hindu LR 675.

Mohan Bantha v. *State of Bihar,* 2001 (2) Crimes 83 (SC).

K. Ramakrishna Reddy v. *K. Padmavathi,* 2001 (1) Andh LT (Cri) 389 (AP): 2001 (4) Rec Cri R 374: 2001 Cr LJ 3424 (AP).

Babban Maurya v. *State of Bihar,* 2007 (3) AIR Jhar R 748: 2007 (2) Pat LJR 157: 2007 Cr LJ 2529 (Pat).

Karan Singh Sudhi v. *Jatender Jeet Kaur,* 2007 (2) Crimes 495 (J&K).

Jaswant Kaur v. *Gurudeep Kaur,* 2007 Cr LJ 4726: 2007 Cg LJ 95: 2007 (2) Crimes 555 (Chatt).

Manish Ratan v. *State,* (2007) 1 SCC 262.

Khetmal Soni v. *State,* 2007 (1) Crimes 719 (Chatt)

Y. Abraham Ajith v. *Inspector of Police, Chennai,* AIR 2004 SC 4286: 2004 AIR SCW 4788: 2004 Cr LJ 4180.

Syed Khaja Mohiuddni v. *State,* 2005 (3) Crimes 683 (AP).

CHAPTER 7

AFFIDAVIT SWORN BY THE ACCUSED

Sub-section (2) of section 265B of the Code says that the application under section 265B(1) of the Code shall contain a brief description of the case relating to which the application is filed including the offence to which the case relates and shall be accompanied by an affidavit sworn by the accused stating therein that he has voluntarily preferred, after understanding the nature and extent of punishment provided under the law for the offence, the plea bargaining in his case and that he has not been convicted previously by a court in a case in which he had been charged with the same offence. The filing of affidavit as contemplated by this provision, is for the purposes specified therein.

In *Vali Basha* v. *Mohd. Bashu*, 2008 (2) All Cri LR 621: 2008 (3) Cur Cri R 153: 2008 Cr LJ 1011 (Kant) it was held that affidavits are not included in the definition of Evidence under the Indian Evidence Act, 1872 and can be used only if the court permits it to be used for sufficient reasons. See *Sant Lal* v. *State of Uttar Pradesh*, 2005 (53) All Cri C 683: 2006 (1) All Cri R 217: 2006 Cr LJ 690 (All); *See* also *Gurdev Raj* v. *State of Punjab*, 2007 AIR SCW 6489: (2007) 13 SCC 380: 2008 Cr LJ 382 (SC); *Sakatar Singh* v. *State of Punjab*, 2005 (2) EFR 596: 2005 (3) Rec Cri R 896: 2005 Cr LJ 4772 (P&H).

See section 145 N.I. Act.

Indo-International Ltd. v. *State of Maharashtra*, 2006 (2) All Cri LR 312: 2006 (2) Rec Cri R 4: 2006 Cr LJ 208 (Bom).

Panda Leasing and Properties Ltd. v. *Hemant Kumar Moharana*, 2006 (2) Crimes 220 (Ori).

Vinod Singh Negi v. *State of Uttaranchal*, 2006 (3) Bank Cas 588: 2006 (2) Cur Cri R 625: 2005 Cr LJ 3827 (Uttra).

Peacock Industries Ltd. v. *Budhrani Finance Ltd.*, 2007 (1) Crimes 271 (Bom).

Indraprastha Holdings Ltd. v. *Vijay J. Shah*, 2006 (3) Civ LJ 692: 2006 (1) CCC 435: 2006 Cr LJ 574 (Bom).

Chapter III of the Indian Penal Code deals with of punishments. Sections 53 to 75 of the Indian Penal Code read:

> *53. Punishments.*—The punishments to which offenders are liable under the provisions of this Code are—
>
> *First.*—Death;

Secondly.—Imprisonment for life;

Fourthly.—Imprisonment, which is of two descriptions, namely:—

(1) Rigorous, that is, with hard labour;

(2) Simple;

Fifthly.—Forfeiture of property;

Sixthly.—Fine.

53A. Construction of reference to transportation.—(1) Subject to the provisions of sub-section (2) and sub-section (3), any reference to "transportation for life" in any other law for the time being in force or in any instrument or order having effect by virtue of any such law or of any enactment repealed shall be construed as a reference to "imprisonment for life".

(2) In every case in which a sentence of transportation for a term has been passed before the commencement of the Code of Criminal Procedure (Amendment) Act, 1955 (26 of 1955), the offender shall be dealt with in the same manner as if sentenced to rigorous imprisonment for the same term.

(3) Any reference to transportation for a term or to transportation for any shorter term (by whatever name called) in any other law for the time being in force shall be deemed to have been omitted.

(4) Any reference to "transportation" in any other law for the time being in force shall,—

(a) if the expression means transportation for life, be construed as a reference to imprisonment for life;

(b) if the expression means transportation for any shorter term, be deemed to have been omitted.

54. Commutation of sentence of death.—In every case in which sentence of death shall have been passed, the appropriate Government may, without the consent of the offender, commute the punishment for any other punishment provided by this Code.

55. Commutation of sentence of imprisonment for life.—In every case in which sentence of imprisonment for life shall have been passed, the appropriate Government] may, without the consent of the offender, commute the punishment for imprisonment of either description for a term not exceeding fourteen years.

55A. Definition of "appropriate Government".—In sections 54 and 55 the expression "appropriate Government" means,—

(a) in cases where the sentence is a sentence of death or is for an offence against any law relating to a matter to which the executive power of the Union extends, the Central Government; and

(b) in cases where the sentence (whether of death or not) is for an offence against any law relating to a matter to which the executive power of the State extends, the Government of the State within which the offender is sentenced.

56. Sentence of Europeans and Americans to penal servitude. Proviso as to sentence for term exceeding ten years but not for life.—[Rep. by the Criminal Law (Removal of Racial Discriminations) Act, 1949 (17 of 1949), sec. 2 (w.e.f. 6-4-1949).]

57. Fractions of terms of punishment.—In calculating fractions of terms of punishment, imprisonment for life shall be reckoned as equivalent to imprisonment for twenty years.

58. Offenders sentenced to transportation how dealt with until transported.—[Rep. by the Code of Criminal Procedure (Amendment) Act, 1955 (26 of 1955), sec. 117 and Sch. (w.e.f. 1-1-1956).]

59. Transportation instead of imprisonment.—[Rep. by the Code of Criminal Procedure (Amendment) Act, 1955 (26 of 1955), sec. 117 and Sch. (w.e.f. 1-1-1956).]

60. Sentence may be (in certain cases of imprisonment) wholly or partly rigorous or simple.—In every case in which an offender is punishable with imprisonment which may be of either description, it shall be competent to the Court which sentences such offender to direct in the sentence that such imprisonment shall be wholly rigorous, or that such imprisonment shall be wholly simple, or that any part of such imprisonment shall be rigorous and the rest simple.

61. Sentence of forfeiture of property.—[Rep. by the Indian Penal Code (Amendment) Act, 1921 (16 of 1921), sec. 4.]

62. Forfeiture of property in respect of offenders punishable with death, transportation or imprisonment.—[Rep. by the Indian Penal Code (Amendment) Act, 1921 (16 of 1921) sec. 4.]

63. Amount of fine.—Where no sum is expressed to which a fine may extend, the amount of fine to which the offender is liable is unlimited, but shall not be excessive.

64. Sentence of imprisonment for non-payment of fine.—In every case, of an offence punishable with imprisonment as well as fine, in which the offender is sentenced to a fine, whether with or without imprisonment,

and in every case of an offence punishable with imprisonment or fine, or with fine only, in which the offender is sentenced to a fine,

it shall be competent to the Court which sentences such offender to direct by the sentence that, in default of payment of the fine, the offender shall suffer imprisonment for a certain term, in which imprisonment shall be in excess of any other imprisonment to which he may have been sentenced or to which he may be liable under a commutation of a sentence.

65. Limit to imprisonment for non-payment of fine, when imprisonment and fine awardable.—The term for which the Court directs the offender to be imprisoned in default of payment of a fine shall not exceed one-fourth of the term of imprisonment which is the maximum fixed for the offence, if the offence be punishable with imprisonment as well as fine.

66. Description of imprisonment for non-payment of fine.—The imprisonment which the Court imposes in default of payment of a fine may be of any description to which the offender might have been sentenced for the offence.

67. Imprisonment for non-payment of fine, when offence punishable with fine only.—If the offence be punishable with fine only, the imprisonment which the Court imposes in default of payment of the fine shall be simple, and the term for which the Court directs the offender to be imprisoned, in default of payment of fine, shall not exceed the following scale, that is to say, for any term not exceeding two months when the amount of the fine shall not exceed fifty rupees, and for any term not exceeding four months when the amount shall not exceed one hundred rupees, and for any term not exceeding six months in any other case.

68. Imprisonment to terminate on payment of fine.—The imprisonment which is imposed in default of payment of a fine shall terminate whenever that fine is either paid or levied by process of law.

69. Termination of imprisonment on payment of proportional part of fine.—If, before the expiration of the term of imprisonment fixed in default of payment, such a proportion of the fine be paid or levied that the term of imprisonment suffered in default of payment is not less than proportional to the part of the fine still unpaid, the imprisonment shall terminate.

Illustration

A is sentenced to a fine of one hundred rupees and to four months' imprisonment in default of payment. Here, if seventy-five rupees of the fine be paid or levied before the expiration of one month of the imprisonment, A will be discharged as soon as the first month has expired. If seventy-five rupees be paid or levied at the time of the expiration of the first month, or at any later time while A continues in imprisonment, A will be immediately discharged. If fifty rupees of the fine be paid or levied before the expiration of two months of the imprisonment, A will be discharged as soon as the two months are completed. If fifty rupees be paid or levied at the time of the expiration of those two months, or at any later time while A continues in imprisonment, A will be immediately discharged.

70. Fine leviable within six years, or during imprisonment—Death not to discharge property from liability.—The fine, or any part thereof which remains unpaid, may be levied at any time within six years after the passing of the sentence, and if, under the sentence, the offender be liable to imprisonment for a longer period than six years, then at any time previous to the expiration of that period; and the death of the offender does not discharge from the liability any property which would, after his death, be legally liable for his debts.

71. Limit of punishment of offence made up of several offences.—Where anything which is an offence is made up of parts, any of which parts is itself an offence, the offender shall not be punished with the punishment of more than one of such his offences, unless it be so expressly provided.

Where anything is an offence falling within two or more separate definitions of any law in force for the time being by which offences are defined or punished, or

where several acts, of which one or more than one would by itself or themselves constitute an offence, constitute, when combined, a different offence,

the offender shall not be punished with a more severe punishment than the Court which tries him could award for any one of such offences.

Illustrations

(a) A gives Z fifty strokes with a stick. Here A may have committed the offence of voluntarily causing hurt to Z by the whole beating, and also by each of the blows which make up the whole beating. If A were liable to punishment for every blow, he might be imprisoned for fifty years, one for each blow. But he is liable only to one punishment for the whole beating.

(b) But if, while A is beating Z, Y interferes, and A intentionally strikes Y, here, as the blow given to Y is no part of the act whereby A voluntarily causes hurt to Z, A is liable to one punishment for voluntarily causing hurt to Z, and to another for the blow given to Y.

72. Punishment of person guilty of one of several offences, the judgment stating that it is doubtful of which.—In all cases in which judgment is given that a person is guilty of one of several offences specified in the judgment, but that it is doubtful of which of these offences, he is guilty, the offender shall be punished for the offence for which the lowest punishment is provided if the same punishment is not provided for all.

73. Solitary confinement.—Whenever any person is convicted of an offence for which under this Code the Court has power to sentence him to rigorous imprisonment, the Court may, by its sentence, order that the offender shall be kept in solitary confinement for any portion or portions of the imprisonment to which he is sentenced, not exceeding three months in the whole, according to the following scale, that is to say—

a time not exceeding one month if the term of imprisonment shall not exceed six months;

a time not exceeding two months if the term of imprisonment shall exceed six months and shall not exceed one year;

a time not exceeding three months if the term of imprisonment shall exceed one year.

74. Limit of solitary confinement.—In executing a sentence of solitary confinement, such confinement shall in no case exceed fourteen days at a time, with intervals between the periods of solitary confinement of not less duration than such periods; and when the imprisonment awarded shall exceed three months, the solitary confinement shall not exceed seven days in any one month of the whole imprisonment awarded, with intervals between the periods of solitary confinement of not less duration than such periods.

75. Enhanced punishment for certain offences under Chapter XII or Chapter XVII after previous conviction.—Whoever, having been convicted,—

(a) by a Court in India, of an offence punishable under Chapter XII or Chapter XVII of this Code with imprisonment of either description for a term of three years or upwards,

shall be guilty of any offence punishable under either of those Chapters with like imprisonment for the like term, shall be subject for every such subsequent offence to imprisonment for life, or to imprisonment of either description for a term which may extend to ten years.

See

P. Jebac Angel Martin v. *State,* 2008 (6) AIR Bom R 1073 (NOC): 2008 Cr LJ 3147 (Mad).

Md. Munna v. *Union of India,* 2005 Cr LJ 4124: AIR 2005 SC 3440: 2005 (4) Crimes 48 (SC).

Shailesh Jasvantbhai v. *State of Gujarat,* (2006) 2 SCC 359: 2006 Cr LJ 1132: 2006 AIR SCW 436.

Subash Chander v. *Kishan Lal,* 2001 AIR SCW 1492: AIR 2001 SC 1903: 2001 Cr LJ 1825.

Reddy Sampath Kumar v. *State of Andhra Pradesh,* 2005 AIR SCW 4620: AIR 2005 SC 3478: 2005 Cr LJ 4131: 2005 (4) Crimes 1 (SC).

K.V. Chacko v. *State of Kerala,* 2004 (2) All Cri LR 49: 2004 (1) Cur Cri R 449: 2004 Cr LJ 481 (Ker).

Phool Kumari v. *Office of the Superintendent Central Jail Tihar, New Delhi,* AIR 2012 SC 3198: 2012 Cr LJ 4261: 2012 AIR SCW 4611.

Guru Basavaray v. *State of Karnataka,* (2012) 8 SCC 734.

Rashid Alam v. *State of West Bengal,* 2008 (3) AIR Jhar (NOC) 975: 2008 (4) All Cri LR 381: 2008 Cr LJ 2861 (Cal).

Caitan Feranandez v. *State,* 2005 (3) Crimes 240 (Bom).

Usman v. *State of Uttar Pradesh,* 2008 (1) AIR Bom R 5 (NOC): 2007 (58) All Cri C 889: 2007 Cr LJ 3868 (All).

State of Assam v. *Sri Bir Bahadur Singh,* 2005 (4) Gau LT 14: 2005 Cr LJ 4345 (Gau).

Shanti Lal v. *State of Madhya Pradesh,* 2007 AIR SCW 6494: (2007) 11 SCC 243: 2008 Cr LJ 386 (SC).

Moideenkutty Kunhankutty Haji v. *State of Kerala,* 2008 (2) Ker LJ 741: 2008 (3) Ker LT 8: 2008 Cr LJ 3402 (Ker).

C. *Ganga* v. *Lakshmi Ammal,* 2008 (2) Ker LJ 25: 2008 (2) Ker LT 306: 2008 Cr LJ 3359 (Ker).

Monica Christy Chikwa v. *State of Punjab,* 2006 (5) AIR Bom R 792 (NOC): 2006 (2) Rec Cri R 290: 2006 Cr LJ 2661 (P&H).

CHAPTER 8

APPEARANCE ON THE DATE FIXED FOR THE CASE

Sub-section (3) of section 265B of the Code says that after receiving the application under sub-section (1), the court shall issue notice to the public prosecutor or the complainant of the case, as the case may be and to the accused to appear on the date fixed for the case. The word "appear" appears in several provisions of the Code. For Appearance *see* sections 204, 205 of the Code.

Bhushan Kumar v. *State, (NCT of Delhi),* AIR 2012 SC 1747: (2012) 5 SCC 424: 2012 Cr LJ 2286.

Raghuvansh Dewanchand Bhasin v. *State of Maharashtra,* AIR 2011 SC 3393: 2011 AIR SCW 5347: 2011 (3) Cur Cri R 489.

Nupur Talwar v. *CBI,* AIR 2012 SC 1921: 2012 (3) Crimes 31: (2012) 5 SCALE 744.

Kulwant Singh v. *Surjit Kaur,* 2002 (2) Marri LJ 491: 2002 (3) Rec Cri R 261: 2002 Cr LJ 3443 (P&H).

Rakesh Devi v. *State of Uttar Pradesh,* 2002 (1) Crimes 540: 2002 (2) Rec Cri R 157: 2002 Cr LJ 1225 (All).

Jancy Nelson D'Souza v. *Nelson D'Souza,* 2004 (2) All Cri LR 361: 2003 All MR (Cri) 1875: 2004 Cr LJ 1690 (Bom).

Shivani Sadanand v. *State,* 2002 (97) DLT 443: 2002 (2) Punj LR 59: 2002 Cr LJ 3384 (Del).

Deva Nand Upadhayay v. *Union of India,* 2005 (3) BLJR 2215: 2006 (2) Cur Cri R 169 2006 Cr LJ 63 (Pat).

S.V. Muzumdar v. *Gujarat State Fertilizer Co. Ltd.,* 2005 Cr LJ 2566: AIR 2005 SC 2436: 2005 AIR SCW 2364.

CHAPTER 9

SATISFACTION OF THE COURT THAT THE APPLICATION HAS BEEN FILED BY THE ACCUSED VOLUNTARILY

Section 265B(4)(a) of the Code says that where the public prosecutor or the complainant of the case, as the case may be, and the accused appear on the date fixed under sub-section (3), the Court shall examine the accused *in camera*, where the other party in the case shall not be present, to satisfy itself that the accused has filed the application voluntarily and where the Court is satisfied that the application has been filed by the accused voluntarily, it shall provide time to the public prosecutor or the complainant of the case, as the case may be, and the accused to work out a mutually satisfactory disposition of the case which may include giving to the victim by the accused the compensation and other expenses during the case and thereafter fix the date for further hearing of the case.

In *Roy Fernandes* v. *State of Goa,* AIR 2012 SC 1030: (2012) 3 SCC 221: 2012 Cr LJ 1542 it was held that section 357 of the Code embodies the concept of compensation to the victim of a crime and empowers the Courts to award suitable amount and this power shall be exercised by Courts having regard to the nature of injury or loss suffered by the victim as also the paying capacity of the accused.

In *R. Mohan* v. *A.K. Vijaya Kumar,* 2012 Cr LJ 3953: 2012 AIR SCW 4085: (2012) 8 SCC 721 it was held that the idea behind directing the accused to pay compensation to the complainant is to give him immediate relief so as to alleviate his grievance and in terms of section 357(3) of the Code compensation is awarded for the loss or injury suffered by the person due to the act of the accused for which he is sentenced.

See

R. Vijayan v. *Baby,* AIR 2012 SC 528: 2012 Cr LJ 846: 2012 AIR SCW 438.

State of Punjab v. *Gurmej Singh,* AIR 2002 SC 2811: 2002 Cr LJ 3741: (2002) 6 SCC 663.

Siva Suriyan v. *Jhangavelu,* (2004) 13 SCC 795.

Damodar S. Prabhu v. *Sayed Babalal H.,* (2010) 5 SCC 663: 2010 Cr LJ 2860: AIR 2010 SC 1907.

K. Bhaskaran v. *Sankaran Vaidhyan Balan,* AIR 1999 SC 3762: 1999 AIR SCW 3809: (1999) 7 SCC 510.

Vijayan v. *Sadanandan K.*, AIR 2009 SC (Supp) 1435: (2009) 6 SCC 652: 2009 Cr LJ 2957: 2009 AIR SCW 3469.

Hari Kishan v. *Sukhbir Singh*, AIR 1988 SC 2127: 1989 Cr LJ 116: (1988) 4 SCC 551.

K.A. Abbas v. *Subu Joseph*, (2010) 6 SCC 230: AIR 2011 SC (Cri) 1093: 2010 AIR SCW 3398.

Suganthi Suresh Kumar v. *Jagdeeshan*, 2002 Cr LJ 1003: (2002) 2 SCC 420: AIR 2002 SC 681.

Subhojit Datta v. *State of Bihar*, 2007 (56) All Ind Cas 709: 2007 (4) East Cri C 121: 2008 Cr LJ 872 (Pat).

Lal Singh Bhikhabhai Chaudhary v. *State of Gujarat*, 2004 (4) Crimes 542: 2004 (4) Guj LR 3466: 2004 Cr LJ 3292 (Guj).

Dilip S. Dahanukar v. *Kotak Mahindra Co. Ltd.*, 2007 Cr LJ 2417: 2007 AIR SCW 2425: 2007 (2) Crimes 435 (SC).

Mangu Lal v. *State of Madhya Pradesh*, AIR 2004 SC 1280: 2004 AIR SCW 137: 2004 Cr LJ 880.

Maheshwar Dattatraya Kale v. *Capt. Atul Wasudeo Divekar*, 2006 (3) CCC 752: 2006 (2) Crimes 248: 2006 Cr LJ 606 (Bom).

Arun Garg v. *State of Punjab*, (2004) 8 SCC 251.

Sathyan Ayyappa Sathyan v. *Yousu*, 2007 (4) Bank Cas 1: 2007 (3) CCC 639: 2007 Cr LJ 2590 (Ker).

Afzal Ahmed v. *Mohd. Faizan*, 2007 (1) AIR Jhar (NOC) 253: 2007 (1) NIJ 51: 2006 Cr LJ 3806 (Uttar).

Inspector of Police v. *R. Jeeva Jothi*, 2007 (2) Mad LJ (Cri) 142: 2007 (1) Mad LW (Cri) 377: 2007 Cr LJ 3003 (Mad).

Gagan Thakur v. *State of Jharkhand*, 2004 (1) BLJR 415: 2004 (2) Cur Cri R 43: 2004 Cr LJ 1910 (Jhar).

K.S. Saji Kumar v. *K. Soman Pillai*, 2007 Cr LJ 2992 (Ker): 2007 (3) Bank Cas 588: 2007 (4) Crimes 229 (Ker).

C. Ganga v. *Lakshmi Ammal*, 2008 (2) Ker LJ 25: 2008 (2) Ker LT 306: 2008 Cr LJ 3359 (Ker).

Mohd. Afiz Khan v. *Anand Finance*, 2004 (2) Crimes 511 (Bom).

Narayan Dass v. *State of Haryana*, 2008 Cr LJ 4000 (P&H).

For *in-Camera*

See

Varadaraju v. *State of Karnataka*, 2005 (4) KCCR 2316: 2006 (5) Kant LJ 616: 2005 Cr LJ 4180 (Kant).

State of Gujarat v. *Rajubhai Dhamirbhai Bariya*, 2004 (1) Guj LH 262: 2004 (1) Guj LR 404: 2004 Cr LJ 771 (Guj).

Sakshi v. *Union of India*, AIR 2004 SC 3566: 2004 AIR SCW 3449: (2004) 5 SCC 518.

It shall Proceed Further in Accordance with the Provisions of this Code from the Stage such Application has been filed under sub-section (1)

Section 265B(4)(b) of the Code says that when the public prosecutor or the complainant of the case, as the case may be, and the accused appear on the date fixed under sub-section (3) the Court shall examine the accused *in-Camera* where the other party in the case shall not be present, to satisfy itself that the accused has filed the application voluntarily and where the Court finds that the application has been filed involuntarily by the accused or he has previously been convicted by a Court in a case in which he had been charged with the same offence, it shall proceed further in accordance with the provisions of this Code from the stage such application has been filed under sub-section (1).

CHAPTER 10

GUIDELINES FOR MUTUALLY SATISFACTORY DISPOSITION

Section 265C of the Code dealing with Guidelines for mutually satisfactory disposition read:

265C. Guidelines for mutually satisfactory disposition.—In working out a mutually satisfactory disposition under clause (a) of sub-section (4) of section 265B, the Court shall follow the following procedure, namely:—

(a) in a case instituted on a police report, the Court shall issue notice to the Public Prosecutor, the police officer who has investigated the case, the accused and the victim of the case to participate in the meeting to work out a satisfactory disposition of the case:

Provided that throughout such process of working out a satisfactory disposition of the case, it shall be the duty of the Court to ensure that the entire process is completed voluntarily by the parties participating in the meeting:

Provided further that the accused, if he so desires, may participate in such meeting with his pleader, if any, engaged in the case;

(b) in a case instituted otherwise than on police report, the Court shall issue notice to the accused and the victim of the case to participate in a meeting to work out a satisfactory disposition of the case:

Provided that it shall be the duty of the Court to ensure, throughout such process of working out a satisfactory disposition of the case, that it is completed voluntarily by the parties participating in the meeting:

Provided further that if the victim of the case or the accused, as the case may be, so desires, he may participate in such meeting with his pleader engaged in the case.

Chapter XIX of the Code deals with trial of warrant cases by Magistrates. Chapter XIXA of the Code dealing with cases instituted on a police Report reads:

244. Evidence for prosecution.—(1) When, in any warrant-case instituted otherwise than on a police report, the accused appears or is brought before a Magistrate, the Magistrate shall proceed to hear the prosecution and take all such evidence as may be produced in support of the prosecution.

(2) The Magistrate may, on the application of the prosecution, issue a summons to any of its witnesses directing him to attend or to produce any document or other thing.

245. When accused shall be discharged.—(1) If, upon taking all the evidence referred to in section 244, the Magistrate considers, for reasons to be recorded, that no case against the accused has been made out which, if unrebutted, would warrant his conviction, the Magistrate shall discharge him.

(2) Nothing in this section shall be deemed to prevent a Magistrate from discharging the accused at any previous stage of the case if, for reasons to be recorded by such Magistrate, he considers the charge to be groundless.

246. Procedure where accused is not discharged.—(1) If, when such evidence has been taken, or at any previous stage of the case, the Magistrate is of opinion that there is ground for presuming that the accused has committed an offence triable under this Chapter, which such Magistrate is competent to try and which, in his opinion, could be adequately punished by him, he shall frame in writing a charge against the accused.

(2) The charge shall then be read and explained to the accused, and he shall be asked whether he pleads guilty or has any defence to make.

(3) If the accused pleads guilty, the Magistrate shall record the plea, and may, in his discretion, convict him thereon.

(4) If the accused refuses to plead, or does not plead or claims to be tried or if the accused is not convicted under sub-section (3), he shall be required to state, at the commencement of the next hearing of the case, or, if the Magistrate for reasons to be recorded in writing so thinks fit, forthwith, whether he wishes to cross-examine any, and if so, which, of the witnesses for the prosecution whose evidence has been taken.

(5) If he says he does so wish, the witnesses named by him shall be recalled and, after cross-examination and re-examination (if any), they shall be discharged.

(6) The evidence of any remaining witnesses for the prosecution shall next be taken and after cross-examination and re-examination (if any), they shall also be discharged.

247. Evidence for defence.—The accused shall then be called upon to enter upon his defence and produce his evidence; and the provisions of section 243 shall apply to the case.

Case Instituted on a Public Report

Section 265C(a) of the Code says that in working out a mutually satisfactory disposition under section 265B(4)(a) of the Code, the court shall follow the following procedure namely in a case instituted on a police report the court shall issue notice to the public prosecutor, the police officer who has investigated the case, the accused and the victim of the case to participate in the meeting to workout a satisfactory disposition of the case. The first proviso says that throughout such process of working out a satisfactory disposition of the case, it shall be the duty of the court to ensure that the entire process is completed voluntarily by the parties participating in the meeting. The second proviso says that the accused, if he so desires may participate in such meeting with his pleader, if any, engaged in the case. For cases instituted on a police report *see* sections 238 to 243 of the Code.

Vinay Kumar Mishra v. *State,* 2005 (3) Crimes 147 (Jhar).

P.R. Ramakrishnan v. *P. Govindarajan,* 2007 (4) AIR Bom R 677 (NOC): 2007 (1) Mad LJ (Cri) 1297: 2007 Cr LJ 1897 (Mad).

State of Karnataka v. *Anne Gowda,* AIR 2006 SC 2641: 2006 AIR SCW 3562: 2006 Cr LJ 3630.

Sheshrao v. *State,* 2002 (3) All Cri LR 80: 2002 (2) Hindu LR 344: 2001 Cr LJ 3805 (Kant).

Hari Babu v. *State of Uttar Pradesh,* 2002 (44) All Cri C 364: 2002 (1) All Cri R 434: 2002 Cr LJ 2213 (All).

State v. *Chandraket Narayan Singh,* 2005 (30) All Ind Cas 694: 2004 (3) Cur Cri R 413: 2004 Cr LJ 3618 (Jhar).

Bipin Shantilal Panchal v. *State of Gujarat,* AIR 2001 SC 1158: 2001 AIR SCW 841: 2001 Cr LJ 1254 (SC).

Banshi Lal v. *State of Rajsthan,* 2002 WLC (Raj) (UC) 150: 2001 Cr LJ 3117 (Raj).

Hariprasad v. *State of Rajasthan,* 2005 Cri LR (Raj) 910: 2005 Cr LJ 3762 (Raj).

State of Karnataka v. *Abdul Rasheem,* 2007 (3) All Cri LR 95: 2006 (46) All Ind Cas 215: 2006 Cr LJ 3169 (Kant).

Kanti Bhadra Shah v. *State of West Bengal,* 2000 Cr LJ 746: 2001 AIR SCW 52: (2000) 1 SCC 722.

Munna Devi v. *State of Rajasthan,* AIR 2002 SC 107: 2002 Cr LJ 225: (2001) 9 SCC 631.

Surjit Kaur v. *D.S. Kapoor,* (2001) 9 SCC 468: 2001 Cr LJ 4699 (SC): 2001 AIR SCW 4070.

A.R. Saravanan v. *State,* 2003 (1) Cur Cri R 203: 2002 (46) Mad LJ (Cri) 1065: 2003 Cr LJ 1140 (Mad).

Ram Kawal Tiwari v. *State of Uttar Pradesh,* 2002 All LJ 437: 2002 (44) All Cri C 241: 2002 Cr LJ 1860 (All).

Deep Narayan Yadav v. *State of Bihar,* 2000 (2) East Cri C 1353: 2000 (2) Pat LJR 628: 2001 Cr LJ 2815 (Pat).

Diamond Cables Ltd. v. *State of Andhra Pradesh,* 2004 (2) ALD (Crl) 305: 2004 (4) Cur Cri R 368: 2004 Cr LJ 4100 (AP).

Dilip Kumar Sarkar v. *State of Jharkhand*, 2003 AIR Jhar HCR 580: 2003 (2) East Cri C 196: 2003 Cr LJ 2086 (Jhar).

H.V. Thimmegowda v. *State*, 2001 (4) Kant LJ 548: 2001 (3) Lab LJ 1183: 2001 Cr LJ 3156 (Kant).

Modalavalasa Shanti Ram Kumar v. *State of Andhra Pradesh*, 2003 (2) ALD (Crl) 28: 2003 (4) Crimes 232: 2003 Cr LJ 3607 (AP).

Tripurari Mohan Prasad v. *Union of India*, 2006 (37) All Ind Cas 430: 2005 (4) East Cri C 187: 2006 Cr LJ 774 (Jhar).

C.K. Kamarudheen v. *P. Shoukat Ali*, 2001 (2) Ker LJ 488: 2001 (3) Ker LT 476: 2002 Cr LJ 1289 (Ker).

Derawar Singh v. *State*, 2006 (4) Crimes 57 (Raj).

Pradip Kr. Sen Gupta v. *State of West Bengal*, 2003 (1) Cal HN 439: 2003 Cr LJ 2345 (Cal).

Thomaskutty v. *Vijaya Kumari*, 2003 (1) Bank Cas 309: 2002 (2) Crimes 368: 2002 Cr LJ 3108 (Ker).

B. Dasarathararamaiah v. *State, Inspector of Police, CID PCR Cell*, 2006 (1) ALD (Crl) 249: 2005 (2) Andh LT (Cri) 198 AP: 2005 Cr LJ 3771 (AP).

Soyi v. *State*, 2006 (2) Crimes 242 (Ker).

Shabra Khatoon v. *State of Jharkhand*, 2005 (34) All Ind Cas 884: 2005 (2) DMC 319: 2005 Cr LJ 3292 (Jhar).

Mohammad Hussain v. *State of Uttar Pradesh*, 2004 (49) All Cri C 311: 2004 (1) All Cri R 882: 2004 Cr LJ 2694 (All).

K. Neelaveni v. *State rep. by Inspector of Police*, AIR 2010 SC 3191: 2010 Cr LJ 2819: 2010 AIR SCW 2760.

Case Instituted Otherwise than in Police Report

Section 265C(b) of the Code says that in working out a mutually satisfactory disposition under section 265B(4)(a) of the Code the court shall follow the following procedure namely in a case instituted otherwise than on police Report the court shall issue notice to the accused and the victim of the case to participate in a meeting to work out a satisfactory disposition of the case. The first proviso says that it shall be the duty of the court to ensure throughout such process of working out a satisfactory disposition of the case, that it is completed, voluntarily by the parties participating in the meeting. The second proviso says that if the victim of the case or the accused, as the case may be, so desires, he may participate in such meeting with his pleader engaged in the case. *See* section 244 to 247 of the Code. *Sadat Ali* v. *State of Tripura*, 2005 (1) Gau LT 132: 2005 (3) Gau LR 510: 2005 Cr LJ 635 (Gau).

Eswara Raddy v. *Adhi Reddy*, 2004 (3) Crimes 307 (AP).

Saranan Chattopadhyaya v. *State of Bihar*, 2006 (38) All Ind Cas 913: 2006 (1) DMC 663: 2006 Cr LJ 921 (Jhar).

Saktipada Dolui v. *Madhabi Dolui*, 2002 (4) All Cri LR 995: 2003 (1) Rec Cri R 525: 2003 Cr LJ 328 (Cal).

Ishwar Saran Shukla v. *State of Uttar Pradesh*, 2001 All LJ 1857: 2001 (3) Crimes 429: 2001 Cr LJ 3903 (All).

Jai Pal Singh v. *State of Uttar Pradesh*, 2001 (43) All Cri C 639: 2002 (1) All Cri LR 179: 2001 Cr LJ 4416 (All).

Public Prosecutor v. *P. Subhash Chandra Reddy*, 2003 (2) ALD (Crl) 6: 2004 (1) Rec Cri R 680: 2003 Cr LJ 4776 (AP).

Dahyabhai Solanki v. *State of Gujarat*, 2003 (1) Guj LH 56: 2003 (1) Guj LR 597: 2003 Cr LJ 767 (Guj).

State of Bihar v. *Baidnath Prasad*, AIR 2002 SC 64: 2002 Cr LJ 208: 2001 AIR SCW 4562.

Cintamani Pandey v. *State of Bihar*, 2007 (4) East Cri C 159: 2007 (3) JLJR 226: 2007 Cr LJ 3577 (Jhar).

Pharmed Chemicals Ltd. v. *Sainath Agencies*, 2004 (2) All Cri LR 900: 2004 (1) Kant LJ 422: 2004 Cr LJ 2253 (Kant).

H. Raghavendra Rao v. *Buckeye Corporation (I) Ltd.*, 2004 (4) Kant LJ 160: 2004 (3) Rec Cri R 900: 2004 Cr LJ 2633 (Kant).

State v. *Jaya Chandran*, 2008 Cr LJ 4591 (Mad).

G. Chandrasekaran v. *C.R. Umapathy*, 2005 (2) Bank Cas 204: 2004 (5) CTC 50: 2005 Cr LJ 1820 (Mad).

Saroj Jaiswal v. *State of Bihar*, 2005 (1) BLJR 484: 2005 (1) East Cri C 556: 2005 Cr LJ 1767 (Jhar).

Manmohan Malhotra v. *P.M. Abdul Salam*, 1995 (1) Cr CJ 6: 1994 (2) Crimes 331: 1994 Cr LJ 1555 (Ker).

Ranvijay Prasad Deo v. *State of Jharkhand*, 2007 (2) AIR Jhar R 971: 2007 (55) All Ind Cas 956: 2007 Cr LJ 3553 (Jhar).

Kamla Kant Trivedi v. *State of Bihar*, 2008 (3) AIR Jhar R 311: 2008 Cr LJ 2757 (Pat).

Mahendra Kumar Mishra v. *Chandra Shekhar Prasad Mishra*, 2001 Cri LR (SC and MP) MPJ 280: 2001 Cr LJ 3455 (Kant).

Heera Lal Pandit v. *State of Bihar*, 2003 (3) East Cri C 59: 2003 (4) Pat LJR 452: 2003 Cr LJ 2976 (Pat).

Report of the Mutually Satisfactory Disposition to be Submitted before the Court

Section 265D of the code dealing with Report of the mutually satisfactory disposition to be submitted before the court reads.

> *265D. Report of the mutually satisfactory disposition to be submitted before the Court.*—Where in a meeting under section 265C, a satisfactory disposition of the case has been worked out, the Court shall prepare a report of such disposition which shall be signed by the presiding officer

of the Court and all other persons who participated in the meeting and if no such disposition has been worked out, the Court shall record such observation and proceed further in accordance with the provisions of this Code from the stage the application under sub-section (1) of section 265B has been filed in such case.

Working out of a Satisfactory Disposition of the Case

In a meeting under section 265C of the Code if a satisfactory disposition of the case has been worked out, the court shall prepare a Report of such disposition which shall be signed by the presiding officer of the court and all other persons who participated in the meeting.

If Disposition has not been Worked Out

If no such disposition has been worked out, the court shall record such observation and proceed further in accordance with the provisions of this Code from the stage the application under section 265B(1) of the Code has been filed in such case.

CHAPTER 11
DISPOSAL OF THE CASE

Section 265(E) of the Code dealing with disposal of the case reads:

265E. Disposal of the case.—Where a satisfactory disposition of the case has been worked out under section 265D, the Court shall dispose of the case in the following manner, namely:—

(a) the Court shall award the compensation to the victim in accordance with the disposition under section 265D and hear the parties on the quantum of the punishment, releasing of the accused on probation of good conduct or after admonition under section 360 or for dealing with the accused under the provisions of the Probation of Offenders Act, 1958 (20 of 1958) or any other law for the time being in force and follow the procedure specified in the succeeding clauses for imposing the punishment on the accused;

(b) after hearing the parties under clause (a), if the Court is of the view that section 360 or the provisions of the Probation of Offenders Act, 1958 (20 of 1958) or any other law for the time being in force are attracted in the case of the accused, it may release the accused on probation or provide the benefit of any such law, as the case may be;

(c) after hearing the parties under clause (b), if the Court finds that minimum punishment has been provided under the law for the offence committed by the accused, it may sentence the accused to half of such minimum punishment;

(d) in case after hearing the parties under clause (b), the Court finds that the offence committed by the accused is not covered under clause (b) or clause (c), then, it may sentence the accused to one-fourth of the punishment provided or extendable, as the case may be, for such offence.

Section 360 of the Code dealing with order to release on probation of good conduct or after admonition reads:

360. Order to release on probation of good conduct or after admonition.—(1) When any person not under twenty-one years of age is convicted of an offence punishable with fine only or with imprisonment for a term of seven years or less, or when any person under twenty-one years of age or any woman is convicted of an offence not punishable with death or imprisonment for life, and no previous conviction is proved against the offender, if it appears to the Court before which he is convicted, regard being had to the age, character or antecedents of the offender, and to the circumstances in which the offence was committed, that it is expedient that the offender should be released on probation of good conduct, the Court may, instead of sentencing him at once to any punishment, direct that he be released on his entering into a bond, with or without sureties, to appear and receive sentence when called upon during such period (not exceeding three years) as the Court may direct and in the meantime to keep the peace and be of good behaviour:

Provided that where any first offender is convicted by a Magistrate of the second class not specially empowered by the High Court, and the Magistrate is of opinion that the powers conferred by this section should be exercised, he shall record his opinion to that effect, and submit the proceedings to a Magistrate of the first class forwarding the accused to or taking bail for his appearance before, such Magistrate, who shall dispose of the case in the manner provided by sub-section (2).

(2) Where proceedings are submitted to a Magistrate of the first class as provided by sub-section (1), such Magistrate may thereupon pass such sentence or make such order as he might have passed or made if the case had originally been heard by him, and, if he thinks further inquiry or additional evidence on any point to be necessary, he may make such inquiry or take such evidence himself or direct such inquiry or evidence to be made or taken.

(3) In any case in which a person is convicted of theft, theft in a building, dishonest misappropriation, cheating or any offence under the Indian Penal Code (45 of 1860) punishable with not more than two years' imprisonment or any offence punishable with fine only and no previous conviction is proved against him, the Court before which he is so convicted may, if it thinks fit, having regard to the age, character, antecedents or physical or mental condition of the offender and to the trivial nature of the offence or any extenuating circumstances under which the offence was committed, instead of sentencing him to any punishment, release him after due admonition.

(4) An order under this section may be made by any Appellate Court or by the High Court or Court of Session when exercising its powers of revision.

(5) When an order has been made under this section in respect of any offender, the High Court or Court of Session may, on appeal when there is a right of appeal to such Court, or when exercising its powers of revision, set aside such order, and in lieu thereof pass sentence on such offender according to law:

Provided that the High Court or Court of Session shall not under this sub-section inflict a greater punishment than might have been inflicted by the Court by which the offender was convicted.

(6) The provisions of sections 121, 124 and 373 shall, so far as may be apply in the case of sureties offered in pursuance of the provisions of this section.

(7) The Court, before directing the release of an offender under sub-section (1) shall be satisfied that an offender or his surety (if any) has a fixed place of abode or regular occupation in the place for which the Court acts or in which the offender is likely to live during the period named for the observance of the conditions.

(8) If the Court which convicted the offender, or a Court which could have dealt with the offender in respect of his original offence, is satisfied that the offender has failed to observe any of the conditions of his recognizance, it may issue a warrant for his apprehension.

(9) An offender, when apprehended on any such warrant, shall be brought forthwith before the Court issuing the warrant, and such Court may either remand him in custody until the case is heard or admit him to bail with a sufficient surety conditioned on his appearing for sentence and such Court may after hearing the case, pass sentence.

(10) Nothing in this section shall affect the provisions of the Probation of Offenders Act, 1958 (20 of 1958), or the Children Act, 1960 (60 of 1960), or any other law for the time being in force for the treatment , training or rehabilitation of youthful offenders.

See the provisions of the Probation of Offenders Act, 1958 and the Children Act, 1960.

See also sections 250, 357, 357A, 358 of the Code.

See Chapter III of the Indian Penal Code.

Disposition under section 265D

Section 265(E)(a) of the Code says that where a satisfactory disposition of the case has been worked out under section 265D, the court shall dispose of the case in the following manner namely the court shall award the compensation to the victim in accordance with the disposition under section 265D and hear the parties on the quantum of the punishments releasing the accused on probation of good conduct or after admonition under section 360 or for dealing with the accused under the provisions of the Probation of Offenders Act, 1958 or any other law for the time being in force and follow the procedure specified in the succeeding clauses for imposing the punishment on the accused. In *Roy Fernandes* v. *State of Goa,* AIR 2012 SC 1030: (2012) 3 SCC 221: 2012 Cr LJ 1542, it was held that section 357 of the Code embodies the Concept of Compensating the victim of a crime and empowers the Courts to award suitable amount.

In *R. Mohan* v. *A.K. Vijaya Kumar*, 2012 Cr LJ 3953: 2012 AIR SCW 4085: (2012) 8 SCC 721, it was held that the idea behind directing the accused to pay compensation to the complainant is to give him immediate relief so as to alleviate his grievance.

See

Damodar S. Prabhu v. *Sayed Babalal*, (2010) 5 SCC 663: AIR 2010 SC 1907: 2010 Cr LJ 2860.

State of Punjab v. *Gurmej Singh*, AIR 2002 SC 2811: 2002 Cr LJ 3741: (2002) 6 SCC 663.

Suva Surjan v. *Jhangavelu*, (2004) 13 SCC 795.

K. Bhaskaran v. *Sankaran Vaidhyan Balan*, AIR 1999 SC 3762: 1999 AIR SCW 3809: (1999) 7 SCC 510.

Vijayan v. *Sadanandan K.*, AIR 2009 SC (Supp) 1435: (2009) 6 SCC 652: 2009 Cr LJ 2957: 2009 AIR SCW 3469.

Hari Kishan v. *Sukhbir Singh*, AIR 1988 SC 2127: 1989 Cr LJ 116: (1988) 4 SCC 551.

K.A. Abbas v. *Subu Joseph*, (2010) 6 SCC 230: AIR 2011 SC (Cri) 1093: 2010 AIR SCW 3398.

Suganthi Suresh Kumar v. *Jagdeeshan*, AIR 2002 SC 681: 2002 Cr LJ 1003: (2002) 2 SCC 420.

In *Md. Jiaur Rahman* v. *State of Assam*, 2006 (54) All Cri C 22 (SOC): 2006 (37) All Ind Cas 844: 2005 Cr LJ 4245 (Gau), it was held that where show cause notice was issued but an order for compensation was made without considering the reply, such order for compensation is in violation of principle of Natural Justice and Fair play. The non-application of mind in issuing show cause notice to the complaint to pay compensation for filing false complaint, had fallen for consideration in *Mehta Prafulchandra Kalidas* v. *Patel Chejibhai Kalidas*, 2006 (1) Bank J 263: 2006 (4) CCC 563: 2006 Cr LJ 1660 (Gau).

In *Mangu Lal* v. *State of Madhya Pradesh*, AIR 2004 SC 1280: 2004 AIR SCW 137: 2004 Cr LJ 880, it was held that the Appellate Court or Revisional Court may award compensation to the victim only after giving an opportunity of hearing to the accused on question of quantum of compensation. For awarding of compensation.

See:

Surender v. *Commissioner and Secretary NCT*, 2005 (123) DLT 517: 2006 (3) Rec Cri R 403: 2006 Cr LJ 1978 (Del).

Arun Garg v. *State of Punjab*, (2004) 8 SCC 251.

Manish Jalan v. *State of Karnataka*, 2008 AIR SCW 5160: AIR 2008 SC 3074: 2008 Cr LJ 3941 (SC).

Sube Singh v. *State of Haryana*, AIR 2006 SC 1117: 2006 Cr LJ 1242: 2006 AIR SCW 779.

State Rep. by Inspector of Police v. *N.M.T. Joy Immaculate*, AIR 2004 SC 2282: 2004 AIR SCW 2828: 2004 Cr LJ 2515.

Vidya Prakash Goud v. *State*, 2003 (2) An LJ (Cri) 214.

C. Thekkamalai v. *State of Tamil Nadu*, 2006 (1) Mad LJ 108: 2006 (1) Rec Cri R 520: 2006 Cr LJ 1997 (Mad).

Jonnadula Mallikarjuna Rao v. *Dodda Venkata Subbareddy*, 2000 (2) Andh WR 19: 2001 (3) Civ LJ 706: 2001 Cr LJ 2008 (AP).

Surendra Choudhary v. *State of Bihar*, 2002 (4) Pat LJR 691: 2003 Cr LJ 2596 (Pat).

Bipin Bihari v. *State of Madhya Pradesh*, 2005 (1) MPHT 285: 2005 (2) MPLJ 514: 2005 Cr LJ 2048 (MP).

Nehru Jain v. *State*, 2005 (1) Crimes 521 (Del).

State of Karnataka v. *Narasanna*, 2004 AIR Kant HCR 1173: 2004 Cr LJ 1973 (Kant).

Rachhpal Singh v. *State of Punjab*, AIR 2002 SC 2710: 2002 AIR SCW 3053: 2002 Cr LJ 3540.

V. Prasada Rao v. *State of Andhra Pradesh*, 2001 (2) Andh LT (Cri) 348 AP: 2002 Cr LJ 395 (AP).

State v. *Srikanth*, 2003 (1) DMC 268: 2002 (2) Hindu LR 618: 2002 Cr LJ 3605 (Kant).

M.R. Patel v. *R.K. Synthetics & Fibres Pvt. Ltd.*, 2003 (4) All Cri LR 466: 2003 (3) Bank Cas 569: 2003 Cr LJ 3218 (Kant).

Pankajbhai Nagjibhai Patel v. *State of Gujarat*, AIR 2001 SC 567: 2001 AIR SCW 184: 2001 Cr LJ 950 (SC).

Maheshwar Dattatraya Kale v. *Capt. Atul Wasudeo Divekar*, 2006 (3) CCC 752: 2006 (2) Crimes 248: 2006 Cr LJ 606 (Bom).

Dilip S. Dahanukar v. *Kotak Mahindra Co. Ltd.*, (2007) 6 SCC 528: 2007 Cr LJ 2417: 2007 (2) Crimes 435 (SC).

State of Karnataka v. *Thimmappa*, 2004 AIR Kant HCR 1241: 2004 Cr LJ 1968 (Kant).

N.E. Varghese v. *State of Kerala*, 2002 (1) Ker LJ 109: 2002 (1) Ker LT 488: 2002 Cr LJ 1712 (Ker).

Subhojit Datta v. *State of Bihar*, 2007 (56) All Ind Cas 709: 2007 (4) East Cri C 121: 2008 Cr LJ 872 (Pat).

Shaila P. Prabhu v. *Nagendra K. Mallya*, 2007 (1) Bank Cas 377: 2006 (3) Cur Cri R 372: 2006 Cr LJ 1554 (Kant).

K.S. Saji Kumar v. *K. Soman Pillai*, 2007 Cr LJ 2992: 2007 (3) Bank Cas 588: 2007 (4) Crimes 229 (Ker).

C. Ganga v. *Lakshmi Ammal*, 2008 (2) Ker LJ 25: 2008 (2) Ker LT 306: 2008 Cr LJ 3359 (Ker).

Mohd. Afiz Khan v. *Anand Finance*, 2004 (2) Crimes 511 (Bom).

Narayan Dass v. *State of Haryana*, 2008 Cr LJ 4000 (P&H).

Lalsingh Bhikhabhai Chaudhary v. *State of Gujarat*, 2004 (4) Crimes 542: 2004 (4) Guj LR 3466: 2004 Cr LJ 3292 (Guj).

Inspector of Police v. *R. Jeeva Jothi*, 2007 (2) Mad LJ (Cri) 142: 2007 (1) Mad LW (Cri) 377: 2007 Cr LJ 3003 (Mad).

Sathyan Ayyappa Sathyan v. *Yousu*, 2007 (4) Bank Cas 1: 2007 (3) CCC 639: 2007 Cr LJ 2590 (Ker).

Sajeev v. *Triveni Credit Corp.*, 2006 (4) Crimes 475 (Ker).

Afzal Ahmed v. *Mohd. Faizan*, 2007 (1) AIR Jhar (NOC) 253: 2007 (1) NIJ 51: 2006 Cr LJ 3806 (Uttar).

Section 360 or the Provisions of the Probation of Offenders Act, 1958 (20 of 1958) or any Other Law for the Time Being in Force are Attracted in the Case of the Accused

Section 265E(b) of the Code says that where a satisfactory disposition of the case has been worked out under section 265D, the court shall dispose of the case in the following manner namely, after being the parties under clause (a) if the court is of the view that section 360 or the provisions of the Probation of Offenders Act, 1958 (20 of 1958) or any other law for the time being in force are attracted in the case of the accused, it may release the accused on probation or provide the benefit of any such law, as the case may be. In *State of Punjab* v. *Balwinder Singh*, AIR 2012 SC 861: (2012) 2 SCC 182: 2012 Cr LJ 1066, it was held that where death was caused by rash and negligent drawing, the provisions of Probation of Offenders Act, 1958 cannot be made applicable. See *Dalbir Singh* v. *State of Haryana*, (2000) 5 SCC 82: AIR 2000 SC 1677: 2000 Cr LJ 2283.

B. Nagabhushanam v. *State of Karnataka*, (2008) 5 SCC 730: 2008 AIR SCW 3573: AIR 2008 SC 2557.

Munna Khan v. *State of Madhya Pradesh*, 2003 (8) All Ind Cas 298: 2003 (2) MPHT 29: 2004 Cr LJ 525 (MP).

See also *Rakesh Singh* v. *State*, 2004 (2) Crime 170 (Del).

In *State* v. *Parthiban*, 2006 (4) Crimes 158 (SC), it was held that the provisions of Probation of Offenders Act, 1958 cannot be invoked in a case of conviction for an offence under section 13(2) of the Prevention of Corruption Act. In *State of Orissa* v. *Kusa Barik*, 2007 (38) OCR 277: 2007 Cr LJ 4096 (Ori). It was held that the provisions of the Probation of Offenders Act, 1958 cannot be invoked in the case of conviction for any of the offenders affecting the Human Body. Where the accused was eighteen years and was convicted under section 15 of NDPS Act, he may be released on Probation, held in *Raj Mohammed* v. *State of Himachal Pradesh*, 2002 Cr LJ 2091: 2003 (2) All Cri LR 321: 2001 (2) Shim LC 81.

An offence punishable with death or imprisonment for life is beyond the scope of the Probation of Offenders Act, 1958 held in *State of Uttar Pradesh* v. *Surjeet Singh*, 2005 (2) All Cri R 1161: 2005 (3) Rec Cri R 283: 2005 Cr LJ 2778 (All). For the principles to give benefit of probation see *State* v. *Subash Pagi*, (2004) 4 Crimes 343 (Bom).

Gulzar v. *State of Madhya Pradesh*, (2007) 1 SCC 619: 2007 (1) Crimes 117 (SC).

Munna v. *State*, 2005 (1) Crimes 464 (MP).

Sanjay v. *State*, 2004 (4) Crimes 527 (Del): 2004 Cr LJ 4761: 2004 (114) DLT 132.

State v. *Mahaboobali*, 2003 Cr LJ 4145 (Kant): 2004 (1) All Cri LR 763: 2005 (2) Rec Cri R 753.

Kailash v. *State of Haryana*, 2003 (3) Rec Cri R 462: 2004 Cr LJ 310 (P&H).

Pawan Kumar v. *State*, 2004 Cr LJ 2310 (Del): 2004 (110) DLT 611: 2004 (3) Rec Cri R 643.

Raghunath Pradhan v. *State of Orissa*, 2007 (1) AIR Jhar (NOC) 134: 2006 (34) OCR 611: 2006 Cr LJ 3211 (Ori).

Sitaram Paswan v. *State of Bihar*, 2005 Cr LJ 4135: AIR 2005 SC 3534: 2005 (4) Crime 22 (SC).

Rakesh Singh v. *State*, 2004 (2) Crime 170 (Del).

Deepak Kumar v. *State*, 2005 (4) Crime 617 (Del).

Bharat Pandharinath More v. *State of Maharashtra*, 2004 All MR (Cri) 136: 2004 (1) Bom CR (Cri) 958: 2004 Cr LJ 205 (Bom).

Suraj Mal v. *State of Rajasthan*, 2006 (3) Raj Cri C 1495: 2006 (2) Raj LW 1680: 2006 Cr LJ 2663 (Raj).

Virender Singh v. *State*, 2004 (110) DLT 632: 2004 (74) DRJ 60: 2004 Cr LJ 2321 (Del).

Shri Shantanu Chakraborty v. *State of Tripura*, 2006 Gau LT (Supp) 115: 2005 Cr LJ 4333 (Gau).

Motty Philipose v. *State of Kerala*, 2006 (4) East Cri C 495: 2006 (1) Ker LT 732: 2006 Cr LJ 2271 (Ker).

Raj Kumar v. *State*, 2004 (2) JKJ 382: 2005 Cr LJ 1322 (J&K).

State v. *Kaptan Singh*, 2008 (1) DLT (Crl) 405: 2008 (1) JCC 397: 2008 Cr LJ 1459 (Del).

Ramesh Dass v. *Raghu Nath*, AIR 2008 SC 1298: 2008 AIR SCW 1349: 2008 Cr LJ 1945 (SC).

Bholi v. *State of Orissa*, 2005 (31) OCR 95: 2005 Cr LJ 2785 (Ori).

Ram Pratap v. *State of Rajasthan*, 2002 FAJ 207: 2002 Cr LJ 502 (Raj).

State of Himachal Pradesh v. *Sukh Ram*, 2003 (1) Cur Cri R 447: 2003 Cr LJ 219 (HP).

Sujya v. *State of Rajasthan,* 2002 (3) Raj LR 822: 2003 Cr LJ 1612 (Raj).

Balbir v. *State,* 2006 (3) Crime 230 (P&H).

Bhajan Singh v. *State of Himachal Pradesh,* 2009 (2) AIR Bom R 304 (NOC): 2008 Cr LJ 4702 (HP).

Basant Kumar v. *State of Chhattisgarh,* 2008 (2) Cur Cri R 427: 2008 (2) MPHT 41: 2008 Cr LJ 1740 (Chhat).

Sudesh Kumar v. *State of Uttarakhand,* AIR 2008 SC 1120: 2008 AIR SCW 996: 2008 Cr LJ 1604 (SC).

Upendra Nath Chaudhary v. *High Court of Judicature at Patna,* 2007 (57) All Ind Cas 389: 2007 (2) Pat LJR 554: 2007 Cr LJ 2913 (Pat).

In *Daljit Singh* v. *State of Punjab,* (2006) 6 SCC 159: 2006 (9) Supreme 804 it was held that where the provisions of the Probation of Offenders Act, 1958 are applied, the provisions of section 360 of the Code cannot be employed and the scope of Probation of Offenders Act, 1958 is much wider.

For benefit under section 360 of the Code.

See *Manjappa* v. *State of Karnataka,* (2007) 6 SCC 231: 2007 AIR SCW 3586: 2007 Cr LJ 3220 (SC).

Ramesh Manohar v. *State,* 2006 (1) Crimes 486 (Bom).

Chhanni v. *State of Uttar Pradesh,* 2006 Cr LJ 4068: AIR 2006 SC 3051: 2006 (3) Crimes 57 (SC).

Gulzar v. *State of Madhya Pradesh,* (2007) 1 SCC 619: 2007 (1) Crimes 117 (SC).

Laxmi Devi v. *State of Jharkhand,* 2006 (1) AIR Jhar R 261: 2006 (1) East Cri C 2962: 2006 Cr LJ 1590 (Jhar).

Commandant 20 BN ITB Police v. *Sanjay Binjoa,* (2001) 5 SCC 317: AIR 2001 SC 2058: 2001 Cr LJ 2349 (SC).

Sentence of the Accused to Half of Such Minimum Punishment

Section 265E(c) of the Code says that where a satisfactory disposition of the case has been worked out under section 265D, the court shall dispose of the case in the following manner namely after hearing the parties under clause (b) if the court finds that minimum punishment has been provided under the law for the offence committed by the accused, it may sentence the accused to half of such minimum punishment.

See

Md. Munna v. *Union of India,* 2005 Cr LJ 4124: AIR 2005 SC 3440: 2005 (4) Crimes 48 (SC).

Shailesh Jasvantbhai v. *State of Gujarat,* (2006) 2 SCC 359: 2006 Cr LJ 1132: 2006 AIR SCW 436.

P. Jebac Angel Martin v. *State,* 2008 (6) AIR Bom R 1073 (NOC): 2008 Cr LJ 3147 (Mad).

Sentence of the Accused to One-fourth of the Punishment

Section 265E(d) of the Code says that where a satisfactory disposition of the case has been worked out under section 265D, the court shall dispose of the case in the following manner namely in case after hearing the parties under clause (b), the court finds that the offence committed by the accused is not covered under clause (b) or clause (c), then, it may sentence the accused to one-fourth of the punishment provided or extendable, as the case may be, for such offence.

See

Subash Chander v. *Kishan Lal,* 2001 AIR SCW 1492: AIR 2001 SC 1903: 2001 Cr LJ 1825.

Reddy Sampath Kumar v. *State of Andhra Pradesh,* 2005 AIR SCW 4620: AIR 2005 SC 3478: 2005 Cr LJ 4131: 2005 (4) Crimes 1 (SC).

K.V. Chacko v. *State of Kerala,* 2004 (2) All Cri LR 49: 2004 (1) Cur Cri R 449: 2004 Cr LJ 481 (Ker).

CHAPTER 12

JUDGMENT OF THE COURT

Section 265F of the Code dealing with Judgment of the court reads:

> *265F. Judgment of the Court.*—The Court shall deliver its judgment in terms of section 265E in the open Court and the same shall be signed by the presiding officer of the Court.

Chapter XXVII of the Code deals with the Judgment. Section 353 of the Code dealing with Judgment says:

> *353. Judgment.*—(1) The judgment in every trial in any Criminal Court of original jurisdiction shall be pronounced in open Court by the presiding officer immediately after the termination of the trial or at some subsequent time of which notice shall be given to the parties or their pleaders,—
>
> (a) by delivering the whole of the judgment; or
>
> (b) by reading out the whole of the judgment; or
>
> (c) by reading out the operative part of the judgment and explaining the substance of the judgment in a language which is understood by the accused or his pleader.
>
> (2) Where the judgment is delivered under clause (a) of sub-section (1), the presiding officer shall cause it to be taken down in short-hand, sign the transcript and every page thereof as soon as it is made ready, and write on it the date of the delivery of the judgment in open Court.
>
> (3) Where the judgment or the operative part thereof is read out under clause (b) or clause (c) of sub-section (1), as the case may be, it shall be dated and signed by the presiding officer in open Court, and if it is not written with his own hand, every page of the judgment shall be signed by him.
>
> (4) Where the judgment is pronounced in the manner specified in clause (c) of sub-section (1), the whole judgment or a copy thereof shall be immediately made available for the perusal of the parties or their pleaders free of cost.
>
> (5) If the accused is in custody, he shall be brought up to hear the judgment pronounced.
>
> (6) If the accused is not in custody, he shall be required by the Court to attend to hear the judgment pronounced, except where his personal

attendance during the trial has been dispensed with and the sentence is one of fine only or he is acquitted:

Provided that, where there are more accused than one, and one or more of them do not attend the Court on the date on which the judgment is to be pronounced, the presiding officer may, in order to avoid undue delay in the disposal of the case, pronounce the judgment notwithstanding their absence.

(7) No judgment delivered by any Criminal Court shall be deemed to be invalid by reason only of the absence of any party or his pleader on the day or from the place notified for the delivery thereof, or of any omission to serve, or defect in serving, on the parties or their pleaders, or any of them, the notice of such day and place.

(8) Nothing in this section shall be construed to limit in any way the extent of the provisions of section 465.

Section 354 of the code dealing with language and contents of Judgment says:

354. Language and contents of judgment.—(1) Except as otherwise expressly provided by this Code, every judgment referred to in section 353,—

(a) shall be written in the language of the Court;

(b) shall contain the point or points for determination, the decision thereon and the reasons for the decision;

(c) shall specify the offence (if any) of which, and the section of the Indian Penal Code (45 of 1860) or other law under which, the accused is convicted and the punishment to which he is sentenced;

(d) if it be a judgment of acquittal, shall state the offence of which the accused is acquitted and direct that he be set at liberty.

(2) When the conviction is under the Indian Penal Code (45 of 1860) and it is doubtful under which of two sections, or under which of two parts of the same section, of that Code the offence falls, the Court shall distinctly express the same, and pass judgment in the alternative.

(3) When the conviction is for an offence punishable with death or, in the alternative, with imprisonment for life or imprisonment for a term of years, the judgment shall state the reasons for the sentence awarded, and, in the case of sentence of death, the special reasons for such sentence.

(4) When the conviction is for an offence punishable with imprisonment for a term of one year or more, but the Court imposes a sentence of imprisonment for a term of less than three months, it shall record its reasons for awarding such sentence, unless the sentence is one of imprisonment till the rising of the Court or unless the case was tried summarily under the provisions of this Code.

(5) When any person is sentenced to death, the sentence shall direct that he be hanged by the neck till he is dead.

(6) Every order under section 117 or sub-section (2) of section 138 and every final order made under section 125, section 145 or section 147 shall contain the point or points for determination, the decision thereon and the reasons for the decision.

Section 355 of the Code dealing with Metropolitan Magistrates Judgment reads:

355. Metropolitan Magistrate's judgment.—Instead of recording a judgment in the manner hereinbefore provided, a Metropolitan Magistrate shall record the following particulars, namely:—

(a) the serial number of the case;

(b) the date of the commission of the offence;

(c) the name of the complainant (if any);

(d) the name of the accused person, and his parentage and residence;

(e) the offence complained of or proved;

(f) the plea of the accused and his examination (if any);

(g) the final order;

(h) the date of such order;

(i) in all cases in which an appeal lies from the final order either under section 373 or under sub-section (3) of section 374, a brief statement of the reasons for the decision.

Judgment to be Signed by the Presiding Officer of the Court

Section 265F of the Code contemplates:

(1) Delivery of Judgment in open Court;

(2) The Presiding Officer of the court to sign the judgment.

See Order XX, rule 3 of the Code of Civil Procedure.

State Bank of India v. *S.N. Goyal*, 2008 (1) SCJ 104: AIR 2008 SC 2594: (2008) 8 SCC 92.

Kalyan Singh v. *Vakil Singh*, AIR 1990 MP 295.

Surendra v. *State of Uttar Pradesh*, AIR 1977 SC 709: 1977 Cr LJ 351: (1976) 4 SCC 232.

Vinod Kumar Singh v. *Banaras Hindu University*, AIR 1988 SC 371: JT 1987 (5) SC 304: (1988) 1 SCC 80.

Phool Kumari v. *Nandu Ram (dead) by LRs*, AIR 2003 HP 75: 2003 (2) Civ LJ 855: 2003 (1) Shim LC 284.

See also section 353 to 355 of the Code supra. *See* further the undernoted decisions

Anil Rai v. *State of Bihar*, (2001) 7 SCC 318: AIR 2001 SC 3173: 2001 AIR SCW 2833.

Heera Lal v. *State of Uttar Pradesh*, 2001 (43) All Cri C 18: 2001 (2) All Cri R 1119: 2001 Cr LJ 2849 (All).

J.R. Kulkarni v. *Directorate of Health Services*, 2003 (3) All Cri LR 660: 2003 (2) Rec Cri R 660: 2003 Cr LJ 1203 (Bom).

Amina Ahmed v. *State of Maharashtra*, AIR 2001 SC 656: 2001 AIR SCW 291: 2001 Cr LJ 965 (SC).

Yelchuri Manohar v. *State of Andhra Pradesh*, 2005 (2) ALD (Crl) 758: 2005 (3) Andh LT (Cri) 386 (AP): 2005 Cr LJ 4593 (AP).

State of Himachal Pradesh v. *Chet Ram*, 2003 Cr LJ 236 (HP).

K.G. Premshankar v. *Inspector of Police*, 2002 AIR SCW 3930: 2002 Cr LJ 4343: AIR 2002 SC 3372.

Arun Kumar Ojha v. *Asaf Ali*, 2006 (34) OCR 817: 2006 Cr LJ 4360 (Ori).

Krishna Mochi v. *State of Bihar*, AIR 2002 SC 1965: 2002 AIR SCW 1909: 2002 Cr LJ 2645 (SC).

Baby Kumar v. *State of Karnataka*, 2003 (2) All Cri LR 954: 2003 (2) Cur Cri R 105: 2003 Cr LJ 1425 (Kant).

State of Himachal Pradesh v. *Surat Singh*, 2003 (1) Cur Cri R 429: 2003 (1) Rec Cri R 529: 2003 Cr LJ 386 (HP).

Kalthuri Mallikarjuna v. *State of Andhra Pradesh*, 1995 APLJ (Cri) 263: 1995 (1) LS AP 335: 1995 Cr LJ 3100 (AP).

Ram Bali v. *State of Uttar Pradesh*, 2004 Cr LJ 2490: AIR 2004 SC 2329: 2004 AIR SCW 2748.

Tessta Setalvad v. *State of Gujarat*, AIR 2004 SC 1979: 2004 Cr LJ 2022: 2004 AIR SCW 2113.

Bhupinder Sharma v. *State of Himachal Pradesh*, AIR 2003 SC 4684: 2003 AIR SCW 5493: 2004 Cr LJ 1 (SC).

Jagannath Choudhary v. *Ramayan Singh*, 2002 Cr LJ 2945: AIR 2002 SC 2229: 2002 AIR SCW 2338.

State v. *Sushil Sharma*, 2007 (3) All Cri LR 47: 2007 (1) Cur Cri R 326: 2007 Cr LJ 4008 (Del).

Shyamlal v. *State of Chhattisgarh*, 2006 Cr LJ 4743 (Chhatt).

Ram Singh v. *State of Chhattisgarh*, 2004 (1) MPHT 1: 2003 Cr LJ 4692 (Chhatt).

Finality of the Judgment

Section 265G of the Code dealing with Finality of the Judgment reads:

> *265G. Finality of the judgment.*—The judgment delivered by the Court under section 265G shall be final and no appeal (except the special leave petition under Article 136 and writ petition under articles 226 and 227 of the Constitution) shall lie in any Court against such judgment.

Article 136 of the Constitution of India dealing with special leave to appeal by the Supreme Court says:

> *136. Special leave to appeal by the Supreme Court.*—(1) Notwithstanding anything in this Chapter, the Supreme Court may, in its discretion, grant special leave to appeal from any judgment, decree, determination, sentence or order in any cause or matter passed or made by any court or tribunal in the territory of India.
>
> (2) Nothing in clause (1) shall apply to any judgment, determination, sentence or order passed or made by any court or tribunal constituted by or under any law relating to the Armed Forces.

Article 226 of the Constitution of India dealing with power of High Courts to issue certain writs says:

> *226. Power of High Courts to issue certain writs.*—(1) Notwithstanding anything in article 32, every High Court shall have powers, throughout the territories in relation to which it exercises jurisdiction, to issue to any person or authority, including in appropriate cases, any Government, within those territories directions, orders or writs, including writs in the nature of *habeas corpus, mandamus, prohibition, quo warranto* and *certiorari,* or any of them, for the enforcement of any of the rights conferred by Part III and for any other purpose.
>
> (2) The power conferred by clause (1) to issue directions, orders or writs to any Government, authority or person may also be exercised by any High Court exercising jurisdiction in relation to the territories within which the cause of action, wholly or in part, arises for the exercise of such power, notwithstanding that the seat of such Government or authority or the residence of such person is not within those territories.
>
> (3) Where any party against whom an interim order, whether by way of injunction or stay or in any other manner, is made on, or in any proceedings relating to, a petition under clause (1), without—
>
> (a) furnishing to such party copies of such petition and all documents in support of the plea for such interim order; and
>
> (b) giving such party an opportunity of being heard,
>
> makes an application to the High Court for the vacation of such order and furnishes a copy of such application to the party in whose favour such order has been made or the counsel of such party, the High Court shall dispose of the application within a period of two weeks from the date on which it is received or from the date on which the copy of such application is so furnished, whichever is later, or where the High Court is closed on the last day of that period, before the expiry of the next day afterwards on which the High Court is open; and if the application is not so disposed of, the interim order shall, on the expiry of that period, or, as the case may be, the expiry of the said next day, stand vacated.

(4) The power conferred on a High Court by this article shall not be in derogation of the power conferred on the Supreme Court by clause (2) of article 32.

Article 227 of the Constitution of India dealing with power of superintendence over all courts by the High Court says:

227. Power of superintendence over all courts by the High Court.—(1) Every High Court shall have superintendence over all courts and tribunals throughout the territories in relation to which it exercises jurisdiction.

(2) Without prejudice to the generality of the foregoing provisions, the High Court may—

(a) call for returns from such courts;

(b) make and issue general rules and prescribe forms for regulating the practice and proceedings of such courts; and

(c) prescribe forms in which books, entries and accounts shall be kept by the officers of any such courts.

(3) The High Court may also settle tables of fees to be allowed to the sheriff and all clerks and officers of such courts and to attorneys, advocates and pleaders practising therein:

Provided that any rules made, forms prescribed or tables settled under clause (2) or clause (3) shall not be inconsistent with the provision of any law for the time being in force, and shall require the previous approval of the Governor.

(4) Nothing in this article shall be deemed to confer on a High Court powers of superintendence over any court or tribunal constituted by or under any law relating to the Armed Forces.

CHAPTER 13

SPECIAL LEAVE PETITION UNDER ARTICLE 136 AND WRIT PETITION UNDER ARTICLES 226 AND 227 OF THE CONSTITUTION

Judgment delivered by the court shall be final and no appeal except the special leave petition under article 136 and writ petition under articles 226 and 227 of the Constitution of India, shall be in any court against such judgment. Thus it is clear from the language of the provision that except for the constitutional remedies which cannot be taken away by a statute, the Judgment delivered by the court under section 265G of the Code shall be final.

See the undernoted decisions

Mano Dutt v. *State of Uttar Pradesh,* (2012) 4 SCC 79: (2012) 3 SCALE 219.

Madhu v. *State of Kerala,* (2012) 2 SCC 399: AIR 2012 SC 664: 2012 Cr LJ 1230.

Rohtash v. *State of Haryana,* (2012) 6 SCC 589: 2012 Cr LJ 3189: AIR 2012 SC 2297.

State of Rajasthan v. *Shera Ram,* AIR 2012 SC 1: (2012) 1 SCC 602: 2011 (4) Crimes 303.

Ranjitham v. *Basavaraj,* AIR 2012 SC 1856: 2012 Cr LJ 2135: 2012 AIR SCW 2205.

State of Haryana v. *Shakuntla,* AIR 2012 SC 2123: 2012 AIR SCW 2952: 2012 Cr LJ 2850.

Khela Banerjee v. *City Montessori School,* (2012) 7 SCC 261: AIR 2012 SC 3776: 2012 AIR SCW 4150.

Allied Motors Ltd. v. *Bharat Petroleum Corpn. Ltd.,* AIR 2012 SC 709: 2012 AIR SCW 513: (2012) 2 SCC 1.

Rasik Lal Masuck Chand Dharuwal v. *M.S.S. Food Products,* (2012) 2 SCC 196.

Delhi Race Club Ltd. v. *Union of India,* AIR 2012 SC 3408: 2012 AIR SCW 4096: (2012) 8 SCC 680.

Uma Sashi Devi v. *Dibakar Banerjee,* AIR 2012 SC 3153: 2012 AIR SCW 4415: (2012) 6 SCALE 602.

Delhi Development Authority v. *Skipper Construction,* (2010) 15 SCC 447.

Raghunathan v. *New Bridge Holdings*, (2012) 11 SCC 311.

State of Madhya Pradesh v. *Bheru Singh*, AIR 2012 SC 1062: 2012 AIR SCW 1398: (2012) 3 SCC 287.

Indian Pharmacy Graduates Association v. *Government of India*, (2012) 11 SCC 613.

Geeta Mehrotra v. *State of Uttar Pradesh*, (2012) 10 SCC 741.

Ahmedsaheb v. *Sayed Ismail*, AIR 2012 SC 3320: 2012 AIR SCW 4287: (2012) 8 SCC 516.

Haryana SEB v. *Raj Bir Singh*, (2010) 15 SCC 649.

Kunhayammed v. *State of Kerala*, (2000) 6 SCC 359: AIR 2000 SC 2587: 2000 AIR SCW 2608.

State of Punjab v. *Davinder Pal Singh Bhullar*, AIR 2012 SC 364: 2012 AIR SCW 207: 2012 Cr LJ 1001.

Jalpat Rai v. *State of Haryana*, AIR 2011 SC 2719: 2011 Cr LJ 4295: 2011 AIR SCW 4222.

Jitender Kumar v. *State of Haryana*, AIR 2012 SC 2488: 2012 Cr LJ 3085: 2012 AIR SCW 3285.

Manohar Joshi v. *State of Maharashtra*, AIR 2012 SC 2043: 2012 AIR SCW 3088: (2011) 11 SCALE 676.

Zafruddin Khan v. *Aligarh Muslim University*, (2011) 14 SCC 127.

Surendra Dehri v. *State of Jharkhand*, (2010) 15 SCC 401.

Secretary, Ministry of Defence v. *Prabhash Chandra Mirdha*, AIR 2012 SC 2250: 2012 Lab IC 2838: 2012 AIR SCW 3470.

Arumugam Servai v. *State of Tamil Nadu*, AIR 2011 SC 1859: 2011 Cr LJ 2899: 2011 AIR SCW 2863.

A.P.S.R.T.C. v. *G. Srinivas Reddy*, AIR 2006 SC 1465: 2006 Lab IC 1302: 2006 AIR SCW 1108.

Food Corporation of India v. *Seil Ltd.*, AIR 2008 SC 1101: 2008 AIR SCW 932: (2008) 3 SCC 440.

Divine Retreat Centre v. *State of Kerala*, AIR 2008 SC 1614: 2008 Cr LJ 1891: 2008 AIR SCW 1793.

CHAPTER 14

POWER OF THE COURT IN PLEA BARGAINING

Section 265H of the Code dealing with power of the court in plea bargaining reads:

265H. Power of the Court in plea bargaining.—A Court shall have, for the purposes of discharging its functions under this Chapter, all the powers vested in respect of bail, trial of offences and other matters relating to the disposal of a case in such Court under this Code.

Section 436 to section 450 of the Code read:

436. In what cases bail to be taken.—(1) When any person other than a person accused of a non-bailable offence is arrested or detained without warrant by an officer in charge of a police station, or appears or is brought before a Court, and is prepared at any time while in the custody of such officer or at any stage of the proceeding before such Court to give bail, such person shall be released on bail:

Provided that such officer or Court, if he or it thinks fit, may, and shall, if such person is indigent and is unable to furnish surety, instead of taking bail from such person, discharge him on his executing a bond without sureties for his appearance as hereinafter provided:

Explanation.—Where a person is unable to give bail within a week of the date of his arrest, it shall be a sufficient ground for the officer or the Court to presume that he is an indigent person for the purposes of this proviso:

Provided further that nothing in this section shall be deemed to affect the provisions of sub-section (3) of section 116 or section 446A.

(2) Notwithstanding anything contained in sub-section (1), where a person has failed to comply with the conditions of the bail-bond as regards the time and place of attendance, the Court may refuse to release him on bail, when on a subsequent occasion in the same case he appears before the Court or is brought in custody and any such refusal shall be without prejudice to the powers of the Court to call upon any person bound by such bond to pay the penalty thereof under section 446.

436A. Maximum period for which an undertrial prisoner can be detained.—Where a person has, during the period of investigation, inquiry or trial under this Code of an offence under any law (not being an offence for which the punishment of death has been specified as one of the punishments under that law) undergone detention for a period extending up to one-half of the maximum period of imprisonment specified for that offence under that law, he shall be released by the Court on his personal bond with or without sureties:

Provided that the Court may, after hearing the Public Prosecutor and for reasons to be recorded by it in writing, order the continued detention of such person for a period longer than one-half of the said period or release him on bail instead of the personal bond with or without sureties:

Provided further that no such person shall in any case be detained during the period of investigation, inquiry or trial for more than the maximum period of imprisonment provided for the said offence under that law.

Explanation.—In computing the period of detention under this section for granting bail, the period of detention passed due to delay in proceeding caused by the accused shall be excluded.

437. When bail may be taken in case of non-bailable offence.—(1) When any person accused of, or suspected of, the commission of any non-bailable offence is arrested or detained without warrant by an officer in charge of a police station or appears or is brought before a Court other than the High Court or Court of Session, he may be released on bail, but—

(i) such person shall not be so released if there appear reasonable grounds for believing that he has been guilty of an offence punishable with death or imprisonment for life;

(ii) such person shall not be so released if such offence is a cognizable offence and he had been previously convicted of an offence punishable with death, imprisonment for life or imprisonment for seven years or more, or he had been previously convicted on two or more occasions of a cognizable offence punishable with imprisonment for three years or more but not less than seven years:

Provided that the Court may direct that a person referred to in clause (i) or clause (ii) be released on bail if such person is under the age of sixteen years or is a woman or is sick or infirm:

Provided further that the Court may also direct that a person referred to in clause (ii) be released on bail if it is satisfied that it is just and proper so to do for any other special reason:

Provided also that the mere fact that an accused person may be required for being identified by witnesses during investigation shall not be sufficient ground for refusing to grant bail if he is otherwise entitled to be released on bail and gives an undertaking that he shall comply with such directions as may be given by the Court:

Provided also that no person shall, if the offence alleged to have been committed by him is punishable with death, imprisonment for life, or imprisonment for seven years or more, be released on bail by the Court under this sub-section without giving an opportunity of hearing to the Public Prosecutor.

(2) If it appears to such officer or Court at any stage of the investigation, inquiry or trial as the case may be, that there are no reasonable grounds for believing that the accused has committed a non-bailable offence, but that there are sufficient grounds for further inquiry into his guilt, the accused shall, subject to the provisions of section 446A and pending such inquiry, be released on bail, or, at the discretion of such officer or Court, on the execution by him of a bond without sureties for his appearance as hereinafter provided.

(3) When a person accused or suspected of the commission of an offence punishable with imprisonment which may extend to seven years or more or of an offence under Chapter VI, Chapter XVI or Chapter XVII of the Indian Penal Code (45 of 1860) or abetment of, or conspiracy or attempt to commit, any such offence, is released on bail under sub-section (1) the Court shall impose the conditions,—

(a) that such person shall attend in accordance with the conditions of the bond executed under this Chapter,

(b) that such person shall not commit an offence similar to the offence of which he is accused, or suspected, of the commission of which he is suspected, and

(c) that such person shall not directly or indirectly make any inducement, threat or promise to any person acquainted with the facts of the case so as to dissuade him from disclosing such facts to the Court or to any police officer or tamper with the evidence,

and may also impose, in the interests of justice, such other conditions as it considers necessary.

(4) An officer or a Court releasing any person on bail under sub-section (1), or sub-section (2), shall record in writing his or its reasons or special reasons for so doing.

(5) Any Court which has released a person on bail under sub-section (1), or sub-section (2), may, if it considers it necessary so to do, direct that such person be arrested and commit him to custody.

(6) If, in any case triable by a Magistrate, the trial of a person accused of any non-bailable offence is not concluded within a period of sixty days from the first date fixed for taking evidence in the case, such person shall, if he is in custody during the whole of the said period, be released on bail to the satisfaction of the Magistrate, unless for reasons to be recorded in writing, the Magistrate otherwise directs.

(7) If, at any time after the conclusion of the trial of a person accused of a non-bailable offence and before judgment is delivered the Court is of opinion that there are reasonable grounds for believing that the accused is not guilty of any such offence, it shall release the accused, if he is in custody, on the execution by him of a bond without sureties for his appearance to hear judgment delivered.

437A. Bail to require accused to appear before next appellate Court.—(1) Before conclusion of the trial and before disposal of the appeal, the Court trying the offence or the Appellate Court, as the case may be, shall require the accused to execute bail bonds with sureties, to appear before the higher Court as and when such Court issues notice in respect of any appeal or petition filed against the judgment of the respective Court and such bail bonds shall be in force for six months.

(2) If such accused fails to appear, the bond stand forfeited and the procedure under section 446 shall apply.

438. Direction for grant of bail to person apprehending arrest.—(1) Where any person has reason to believe that he may be arrested on accusation of having committed a non-bailable offence, he may apply to the High Court or the Court of Session for a direction under this section that in the event of such arrest he shall be released on bail; and that Court may, after taking into consideration, *inter alia*, the following factors, namely:—

(i) the nature and gravity of the accusation;

(ii) the antecedents of the applicant including the fact as to whether he has previously undergone imprisonment on conviction by a Court in respect of any cognizable offence;

(iii) the possibility of the applicant to flee from justice; and

(iv) where the accusation has been made with the object of injuring or humiliating the applicant by having him so arrested,

either reject the application forthwith or issue an interim order for the grant of anticipatory bail:

Provided that, where the High Court or, as the case may be, the Court of Session, has not passed any interim order under this sub-section or has rejected the application for grant of anticipatory bail, it shall be open to an officer in-charge of a police station to arrest, without warrant the applicant on the basis of the accusation apprehended in such application.

(1A) Where the Court grants an interim order under sub-section (1), it shall forthwith cause a notice being not less than seven days notice, together with a copy of such order to be served on the Public Prosecutor and the Superintendent of Police, with a view to give the Public Prosecutor a reasonable opportunity of being heard when the application shall be finally heard by the Court.

(1B) The presence of the applicant seeking anticipatory bail shall be obligatory at the time of final hearing of the application and passing of final order by the Court, if on an application made to it by the Public Prosecutor, the Court considers such presence necessary in the interest of justice.

(2) When the High Court or the Court of Session makes a direction under sub-section (1), it may include such conditions in such directions in the light of the facts of the particular case, as it may thinks fit, including—

(i) a condition that the person shall make himself available for interrogation by a police officer as and when required;

(ii) a condition that the person shall not, directly or indirectly, make any inducement, threat or promise to any person acquainted with the facts of the case so as to dissuade him from disclosing such facts to the Court or to any police officer;

(iii) a condition that the person shall not leave India without the previous permission of the Court;

(iv) such other condition as may be imposed under sub-section (3) of section 437, as if the bail were granted under that section.

(3) If such person is thereafter arrested without warrant by an officer in charge of a police station on such accusation, and is prepared either at the time of arrest or at any time while in the custody of such officer to give bail, he shall be released on bail, and if a Magistrate taking cognizance of such offence decides that a warrant should issue in the first instance against that person, he shall issue a bailable warrant in conformity with the direction of the Court under sub-section (1).

439. Special powers of High Court or Court of Session regarding bail.—(1) A High Court or Court of Session may direct—

(a) that any person accused of an offence and in custody be released on bail, and if the offence is of the nature specified in sub-section (3) of section 437, may impose any condition which it considers necessary for the purposes mentioned in that sub-section;

(b) that any condition imposed by a Magistrate when releasing any person on bail be set aside or modified:

Provided that the High Court or the Court of Session shall, before granting bail to a person who is accused of an offence which is triable exclusively by the Court of Session or which, though not so triable, is punishable with imprisonment for life, give notice of the application for bail to the Public Prosecutor unless it is, for reasons to be recorded in writing, of opinion that it is not practicable to give such notice.

(2) A High Court or Court of Session may direct that any person who has been released on bail under this Chapter be arrested and commit him to custody.

440. Amount of bond and reduction thereof.—(1) The amount of every bond executed under this Chapter shall be fixed with due regard to the circumstances of the case and shall not be excessive.

(2) The High Court or Court of Session may direct that the bail required by a police officer or Magistrate be reduced.

441. Bond of accused and sureties.—(1) Before any person is released on bail or released on his own bond, a bond for such sum of money as the police officer or Court, as the case may be, thinks sufficient shall be executed by such person, and, when he is released on bail, by one or more sufficient sureties conditioned that such person shall attend at the time and place mentioned in the bond, and shall continue so to attend until otherwise directed by the police officer or Court, as the case may be.

(2) Where any condition is imposed for the release of any person on bail, the bond shall also contain that condition.

(3) If the case so requires, the bond shall also bind the person released on bail to appear when called upon at the High Court, Court of Session or other Court to answer the charge.

(4) For the purpose of determining whether the sureties are fit or sufficient, the Court may accept affidavits in proof of the facts contained therein relating to the sufficiency or fitness of the sureties, or, if it considers necessary, may either hold an inquiry itself or cause an inquiry to be made by a Magistrate subordinate to the Court, as to such sufficiency or fitness.

441A. Declaration by sureties.—Every person standing surety to an accused person for his release on bail, shall make a declaration before the Court as to the number of persons to whom he has stood surety including the accused, giving therein all the relevant particulars.

442. Discharge from custody.—(1) As soon as the bond has been executed, the person for whose appearance it has been executed shall be released; and when he is in jail, the Court admitting him to bail shall issue an order of release to the officer in charge of the jail, and such officer on receipt of the orders shall release him.

(2) Nothing in this section, section 436 or section 437 shall be deemed to require the release of any person liable to be detained for some matter other than that in respect of which the bond was executed.

443. Power to order sufficient bail when that first taken is insufficient.—If, through mistake, fraud, or otherwise, insufficient sureties have been accepted, or if they afterwards become insufficient, the Court may issue a warrant of arrest directing that the person released on bail be brought before it and may order him to find sufficient sureties, and, on his failing so to do, may commit him to jail.

444. Discharge of sureties.—(1) All or any sureties for the attendance and appearance of a person released on bail may at any time apply to a Magistrate to discharge the bond, either wholly or so far as relates to the applicants.

(2) On such application being made, the Magistrate shall issue his warrant of arrest directing that the person so released be brought before him.

(3) On the appearance of such person pursuant to the warrant, or on his voluntary surrender, the Magistrate shall direct the bond to be discharged either wholly or so far as relates to the applicants, and shall call upon such person to find other sufficient sureties, and, if he fails to do so, may commit him to jail.

445. Deposit instead of recognizance.—When any person is required by any Court or officer to execute a bond with or without sureties, such Court or officer may, except in the case of a bond for good behaviour, permit him to deposit a sum of money or Government promissory notes to such amount as the Court or officer may fix in lieu of executing such bond.

446. Procedure when bond has been forfeited.—(1) Where a bond under this Code is for appearance, or for production of property, before a Court and it is proved to the satisfaction of that Court or of any Court to which the case has subsequently been transferred, that the bond has been forfeited,

or where, in respect of any other bond under this Code, it is proved to the satisfaction of the Court by which the bond was taken, or of any Court to which the case has subsequently been transferred, or of the Court of any Magistrate of the first class, that the bond has been forfeited,

the Court shall record the grounds of such proof, and may call upon any person bound by such bond to pay the penalty thereof or to show cause why it should not be paid.

Explanation.—A condition in a bond for appearance, or for production of property, before a Court shall be construed as including a condition for appearance, or as the case may be, for production of property, before any Court to which the case may subsequently be transferred.

(2) If sufficient cause is not shown and the penalty is not paid, the Court may proceed to recover the same as if such penalty were a fine imposed by it under this Code:

Provided that where such penalty is not paid and cannot be recovered in the manner aforesaid, the person so bound as surety shall be liable, by order of the Court ordering the recovery of the penalty, to imprisonment in civil jail for a term which may extend to six months.

(3) The Court may, after recording its reasons for doing so, remit any portion of the penalty mentioned and enforce payment in part only.

(4) Where a surety to a bond dies before the bond is forfeited, his estate shall be discharged from all liability in respect of the bond.

(5) Where any person who has furnished security under section 106 or section 117 or section 360 is convicted of an offence the commission of which constitutes a breach of the conditions of his bond, or of a bond executed in lieu of his bond under section 448, a certified copy of the judgment of the Court by which he was convicted of such offence may be used as evidence in proceedings under this section against his surety or sureties, and, if such certified copy is so used, the Court shall presume that such offence was committed by him unless the contrary is proved.

446A. Cancellation of bond and bailbond.—Without prejudice to the provisions of section 446, where a bond under this Code is for appearance of a person in a case and it is forfeited for breach of a condition—

(a) the bond executed by such person as well as the bond, if any, executed by one or more of his sureties in that case shall stand cancelled; and

(b) thereafter no such person shall be released only on his own bond in that case, if the Police Officer or the Court, as the case may be, for appearance before whom the bond was executed, is satisfied that there was no sufficient cause for the failure of the person bound by the bond to comply with its condition:

Provided that subject to any other provision of this Code he may be released in that case upon the execution of a fresh personal bond for such sum of money and bond by one or more of such sureties as the Police Officer or the Court, as the case may be, thinks sufficient.

447. Procedure in case of insolvency or death of surety or when a bond is forfeited.—When any surety to a bond under this Code becomes insolvent or dies, or when any bond is forfeited under the provisions of section 446, the Court by whose order such bond was taken, or a Magistrate of the first class may order the person from whom such security was demanded to furnish fresh security in accordance with the directions of the original order, and if such security is not furnished, such Court or Magistrate may proceed as if there had been a default in complying with such original order.

448. Bond required from minor.—When the person required by any Court, or officer to execute a bond is a minor, such Court or officer may accept, in lieu thereof, a bond executed by a surety or sureties only.

449. Appeal from orders under section 446.—All orders passed under section 446, shall be appealable,—

(i) in the case of an order made by a Magistrate, to the Sessions Judge;

(ii) in the case of an order made by a Court of Sessions, to the Court to which an appeal lies from an order made by such Court.

450. Power to direct levy of amount due on certain recognizances.—The High Court or Court of Session may direct any Magistrate to levy the amount due on a bond for appearance or attendance at such High Court or Court of Session.

Sections 6 to 23 of the Code read:

6. Classes of Criminal Courts.—Besides the High Courts and the Courts constituted under any law, other than this Code, there shall be, in every State, the following classes of Criminal Courts, namely:—

(i) Courts of Session;

(ii) Judicial Magistrates of the first class and, in any metropolitan area, Metropolitan Magistrates;

(iii) Judicial Magistrates of the second class; and

(iv) Executive Magistrates.

7. Territorial divisions.—(1) Every State shall be a sessions division or shall consist of sessions divisions; and every sessions division shall, for the purposes of this Code, be a district or consist of districts:

Provided that every metropolitan area shall, for the said purposes, be a separate sessions division and district.

(2) The State Government may, after consultation with the High Court, alter the limits or the number of such divisions and districts.

(3) The State Government may, after consultation with the High Court, divide any district into sub-divisions and may alter the limits or the number of such sub-divisions.

(4) The sessions divisions, districts and sub-divisions existing in a State at the commencement of this Code, shall be deemed to have been formed under this section.

8. Metropolitan areas.—(1) The State Government may, by notification, declare that, as from such date as may be specified in the notification, any area in the State comprising a city or town whose population exceeds one million shall be a metropolitan area for the purposes of this Code.

(2) As from the commencement of this Code, each of the Presidency-towns of Bombay, Calcutta and Madras and the city of Ahmedabad shall be deemed to be declared under sub-section (1) to be a metropolitan area.

(3) The State Government may, by notification, extend, reduce or alter the limits of a metropolitan area but the reduction or alteration shall not be so made as to reduce the population of such area to less than one million.

(4) Where, after an area has been declared, or deemed to have been declared to be, a metropolitan area, the population of such area falls below one million, such area shall, on and from such date as the State Government may, by notification, specify in this behalf, cease to be a metropolitan area; but notwithstanding such cesser, any inquiry, trial or appeal pending immediately before such cesser before any Court or Magistrate in such area shall continue to be dealt with under this Code, as if such cesser had not taken place.

(5) Where the State Government reduces or alters, under sub-section (3), the limits of any metropolitan area, such reduction or alteration shall not affect any inquiry, trial or appeal pending immediately before such reduction or alteration before any Court or Magistrate, and every such inquiry, trial or appeal shall continue to be dealt with under this Code as if such reduction or alteration had not taken place.

Explanation.—In this section, the expression "population" means the population as ascertained at the last preceding census of which the relevant figures have been published.

9. Court of Session.—(1) The State Government shall establish a Court of Session for every sessions division.

(2) Every Court of Session shall be presided over by a Judge, to be appointed by the High Court.

(3) The High Court may also appoint Additional Sessions Judges and Assistant Sessions Judges to exercise jurisdiction in a Court of Session.

(4) The Sessions Judge of one sessions division may be appointed by the High Court to be also an Additional Sessions Judge of another division, and in such case he may sit for the disposal of cases at such place or places in the other division as the High Court may direct.

(5) Where the office of the Sessions Judge is vacant, the High Court may make arrangements for the disposal of any urgent application which is, or may be, made or pending before such Court of Session by an Additional or Assistant Sessions Judge, or, if there be no Additional or Assistant Sessions Judge, by a Chief Judicial Magistrate, in the sessions division; and every such Judge or Magistrate shall have jurisdiction to deal with any such application.

(6) The Court of Sessions shall ordinarily hold its sitting at such place or places as the High Court may, by notification, specify; but, if, in any particular case, the Court of Session is of opinion that it will tend to the general convenience of the parties and witnesses to hold its sittings

at any other place in the sessions division, it may, with the consent of the prosecution and the accused, sit at that place for the disposal of the case or the examination of any witness or witnesses therein.

Explanation.—For the purposes of this Code, "appointment" does not include the first appointment, posting or promotion of a person by the Government to any Service, or post in connection with the affairs of the Union or of a State, where under any law, such appointment, posting or promotion is required to be made by Government.

10. Subordination of Assistant Sessions Judges.—(1) All Assistant Sessions Judges shall be subordinate to the Sessions Judge in whose Court they exercise jurisdiction.

(2) The Sessions Judge may, from time to time, make rules consistent with this Code, as to the distribution of business among such Assistant Sessions Judges.

(3) The Sessions Judge may also make provision for the disposal of any urgent application, in the event of his absence or inability to act, by an Additional or Assistant Sessions Judge, or, if there be no Additional or Assistant Sessions Judge, by the Chief Judicial Magistrate, and every such Judge or Magistrate shall be deemed to have jurisdiction to deal with any such application.

11. Courts of Judicial Magistrates.—(1) In every district (not being a metropolitan area), there shall be established as many Courts of Judicial Magistrates of the first class and of the second class, and at such places, as the State Government may, after consultation with the High Court, by notification, specify:

Provided that the State Government may, after consultation with the High Court, establish, for any local area, one or more Special Courts of Judicial Magistrates of the first class or of the second class to try any particular case or particular class of cases, and where any such Special Court is established, no other Court of Magistrate in the local area shall have jurisdiction to try any case or class of cases for the trial of which such Special Court of Judicial Magistrate has been established.

(2) The presiding officers of such Courts shall be appointed by the High Court.

(3) The High Court may, whenever it appears to it to be expedient or necessary, confer the powers of a Judicial Magistrate of the first class or of the second class on any member of the Judicial Service of the State, functioning as a Judge in a Civil Court.

12. Chief Judicial Magistrate and Additional Chief Judicial Magistrate, etc.—(1) In every district (not being a metropolitan area), the High Court shall appoint a Judicial Magistrate of the first class to be the Chief Judicial Magistrate.

(2) The High Court may appoint any Judicial Magistrate of the first class to be an Additional Chief Judicial Magistrate, and such Magistrate shall have all or any of the powers of a Chief Judicial Magistrate under this Code or under any other law for the time being in force as the High Court may direct.

(3) (a) The High Court may designate any Judicial Magistrate of the first class in any sub-division as the Sub-divisional Judicial Magistrate and relieve him of the responsibilities specified in this section as occasion requires.

(b) Subject to the general control of the Chief Judicial Magistrate, every Sub-divisional Judicial Magistrate shall also have and exercise, such powers of supervision and control over the work of the Judicial Magistrates (other than Additional Chief Judicial Magistrates) in the sub-division as the High Court may, by general or special order, specify in this behalf.

13. Special Judicial Magistrates.—(1) The High Court may, if requested by the Central or State Government so to do, confer upon any person who holds or has held any post under the Government, all or any of the powers conferred or conferrable by or under this Code on a Judicial Magistrate of the first class or of the second class, in respect to particular cases or to particular classes of cases, in any local area, not being a metropolitan area:

Provided that no such power shall be conferred on a person unless he possesses such qualification or experience in relation to legal affairs as the High Court may, by rules, specify.

(2) Such Magistrates shall be called Special Judicial Magistrates and shall be appointed for such term, not exceeding one year at a time, as the High Court may, by general or special order, direct.

(3) The High Court may empower a Special Judicial Magistrate to exercise the powers of a Metropolitan Magistrate in relation to any metropolitan area outside his local jurisdiction.

14. Local Jurisdiction of Judicial Magistrates.—(1) Subject to the control of the High Court, the Chief Judicial Magistrate may, from time to time, define the local limits of the areas within which the Magistrates appointed under section 11 or under section 13 may exercise all or any of the powers with which they may respectively be invested under this Code:

Provided that the Court of a Special Judicial Magistrate may hold its sitting at any place within the local area for which it is established.

(2) Except as otherwise provided by such definition, the jurisdiction and powers of every such Magistrate shall extend throughout the district.

(3) Where the local jurisdiction of a Magistrate, appointed under section 11 or section 13 or section 18, extends to an area beyond the district, or the metropolitan area, as the case may be, in which he ordinarily holds Court, any reference in this Code to the Court of Session, Chief Judicial Magistrate or the Chief Metropolitan Magistrate shall, in relation to such Magistrate, throughout the area within his local jurisdiction, be construed, unless the context otherwise requires, as a reference to the Court of Session, Chief Judicial Magistrate, or Chief Metropolitan Magistrate, as the case may be, exercising jurisdiction in relation to the said district or metropolitan area.

15. Subordination of Judicial Magistrates.—(1) Every Chief Judicial Magistrate shall be subordinate to the Sessions Judge; and every other Judicial Magistrate shall, subject to the general control of the Sessions Judge, be subordinate to the Chief Judicial Magistrate.

(2) The Chief Judicial Magistrate may, from time to time, make rules or give special orders, consistent with this Code, as to the distribution of business among the Judicial Magistrates subordinate to him.

16. Courts of Metropolitan Magistrates.—(1) In every metropolitan area, there shall be established as many Courts of Metropolitan Magistrates, and at such places, as the State Government may, after consultation with the High Court, by notification, specify.

(2) The presiding officers of such Courts shall be appointed by the High Court.

(3) The jurisdiction and powers of every Metropolitan Magistrate shall extend throughout the metropolitan area.

17. Chief Metropolitan Magistrate and Additional Chief Metropolitan Magistrate.—(1) The High Court shall, in relation to every metropolitan area within its local jurisdiction, appoint a Metropolitan Magistrate to be the Chief Metropolitan Magistrate for such metropolitan area.

(2) The High Court may appoint any Metropolitan Magistrate to be an Additional Chief Metropolitan Magistrate, and such Magistrate shall have all or any of the powers of a Chief Metropolitan Magistrate under this Code or under any other law for the time being in force as the High Court may direct.

18. Special Metropolitan Magistrates.—(1) The High Court may, if requested by the Central or State Government so to do, confer upon any person who holds or has held any post under the Government, all or any of the powers conferred or conferrable by or under this Code on a Metropolitan Magistrate, in respect to particular cases or to particular classes of cases in any metropolitan area within its local jurisdiction:

Provided that no such power shall be conferred on a person unless he possesses such qualification or experience in relation to legal affairs as the High Court may, by rules, specify.

(2) Such Magistrates shall be called Special Metropolitan Magistrates and shall be appointed for such term, not exceeding one year at a time, as the High Court may, by general or special order, direct.

(3) The High Court or the State Government, as the case may be, may empower any Special Metropolitan Magistrate to exercise, in any local area outside the metropolitan area, the powers of a Judicial Magistrate of the first class.

19. Subordination of Metropolitan Magistrates.—(1) The Chief Metropolitan Magistrate and every Additional Chief Metropolitan Magistrate shall be subordinate to the Sessions Judge; and every other Metropolitan Magistrate shall, subject to the general control of the Sessions Judge, be subordinate to the Chief Metropolitan Magistrate.

(2) The High Court may, for the purposes of this Code, define the extent of the subordination, if any, of the Additional Chief Metropolitan Magistrates to the Chief Metropolitan Magistrate.

(3) The Chief Metropolitan Magistrate may, from time to time, make rules or give special orders, consistent with this Code, as to the distribution of business among the Metropolitan Magistrates and as to the allocation of business to an Additional Chief Metropolitan Magistrate.

20. Executive Magistrates.—(1) In every district and in every metropolitan area, the State Government may appoint as many persons as it thinks fit to be Executive Magistrates and shall appoint one of them to be the District Magistrate.

(2) The State Government may appoint any Executive Magistrate to be an Additional District Magistrate, and such Magistrate shall have such of the powers of a District Magistrate under this Code or under any other law for the time being in force, as may be directed by the State Government.

(3) Whenever, in consequence of the office of a District Magistrate becoming vacant, any officer succeeds temporarily to the executive administration of the district, such officer shall, pending the orders of the State Government, exercise all the powers and perform all the duties respectively conferred and imposed by this Code on the District Magistrate.

(4) The State Government may place an Executive Magistrate in charge of a sub-division and may relieve him of the charge as occasion requires; and the Magistrate so placed in charge of a sub-division shall be called the Sub-divisional Magistrate.

(4A) The State Government may, by general or special order and subject to such control and directions as it may deem fit to impose, delegate its powers under sub-section (4) to the District Magistrate.

(5) Nothing in this section shall preclude the State Government from conferring under any law for the time being in force, on a Commissioner of Police, all or any of the powers of an Executive Magistrate in relation to a metropolitan area.

21. Special Executive Magistrates.—The State Government may appoint, for such term as it may think fit, Executive Magistrates, to be known as Special Executive Magistrates for particular areas or for the performance of particular functions and confer on such Special Executive Magistrates such of the powers as are conferrable under this Code on Executive Magistrates, as it may deem fit.

22. Local Jurisdiction of Executive Magistrates.—(1) Subject to the control of the State Government, the District Magistrate may, from time to time, define the local limits of the areas within which the Executive Magistrates may exercise all or any of the powers with which they may be invested under this Code.

(2) Except as otherwise provided by such definition, the jurisdiction and powers of every such Magistrate shall extend throughout the district.

23. Subordination of Executive Magistrates.—(1) All Executive Magistrates, other than the Additional District Magistrate, shall be subordinate to the District Magistrate, and every Executive Magistrate (other than the Sub-divisional Magistrate) exercising powers in a sub-division shall also be subordinate to the Sub-divisional Magistrate, subject, however, to the general control of the District Magistrate.

(2) The District Magistrate may, from time to time, make rules or give special orders, consistent with this Code, as to the distribution of business among the Executive Magistrates subordinate to him and as to the allocation of business to an Additional District Magistrate.

See also sections 225 to 265 of the Code sections 272 to 327 of the Code.

CHAPTER 15

POWERS VESTED IN RESPECT OF BAIL TRIAL OF OFFENCES AND OTHER MATTERS

Court for the purposes of discharging its functions under this chapter shall have all powers vested in respect of bail, trial of offences and other matters relating to the disposal of a case in such court under the Code. In *Registrar General* v. *Pandey Gajendra Prasad,* AIR 2012 SC 2319: 2012 Lab IC 2663: 2012 AIR SCW 3383, it was held that Judicial discretion in granting bail to be exercised Judiciously taking into consideration all the relevant facts and circumstances.

See *Sanjay Chandra* v. *CBI,* AIR 2012 SC 830: 2012 Cr LJ 702: 2011 AIR SCW 6838.

Maulana Mohammed Amir Rashadi v. *State of Uttar Pradesh,* (2012) 2 SCC 382.

Ash Mohammad v. *Shiv Raj Singh,* (2012) 9 SCC 446: 2012 AIR SCW 5243.

Prakash Kadam v. *Ramprasad Vishwanath Gupta,* (2011) 6 SCC 189: AIR 2011 SC 1945: 2011 Cr LJ 3585.

Narendra K. Amin v. *State of Gujarat,* (2008) 13 SCC 584: AIR 2008 SC (Supp) 1939: (2008) 6 SCALE 415.

Ram Govind Upadhyay v. *Sudarshan Singh,* (2002) 3 SCC 598: AIR 2002 SC 1475: 2002 Cr LJ 1849.

Prahlad Singh Bhati v. *State (NCT of Delhi),* 2001 AIR SCW 1263: AIR 2001 SC 1444: (2001) 4 SCC 280.

Puran v. *Rambilas,* (2001) 6 SCC 338: AIR 2001 SC 2023: 2001 AIR SCW 1935.

State of Uttar Pradesh v. *Amarmani Tripathi,* (2005) 8 SCC 21: AIR 2005 SC 3490: 2005 AIR SCW 4763.

Prasanta Kumar Sarkar v. *Ashis Chatterjee,* (2010) 14 SCC 496: AIR 2011 SC 274: 2011 Cr LJ 302.

Chaman Lal v. *State of Uttar Pradesh,* (2004) 7 SCC 525: AIR 2004 SC 4267: 2004 Cr LJ 4243.

Pusai v. *State (NCT) of Delhi,* AIR 2004 SC 1184: 2004 Cr LJ 923: 2004 AIR SCW 74.

Sushil Suri v. *State,* 2006 (3) Crimes 421 (Del).

Chowwappa Construction v. *Embassy Construction & Development (P) Ltd.,* 2002 Cr LJ 3863 (Kant): 2002 (4) Kant LJ 532: 2002 (4) Rec Cri R 496.

CHAPTER 16

PERIOD OF DETENTION UNDERGONE BY THE ACCUSED TO BE SET OFF AGAINST THE SENTENCE OF IMPRISONMENT

Section 265(I) of the Code dealing with period of detention undergone by the accused to be set off against the sentence of imprisonment, reads:

> *265-I. Period of detention undergone by the accused to be set off against the sentence of imprisonment.*—The provisions of section 428 shall apply, for setting off the period of detention undergone by the accused against the sentence of imprisonment imposed under this Chapter, in the same manner as they apply in respect of the imprisonment under other provisions of this Code.

Section 428 of the Code dealing with period of detention undergone by the accused to be set off against the sentence of imprisonment says:

> *428. Period of detention undergone by the accused to be set off against the sentence of imprisonment.*—Where an accused person has, on conviction, been sentenced to imprisonment for a term, not being imprisonment in default of payment of fine, the period of detention, if any, undergone by him during the investigation, inquiry or trial of the same case and before the date of such conviction, shall be set off against the term of imprisonment imposed on him on such conviction, and the liability of such person to undergo imprisonment on such conviction shall be restricted to the remainder, if any, of the term of imprisonment imposed on him:
>
> Provided that in cases referred to in section 433A, such period of detention shall be set off against the period of fourteen years referred to in that section.

Section 433A of the Code dealing with restriction on powers of remission or commutation in certain cases says:

> *433A. Restriction on powers of remission or commutation in certain cases.*—Notwithstanding anything contained in section 432, where a sentence of imprisonment for life is imposed on conviction of a person for an offence for which death is one of the punishments provided by laws, or where a sentence of death imposed on a person has been commuted under section 433 into one of imprisonment for life, such person shall not be released from prison unless he had served at least fourteen years of imprisonment.

For setting off the period of Detention undergone by the accused against the sentence of imprisonment imposed under this chapter, section 428 of the Code shall apply in the same manner as they apply in respect of the imprisonment under other provisions of this Code.

For setting off *see*

N.D. Patil v. *State of Karnataka,* 2002 (3) Cur Cri R 534: 2002 (4) Rec Cri R 724: 2002 Cr LJ 3861 (Kant).

Sunil Ojha v. *State of NCT of Delhi,* 2007 (4) All Cri LR 56: 2007 (4) Rec Cri R 311: 2007 Cr LJ 3068 (Del).

Amerika v. *State of Uttar Pradesh,* 2001 (2) All Cri R 1342: 2002 (1) Rec Cri R 494: 2001 Cr LJ 4401 (All).

Advocate-General v. *Chidambara,* 2003 AIR Kant HCR 2916: ILR (Kant) 2003 (4) Kant 3631: 2004 Cr LJ 493 (Kant).

Chandran v. *State of Kerala,* 2008 (1) Ker LJ 59: 2007 (4) Ker LT 890: 2008 Cr LJ 188 (Ker).

Maliyakkal Abdul Azeez v. *Assistant Collector,* AIR 2003 SC 928: 2003 AIR SCW 406: 2003 Cr LJ 1215 (SC).

Salim Nurmohmad Haveliwala v. *State of Gujarat,* 2007 (2) Guj LH 760: 2007 Cr LJ 4564 (Guj).

Raj Kumar v. *State of Haryana,* 2005 (3) All Cri LR 542: 2005 (2) Rec Cri R 960: 2005 Cr LJ 2527 (P&H).

Hitesh Pravinchand Shah v. *State of Maharashtra,* 2004 Cr LJ 523: 2004 (2) Rec Cri R 1462: 2004 (3) Crimes 270 (Bom).

Papaiah v. *State,* 2004 (2) Crimes 324 (Kant).

K.V. Chacko v. *State of Kerala,* 2004 (2) All Cri LR 49: 2004 (1) Cur Cri R 449: 2004 Cr LJ 481 (Ker).

Vinod Kumar v. *Union of India,* 2005 (1) Crimes 443 (Bom).

Mohd. Aslam v. *State of Maharashtra,* (2001) 9 SCC 362: JT 2000 (8) SC 104.

Sachindranath Dey v. *Superintendent, Mumbai Central Prison, Mumbai,* 2004 (4) Bom LR 906: 2004 (4) Mah LJ 648: 2004 Cr LJ 4752 (Bom).

Jai Kishan v. *State of Haryana,* 2002 Cr LJ 412: 2002 (1) All Cri LR 217: 2001 (4) Rec Cri R 250.

Akloo Sada v. *State of Bihar,* 1998 (3) BLJR 1930: 1998 (2) East Cri C 622: 1998 Cr LJ 4345 (Pat).

Benson v. *State of Kerala,* 2007 (3) Ker LJ 264: 2007 (4) Ker LT 180: 2008 Cr LJ 573 (Ker).

State of Maharashtra v. *Nazakat* alias *Mubarak Ali,* AIR 2001 SC 2255: 2001 Cr LJ 2588: (2001) 6 SCC 311.

Atul Manubhai Parekh v. *C.B.I.*, 2010 (4) SCJ 311: 2009 (7) Supreme 659: AIR 2010 SC (Supp) 429.

Champalal Poonjaji Shah v. *State of Maharashtra*, (1982) 1 SCC 507: AIR 1982 SC 791: 1982 Cr LJ 612.

Government of Andhra Pradesh v. *Anne Venkateswara Rao*, AIR 1977 SC 1096: 1977 Cr LJ 935: (1977) 3 SCC 298.

Raghubir Singh v. *State of Haryana*, AIR 1984 SC 1796: (1984) 4 SCC 348: (1984) 2 Crimes 569.

CHAPTER 17
SAVINGS

Section 265J of the Code dealing with savings reads:

265J. Savings.—The provisions of this Chapter shall have effect notwithstanding anything inconsistent therewith contained in any other provisions of this Code and nothing in such other provisions shall be construed to constrain the meaning of any provision of this Chapter.

Explanation.—For the purposes of this Chapter, the expression "Public Prosecutor" has the meaning assigned to it under clause (u) of section 2 and includes an Assistant Public Prosecutor appointed under section 25.

Section 25 of the Code dealing with Assistant Public Prosecutors, says:

25. Assistant Public Prosecutors.—(1) The State Government shall appoint in every district one or more Assistant Public Prosecutors for conducting prosecutions in the Courts of Magistrates.

(1A) The Central Government may appoint one or more Assistant Public Prosecutors for the purpose of conducting any case or class of cases in the Courts of Magistrates.

(2) Save as otherwise provided in sub-section (3), no police officer shall be eligible to be appointed as an Assistant Public Prosecutor.

(3) Where no Assistant Public Prosecutor is available for the purposes of any particular case, the District Magistrate may appoint any other person to be the Assistant Public Prosecutor in charge of that case:

Provided that a police officer shall not be so appointed—

(a) if he has taken any part in the investigation into the offence with respect to which the accused is being prosecuted; or

(b) if he is below the rank of Inspector.

Section 24 of the Code dealing with Public Prosecutors, says:

24. Public Prosecutors.—(1) For every High Court, the Central Government or the State Government shall, after consultation with the High Court, appoint a Public Prosecutor and may also appoint one or more Additional Public Prosecutors, for conducting in such Court, any prosecution, appeal or other proceeding on behalf of the Central Government or State Government, as the case may be.

(2) The Central Government may appoint one or more Public Prosecutors for the purpose of conducting any case or class of cases in any district or local area.

(3) For every district, the State Government shall appoint a Public Prosecutor and may also appoint one or more Additional Public Prosecutors for the district:

Provided that the Public Prosecutor or Additional Public Prosecutor appointed for one district may be appointed also to be a Public Prosecutor or an Additional Public Prosecutor, as the case may be, for another district.

(4) The District Magistrate shall, in consultation with the Sessions Judge, prepare a panel of names of persons, who are, in his opinion fit to be appointed as Public Prosecutors or Additional Public Prosecutors for the district.

(5) No person shall be appointed by the State Government as the Public Prosecutor or Additional Public Prosecutor for the district unless his name appears in the panel of names prepared by the District Magistrate under sub-section (4).

(6) Notwithstanding anything contained in sub-section (5), where in a State there exists a regular Cadre of Prosecuting Officers, the State Government shall appoint a Public Prosecutor or an Additional Public Prosecutor only from among the persons constituting such Cadre:

Provided that where, in the opinion of the State Government, no suitable person is available in such Cadre for such appointment that Government may appoint a person as Public Prosecutor or Additional Public Prosecutor, as the case may be, from the panel of names prepared by the District Magistrate under sub-section (4).

Explanation.—For the purposes of this sub-section,—

(a) "regular Cadre of Prosecuting Officers" means a Cadre of Prosecuting Officers which includes therein the post of a Public Prosecutor, by whatever name called, and which provides for promotion of Assistant Public Prosecutors, by whatever name called, to that post;

(b) "Prosecuting Officer" means a person, by whatever name called, appointed to perform the functions of a Public Prosecutor, an Additional Public Prosecutor or an Assistant Public Prosecutor under this Code.

(7) A person shall be eligible to be appointed as a Public Prosecutor or an Additional Public Prosecutor under sub-section (1) or sub-section (2) or sub-section (3) or sub-section (6), only if he has been in practice as an advocate for not less than seven years.

(8) The Central Government or the State Government may appoint, for the purposes of any case or class of cases, a person who has been in practice as an advocate for not less than ten years as a Special Public Prosecutor:

Provided that the Court may permit the victim to engage an advocate of his choice to assist the prosecution under this sub-section.

(9) For the purposes of sub-section (7) and sub-section (8), the period during which a person has been in practice as a pleader, or has rendered (whether before or after the commencement of this Code) service as a Public Prosecutor or as an Additional Public Prosecutor or Assistant Public Prosecutor or other Prosecuting Officer, by whatever name called, shall be deemed to be the period during which such person has been in practice as an advocate.

The Provisions of this Chapter shall have Effect

Notwithstanding anything inconsistent with the provisions of this Chapter contained in any other provisions of this Code, the provisions of this Chapter shall have effect and nothing in such other provisions shall be construed or constrain the meaning of any provisions of this Chapter.

Explanation

Explanation in section 265J of the Code says that for the purposes of this chapter, the expression "Public Prosecutor" has the meaning assigned to it under section 2(v) of the Code and includes an Assistant Public Prosecutor appointed under section 25 of the Code. In *V.K. Sasikala* v. *State,* (2012) 9 SCC 771: 2012 AIR SCW 5502, it was held that though the primary duty of a Public Prosecutor is to ensure that an accused is punished, his duties extended to ensuring fairness in the proceedings and also to ensure that all relevant facts and circumstances are brought to the notice of the court for a just determination of the truth so that due justice prevails.

See *Rajiv Ranjan Singh Lalan (8)* v. *Union of India,* (2006) 6 SCC 613: 2006 AIR SCW 4287.

Center for Public Interest Litigation v. *Union of India,* (2012) 3 SCC 117: 2012 Cr LJ 1153.

Shiv Reddy v. *State,* 205 (4) Crimes 518 (Kant).

Varada Rama Mohana Rao v. *State of Andhra Pradesh,* AIR 2004 SC 3221: 2004 AIR SCW 3054: 2004 Cr LJ 2829 (SC).

Gulzar Khan v. *State of Karnataka,* 2001 (4) All Cri LR 92: 2001 (4) Rec Cri R 209: 2001 Cr LJ 3586 (Kant).

Badri Vishal Gupta v. *State of Uttar Pradesh,* 2007 (3) MPHT 453: 2007 Cr LJ 4421 (All).

K. Nagappa v. *State of Andhra Pradesh,* 2008 (2) ALD (Crl) 148: 2008 (3) Andh LT 129: 2008 Cr LJ 2147 (AP).

V.K. Rajan v. *State of Kerala,* ILR (2007) 4 Ker 636: 2008 Cr LJ 909 (Ker).

Devineni Seshagiri Rao v. *Government of Andhra Pradesh,* 2004 (1) All Cri LR 107: 2004 (7) Andh LT 988: 2004 Cr LJ 52 (AP).

CHAPTER 18
OTHER PROVISIONS

Statements of accused not to be used

Section 265K of the Code dealing with statements of accused not to be used reads:

> *265K. Statements of accused not to be used.*—Notwithstanding anything contained in any law for the time being in force, the statements or facts stated by an accused in an application for plea bargaining filed under section 265B shall not be used for any other purpose except for the purpose of this Chapter.

Non-application of the Chapter

Section 265L of the Code dealing with Non-application of the chapter reads:

> *265L. Non-application of the Chapter.*—Nothing in this Chapter shall apply to any juvenile or child as defined in clause (k) of section 2 of the Juvenile Justice (Care and Protection of Children) Act, 2000 (56 of 2000).

Special Summons in case of Petty Offence

Section 206 of the Code dealing with special summons in cases of petty offence reads:

> *206. Special summons in cases of petty offence.*—(1) If, in the opinion of a Magistrate taking cognizance of a petty offence, the case may be summarily disposed of under section 260 or section 261, the Magistrate shall, except where he is, for reasons to be recorded in writing of a contrary opinion, issue summons to the accused requiring him either to appear in person or by pleader before the Magistrate on a specified date, or if he desires to plead guilty to the charge without appearing before the Magistrate, to transmit before the specified date, by post or by messenger to the Magistrate, the said plea in writing and the amount of fine specified in the summons or if he desires to appear by pleader and to plead guilty to the charge through such pleader, to authorise, in writing, the pleader to plead guilty to the charge on his behalf and to pay the fine through such pleader:
>
> Provided that the amount of the fine specified in such summons shall not exceed one thousand rupees.
>
> (2) For the purposes of this section, "petty offence" means any offence punishable only with fine not exceeding one thousand rupees, but does

not include any offence so punishable under the Motor Vehicles Act, 1939 (4 of 1939), or under any other law which provides for convicting the accused person in his absence on a plea of guilty.

(3) The State Government may, by notification, specially empower any Magistrate to exercise the powers conferred by sub-section (1) in relation to any offence which is compoundable under section 320 or any offence punishable with imprisonment for a term not exceeding three months, or with fine, or with both where the Magistrate is of opinion that, having regard to the facts and circumstances of the case, the imposition of fine only would meet the ends of justice.

Section 320 of the Code dealing with compounding of offences reads:

320. Compounding of offences.—(1) The offences punishable under the sections of the Indian Penal Code (45 of 1860) specified in the first two columns of the Table next following may be compounded by the persons mentioned in the third column of that Table:—

TABLE

Offence	Section of the Indian Penal Code applicable	Person by whom offence may be compounded
1	2	3
Uttering words, etc., with deliberate intent to wound the religious feelings of any person.	298	The person whose religious feelings are intended to be wounded.
Voluntarily causing hurt.	323	The person to whom the hurt is caused.
Voluntarily causing hurt on provocation	334	The person to whom the hurt is caused.
Voluntarily causing grievous hurt on grave and sudden provocation.	335	The person to whom the hurt is caused.
Wrongfully restraining or confining any person.	341, 342	The person restrained or confined.
Wrongfully confining a person for three days or more	343	The person confined.
Wrongfully confining, a person for ten days or more.	344	The person confined.
Wrongfully confining a person in secret.	346	The person confined.
Assault or use of criminal force.	352, 355, 358	The person assaulted or to whom criminal force is used.
Theft.	379	The owner of the property stolen.
Dishonest misappropriation of property.	403	The owner of the property misappropriated.
Criminal breach of trust by a carrier, wharfinger, etc.	407	The owner of the property in respect of which the breach of trust has been committed.

1	2	3
Dishonestly receiving stolen property knowing it to be stolen.	411	The owner of the property stolen.
Assisting in the concealment or disposal of stolen property, knowing it to be stolen.	414	The owner of the property stolen.
Cheating.	417	The person cheated.
Cheating by personation.	419	The person cheated.
Fraudulent removal or concealment of property, etc., to prevent distribution among creditors.	421	The creditors who are affected thereby.
Fraudulently preventing from being made available for his creditors a debt or demand due to the offender.	422	The creditors who are affected thereby.
Fraudulent execution of deed of transfer containing false statement of consideration.	423	The person affected thereby.
Fraudulent removal or concealment of properly.	424	The person affected thereby.
Mischief, when the only loss or damage caused is loss or damage to a private person.	426, 427	The person to whom the loss or damage is caused.
Mischief by killing or maiming animal.	428	The owner of the animal.
Mischief by killing or maiming cattle, etc.	429	The owner of the cattle or animal.
Mischief by injury to works of irrigation by wrongfully diverting water when the only loss or damage caused is loss or damage to private person.	430	The person to whom the loss or damage is caused.
Criminal trespass.	447	The person in possession of the property trespassed upon.
House-trespass.	448	The person in possession of the property trespassed upon.
House-trespass to commit an offence (other than theft) punishable with imprisonment.	451	The person in possession of the house trespassed upon.
Using a false trade or property mark.	482	The person to whom loss or injury is caused by such use.
Counterfeiting a trade or property mark used by another.	483	The person to whom loss or injury is caused by such use.
Knowingly selling, or exposing or possessing for sale or for manufacturing purpose, goods marked with a counterfeit property mark.	486	The person to whom loss or injury is caused by such use.

1	2	3
Criminal breach of contract of service.	491	The person with whom the offender has contracted.
Adultery.	497	The husband of the woman.
Enticing or taking away or detaining with criminal intent a married woman.	498	The husband of the woman and the woman.
Defamation, except such cases as are specified against section 500 of the Indian Penal Code (45 of 1860) in column 1 of the Table under sub-section (2).	500	The person defamed.
Printing or engraving matter, knowing it to be defamatory.	501	The person defamed.
Sale of printed or engraved substance containing defamatory matter, knowing it to contain such matter.	502	The person defamed.
Insult intended to provoke a breach of the peace.	504	The person insulted.
Criminal intimidation.	506	The person intimidated.
Inducing person to believe himself an object of divine displeasure.	508	The person induced.

(2) The offences punishable under the sections of the Indian Penal Code (45 of 1860) specified in the first two columns of the table next following may, with the permission of the Court before which any prosecution for such offence is pending, be compounded by the persons mentioned in the third column of that table:—

TABLE

Offence	Section of the Indian Penal Code applicable	Person by whom offence may be compounded
1	2	3
Causing miscarriage.	312	The woman to whom miscarriage is caused.
Voluntarily causing grievous hurt.	325	The person to whom hurt is caused.
Causing hurt by doing an act so rashly and negligently as to endanger human life or the personal safety of others.	337	The person to whom hurt is caused.
Causing grievous hurt by doing an act so rashly, and negligently as to endanger human life or the personal safety of others.	338	The person to whom hurt is caused

1	2	3
Assault or criminal force in attempting wrongfully to confine a person.	357	The person assaulted or to whom the force was used.
Theft by clerk or servant of property in possession of master.	381	The owner of the property stolen.
Criminal breach of trust	406	The owner of property in respect of which breach of trust has been committed.
Criminal breach of trust by a clerk or servant.	408	The owner of the property in respect of which the breach of trust has been committed.
Cheating a person whose interest the offender was bound, either by law or by legal contract, to protect.	418	The person cheated.
Cheating and dishonestly inducing delivery of property or the making, alteration or destruction of a valuable security.	420	The person cheated.
Marrying again during the life-time of a husband or wife.	494	The husband or wife of the person so marrying.
Defamation against the President or the Vice-President or the Governor of a State or the Administrator of a Union territory or a Minister in respect of his public functions when instituted upon a complaint made by the Public Prosecutor.	500	The person defamed.
Uttering words or sounds or making gestures or exhibiting any object intending to insult the modesty of a woman or intruding upon the privacy of a woman.	509	The woman whom it was intended to insult or whose privacy was intruded upon.

(3) When an offence is compoundable under this section, the abetment of such offence or an attempt to commit such offence (when such attempt is itself an offence) or where the accused is liable under section 34 or 149 of the Indian Penal Code (45 of 1860) may be compounded in like manner.

(4)(a) When the person who would otherwise be competent to compound an offence under this section is under the age of eighteen years or is an idiot or a lunatic, any person competent to contract on his behalf, may, with the permission of the Court compound such offence.

(b) When the person who would otherwise be competent to compound an offence under this section is dead, the legal representative, as defined in the Code of Civil Procedure, 1908 (5 of 1908) of such person may, with the consent of the Court compound such offence.

(5) When the accused has been committed for trial or when he has been convicted and an appeal is pending, no composition for the offence shall be allowed without the leave of the Court to which he is committed, or, as the case may be, before which the appeal is to be heard.

(6) A High Court or Court of Session acting in the exercise of its powers of revision under section 401 may allow any person to compound any offence which such person is competent to compound under this section.

(7) No offence shall be compounded if the accused is, by reason of a previous conviction, liable either to enhanced punishment or to a punishment of a different kind for such offence.

(8) The composition of an offence under this section shall have the effect of an acquittal of the accused with whom the offence has been compounded.

(9) No offence shall be compounded except as provided by this section.

Even prior to the introduction of the concept of plea bargaining, accused was permitted to plead guilty of petty offences under section 206(1) and (3) of the Code.

For compounding of offences.

See

Rohtas v. *State of Delhi,* 2005 (1) Crimes 549: 2005 (116) DLT 612: 2005 Cr LJ 805 (Del).

Rajendra Kumar Behra v. *State of Orissa,* 2003 Cr LJ 490 (Ori).

Vinay Devanna Nayak v. *Ryot Seva Sahakari Bank Ltd.,* 2007 AIR SCW 7844: AIR 2008 SC 716: 2008 Cr LJ 805 (SC).

Madan Mohan Abbot v. *State of Punjab,* AIR 2008 SC 1969: 2008 AIR SCW 2287: 2008 Cr LJ 2243 (SC).

Y.P. Baiju v. *State of Kerala,* 2008 (2) ALJ (NOC) 570: 2008 (3) AIR Bom R 519 (NOC): 2008 Cr LJ 928 (Ker).

Bankat v. *State of Maharashtra,* 2005 Cr LJ 646: AIR 2005 SC 368: 2004 (4) Crimes 390 (SC).

Subramanian v. *Rajathi,* (2010) 15 SCC 352.

Gian Singh v. *State of Punjab,* (2012) 10 SCC 303.

B.S. Joshi v. *State of Haryana,* 2003 AIR SCW 1824: AIR 2003 SC 1386: (2003) 4 SCC 675.

Nikhil Merchant v. *C.B.I.,* 2008 AIR SCW 7501: AIR 2009 SC 428: (2008) 9 SCC 677.

Manoj Sharma v. *State,* (2008) 16 SCC 1: AIR 2008 SC (Supp) 1171.

Susi Baha Topno v. *State of Jharkhand,* 2008 (2) AIR Jhar R 560: 2008 (4) All Cri LR 526: 2008 Cr LJ 3346 (Jhar).

Dilbag Singh v. *State of Himachal Pradesh,* 2006 (1) Rec Cri R 552: 2005 (3) Shim LC 113: 2005 Cr LJ 4734 (HP).

Ram Kumar Goutam v. *State of Madhya Pradesh,* 2000 (3) Cur Cri R 679: 2000 (2) MPLJ 431: 2001 Cr LJ 1604 (MP).

E.K. Jeevaraj v. *State of Kerala,* ILR (2007) 1 Ker 368: 2007 (1) Ker LJ 18: 2007 Cr LJ 713 (Ker).

Ramesh Babulal Baheti v. *Central Bureau of Investigation,* 2004 (1) Kant LJ 435: 2004 (2) Rec Cri R 930: 2004 Cr LJ 2274 (Kant).

Suryanarayan Murthy v. *State of Andhra Pradesh,* 2000 (2) Andh LT (Cri) 110: 2001 Cr LJ 3072 (AP).

Sindhi Das (Debbarma) v. *Kaizar Debbarma,* 2001 (4) Cur Cri R 205: 2001 (2) DMC 539: 2001 Cr LJ 20 (Gau).

Ramesh v. *State of Madhya Pradesh,* 2007 (1) AIR Jhar (NOC) 255: 2006 Cri LR (SC and MP) MPJ 684: 2006 Cr LJ 3815 (MP).

Guman Kutrya Pawara v. *State of Maharashtra,* 2006 (3) Crimes 63: 2006 (3) Cur Cri R 145: 2006 Cr LJ 1163 (Bom).

Kursheed v. *State of Uttar Pradesh,* 2007 (4) Crimes 105 (SC).

Nikhil Kumar Pattanaik v. *State of Orissa,* 2003 (9) All Ind Cas 583: 2003 (2) Ori LR 61: 2003 Cr LJ 3957 (Ori).

Sailesh Shyam Parsekar v. *Baban,* 2005 AIR SCW 3358: (2005) 4 SCC 162: 2005 Cr LJ 4878 (SC).

Mahendra Singh v. *State,* 2006 (4) Crimes 664 (MP).

State of Karnataka v. *Cyabrial A-1,* 2005 (2) All Cri LR 849: 2006 (1) Crimes 185: 2005 Cr LJ 2352 (Kant).

Santosh v. *State of Kerala,* 2008 (2) Ker LJ 794: 2008 (3) Ker LT 240: 2008 Cr LJ 4103 (Ker).

Biswaroop Ghosh v. *State of Maharashtra,* 2008 (3) AIR Bom R 338: 2008 (3) All Cri LR 755: 2008 Cr LJ 2521 (Bom).

Heeralal Prasad Verma v. *State of Jharkhand,* 2006 (1) Crimes 772: 2006 (1) DMC 187: 2006 Cr LJ 778 (Jhar).

Hariram v. *State of Madhya Pradesh,* 2006 (4) AIR Bom R 598 (NOC): 2006 Cr LJ 387: 2006 Cr LJ 1764 (Chhatt).

Sailesh Bhardwaj Sharma v. *State of Jharkhand,* 2005 (1) DMC 202: 2005 (1) East Cri C 547: 2005 Cr LJ 1763 (Jhar).

Srivant More v. *Ashvini Kumar More,* 2007 (3) Crimes 106 (SC).

Upasana Finance Ltd. v. *S.N. Bagla and Company,* 2006 (2) All Cri LR 720: 2005 (4) Cal HN 39: 2006 Cr LJ 833 (Cal).

Hasi Mohan Barman v. *State of Assam,* AIR 2008 SC 388: 2007 AIR SCW 7123: 2007 (4) Crimes 267 (SC).

Balveer Prasad v. *State of Uttar Pradesh*, 2006 (56) All Cri C 479: 2006 (3) All Cri R 2787: 2007 Cr LJ 196 (All).

Jitender Rana v. *State (NCT of Delhi)*, 2007 (3) AIR Jhar (NOC) 789: 2007 (2) Chand Cri C 405: 2007 Cr LJ 1641 (Del).

Public Prosecutor v. *Banda Gopal Reddy*, 2005 (3) Rec Cri R 3: 2005 Cr LJ 584 (AP).

Rama Paswan v. *State of Jharkhand*, 2007 AIR SCW 2779: 2007 (4) Supreme 771: 2007 Cr LJ 2750 (SC).

Mukesh D. Ambani v. *State of Bihar*, 2007 (3) Pat LJR 389: 2007 Cr LJ 1565 (Pat).

Deepa Finance Corporation v. *A.K. Mohammed*, 2001 (4) Civ LJ 567: 2001 (3) CCC 382: 2001 Cr LJ 3582 (Kant).

Rajan K. Moorthy v. *M. Vijayan*, 2008 (2) All Cri LR 828: AIR 2008 MD 438 (NOC): 2008 Cr LJ 1254 (Mad).

Yesudas v. *Sub-Inspector of Police*, 2008 (1) Ker LJ 237: 2008 (1) Ker LT 245: 2008 Cr LJ 1290 (Ker).

Sridhar Pani v. *State of Orissa*, 2003 (25) OCR 447: 2003 (2) Ori LR 238: 2003 Cr LJ 3952 (Ori).

Manish Jalan v. *State of Karnataka*, 2008 AIR SCW 5160: AIR 2008 SC 3074: 2008 Cr LJ 3941 (SC).

Sabu George v. *Home Secretary*, 2007 (1) Ker J 579: 2007 (1) Ker LT 982: 2007 Cr LJ 1865 (Ker).